GHOSTS
OF
CROOK
COUNTY

ALSO BY RUSSELL COBB

*The Great Oklahoma Swindle: Race, Religion,
and Lies in America's Weirdest State*

GHOSTS
OF
CROOK
COUNTY

AN OIL FORTUNE,
A PHANTOM CHILD,
AND
THE FIGHT FOR
INDIGENOUS LAND

RUSSELL COBB

BEACON PRESS
BOSTON

BEACON PRESS
Boston, Massachusetts
www.beacon.org

Beacon Press books
are published under the auspices of
the Unitarian Universalist Association of Congregations.

27 26 25 24   8 7 6 5 4 3 2 1

This book is printed on acid-free paper that meets the uncoated paper
ANSI/NISO specifications for permanence as revised in 1992.

Text design and composition by Kim Arney

Library of Congress Cataloging-in-Publication Data
Names: Cobb, Russell, 1974– author.
Title: Ghosts of crook county : an oil fortune, a phantom child,
and the fight for indigenous land / Russell Cobb.
Description: Boston : Beacon Press, [2024] | Includes bibliographical
references and index. |
Identifiers: LCCN 2024011493 | ISBN 9780807007372 (hardcover) |
ISBN 9780807012994 (epub)
Subjects: LCSH: Petroleum industry and trade—Corrupt practices—
Oklahoma—History—20th century. | Racism against Indigenous peoples—
Oklahoma—History—20th century. | Indigenous peoples—Crimes
against—Oklahoma—History—20th century. | Oklahoma—History—Land
Rush, 1889. | Oklahoma—History—Land Rush, 1889.
Classification: LCC HD9567.O5 C63 2024 |
DDC 338.2/728209766—dc23/eng/20240429
LC record available at https://lccn.loc.gov/2024011493

To Rachel, August, and Henry.
The only true curse is ignorance.

CONTENTS

THOMAS ATKINS'S CREEK BY BLOOD FAMILY TREE

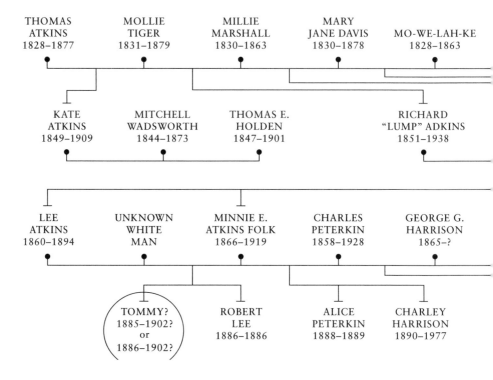

THOMAS
ATKINS
1828–1877

MOLLIE
TIGER
1831–1879

MILLIE
MARSHALL
1830–1863

MARY
JANE DAVIS
1830–1878

MO-WE-LAH-KE
1828–1863

KATE
ATKINS
1849–1909

MITCHELL
WADSWORTH
1844–1873

THOMAS E.
HOLDEN
1847–1901

RICHARD
"LUMP" ADKINS
1851–1938

LEE
ATKINS
1860–1894

UNKNOWN
WHITE
MAN

MINNIE E.
ATKINS FOLK
1866–1919

CHARLES
PETERKIN
1858–1928

GEORGE G.
HARRISON
1865–?

TOMMY?
1885–1902?
or
1886–1902?

ROBERT
LEE
1886–1886

ALICE
PETERKIN
1888–1889

CHARLEY
HARRISON
1890–1977

THOMAS ATKINS'S BLACK CREEK FAMILY TREE

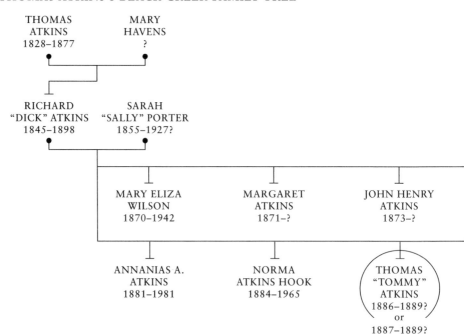

THOMAS
ATKINS
1828–1877

MARY
HAVENS
?

RICHARD
"DICK" ATKINS
1845–1898

SARAH
"SALLY" PORTER
1855–1927?

MARY ELIZA
WILSON
1870–1942

MARGARET
ATKINS
1871–?

JOHN HENRY
ATKINS
1873–?

ANNANIAS A.
ATKINS
1881–1981

NORMA
ATKINS HOOK
1884–1965

THOMAS
"TOMMY"
ATKINS
1886–1889?
or
1887–1889?

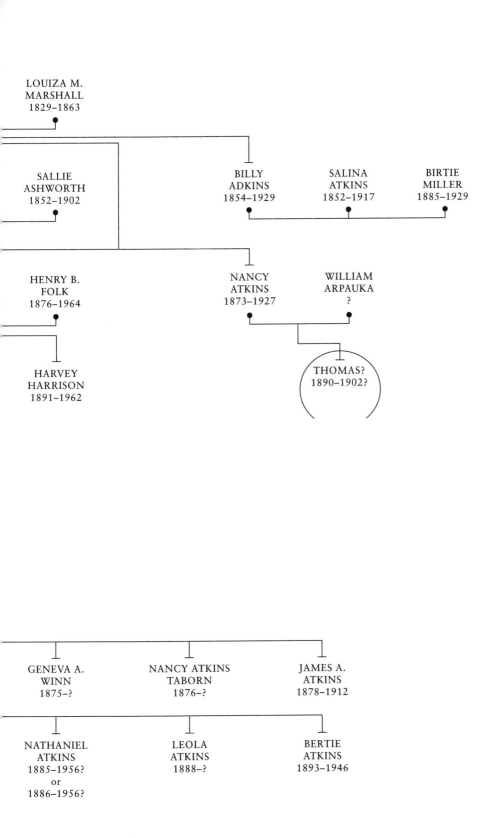

LOUIZA M.
MARSHALL
1829–1863

SALLIE
ASHWORTH
1852–1902

BILLY
ADKINS
1854–1929

SALINA
ATKINS
1852–1917

BIRTIE
MILLER
1885–1929

HENRY B.
FOLK
1876–1964

NANCY
ATKINS
1873–1927

WILLIAM
ARPAUKA
?

HARVEY
HARRISON
1891–1962

THOMAS?
1890–1902?

GENEVA A.
WINN
1875–?

NANCY ATKINS
TABORN
1876–?

JAMES A.
ATKINS
1878–1912

NATHANIEL
ATKINS
1885–1956?
or
1886–1956?

LEOLA
ATKINS
1888–?

BERTIE
ATKINS
1893–1946

GHOSTS
OF
CROOK
COUNTY

"IT WAS DOUBTFUL IF SUCH A PERSON HAD EVER EXISTED"

I grew up in Tulsa, where, on the west side of the Arkansas River, oil refineries hug the riverbank. A breeze occasionally carries notes of sulfur through the leafy neighborhood of Maple Ridge on the east side of the river. In the summer, there's a sweet putridity to the odor. Nobody seems to mind: it is the smell of money.

Tulsa was once known as the Oil Capital of the World, and although it ceased to have a legitimate claim on that title generations ago, oil continues to be the touchstone of life in the city. The most recognizable icon is a seventy-six-foot-high statue of a stern-faced roughneck astride an oil derrick—the *Golden Driller*. It is the fifth-tallest statue in the United States and the official state monument of Oklahoma.

In the 1920s, my great-grandfather, Russell Cobb Sr., drilled for oil west of Tulsa in Creek County. For a brief time, the county was the world's most important source of light sweet petroleum. This stretch of the Mid-Continent oil field, from Tulsa to Glenpool to Cushing, could be considered the foundational land for the modern American oil industry. The oil here powered the Allies to victory in World War I. It made Cushing the nexus of a web of oil pipelines still operating today. The benchmark price for a barrel of oil on the New York Mercantile Exchange refers to the cost for delivery in Cushing, Oklahoma. It is known as the Pipeline Crossroads of the World and holds around 10 percent of the nation's petroleum reserves at any given time. Creek County also got its nickname—"Crook County"—during the boom years. It is an apt description.

My great-grandfather named his business Cobra Oil Company. Cobb was a New Yorker and a Harvard man with an aristocratic

Russian wife named Elena. Her father had been assassinated by Bolsheviks. Cobb's best friend and business partner, Olney Flynn, spoke glowingly about Tulsa—the last, best frontier in America. Flynn got himself elected mayor and Cobb, the city's police and fire commissioner. They were both rich. For the duo, Tulsa was a blank urban canvas to be colored in with golf and tennis clubs, graceful yet subdued white churches, private schools, and housing designs that mimicked the Cape Cods, Dutch Colonials, and Tudor Revivals from back East. The names of the original Muscogee landowners and dusty origins of the place as a cow town were erased. Tulsa's neighborhoods now had names like Bryn Mawr, Maple Ridge, and Forest Hills.

For a while, the money came easy, and Cobb Sr.'s son, Russell Cobb Jr., began to buy oil leases with other people's money, promising spectacular returns and tax write-offs to Hollywood types. Easy money in the Oklahoma oil patch attracted celebrities like Barbra Streisand and Liza Minnelli to invest millions in the Tulsa-based Home-Stake Production Company.[1] The promised tax write-offs turned out to be scams and the returns on investment were based on a Ponzi scheme. Russell Jr. was not the architect of the swindle, but he was a player in this world. He chartered flights to Las Vegas with his friend, hotelier Conrad "Nicky" Hilton. In one stunt, Cobb landed a helicopter on the first hole of a golf green during a PGA event.

In the early 1960s, he went broke just like the famous Hemingway quote: slowly at first, then all at once.[2] Russell Cobb Sr. shot himself in a bathtub in the Hotel Tulsa in 1962. Russell Cobb Jr. died owing hundreds of thousands of dollars to the IRS in 1968. By the time the entire swindle became known to the world, my father, Candler Cobb, was trying to restart the family business in Houston of the 1970s. He was bringing the company back to prosperity without any improprieties when he fell ill with a serious heart disease in 1975. He was a charming young tennis player with a baby boy, me. By the time I was six, he was dead. His twin brother, Russell Cobb III, tried to avert a similar fate by becoming a born-again Christian with the help of the televangelist Richard Roberts. It was no use.

His grieving wife told me there was some sort of curse upon us. She called in Roberts to lift it through prayer. He prayed over us, but Roberts had his own demons. Some Tulsans shook their heads. The Cobbs were good men—we just had bad timing and terrible luck. When people around town ask me if I'm related to that third Russell, I'm always afraid they're going tell me how much money he owes them.

THE OIL CURSE AND THE QUESTION OF LAND OWNERSHIP

The reversals of oil fortunes have touched American families much more prominent than my own—the Gettys and the Rockefellers have their own versions of the oil curse. There is an empirical basis for what might seem like punishment from an angry and capricious god. Called the natural resource curse, or the Dutch disease, it is an explanation for why the general well-being of a people often declines with the discovery of natural resource wealth. Investors chase after riches from nonrenewable resources without investing in basic goods and services.

In Oklahoma, the natural resource curse might be deemed as an intergenerational comeuppance for what historian Angie Debo called "an orgy of exploitation almost beyond belief" during the state's first boom.[3] Only a few years before the likes of Cobra Oil Co. came into possession of petroleum-rich minerals in the 1900s, the land had been owned outright by Native Americans. These Native Americans were the citizens of the Five Civilized Tribes, as they were called—the Cherokee, Muscogee (Creek), Choctaw, Chickasaw, and Seminole—who had been forcibly moved from their traditional homes in the Southeast and relocated to a series of reservations designated by the federal government as Indian Territory, now the state of Oklahoma.* The federal government gave tribal citizens patents to the land there—tens of millions of acres. Citizens of these tribes held title in fee simple—the closest thing in the common law tradition to absolute ownership. But in the years between 1907 and 1922, those lands were passed from Native hands to the portfolios of white oilmen and their companies. Today, only 2 percent of that land remains with Native families. How, exactly, did this happen?

When the US government granted 160-acre land allotments to the members of the Five Tribes, it was part of a sweeping experiment to

---

*Henceforth I refer to this group of nations as the Five Tribes. The word "civilized" is loaded with a host of problematic connotations, including, most important, the idea that other Indigenous nations are "uncivilized."

privatize tribal land and grant it to individual tribal citizens. Private land ownership was not part of the Five Tribes' belief system, but these allotments extended a lucrative invitation for Indians to partake in the American capitalist system.* Like many such projects, it began with a census. Beginning in 1893, the Dawes Commission—a quasi-judicial body appointed by Congress and named after Senator Henry L. Dawes of Massachusetts—worked to document every single citizen of the Five Tribes. Every citizen enrolled by the commission would be entitled to 160 acres of their choosing. Tribal citizens would be able to farm their allotments, drill on them, or even rent them out to sharecroppers or tenant farmers. In exchange, the tribes agreed to the termination of their governments.

But how would a group of white men from outside Indian Country define who was a member of a tribe? The Dawes Commission imposed a European notion of "blood quantum" on the tribes, creating a mathematics for belonging based on a government agent's perception of someone's race. In creating what came to be known as the Dawes Rolls, commissioners often made arbitrary determinations about how much Indian blood a person had. Despite their dubious nature, these determinations had direct consequences for land ownership. "Full-bloods" were considered incompetent under the law and were barred from selling their land. Persons who were less than "one-half-blood quantum" had almost no restrictions on the sale of land. Race was not just a construct imposed on the Oklahoma tribes; it was also a legal tool for determining who owned what land, and how they were able to control it.

The decisions made by the Dawes Commission and the rolls it created remain a legal basis for citizenship in the Five Tribes today. When people claim Cherokee heritage, professional researchers turn not to genetics but to the Dawes Rolls. The Dawes Commission enrolled people of European, Indigenous, and African descent—and all possible mixtures therein. These rolls reflected raw political power—the power

---

*A note on the word "Indian." I use this term in two situations: (1) as a legal descriptor of people or lands covered under the US Constitution with inherent sovereignty and self-government in what US federal law describes as "Indian Country"; and (2) as a reference to historical documentation or terminology from a particular period. Otherwise, I use terms preferred by Native and Indigenous people themselves, which when possible specify the particular nation or tribe.

to issue land deeds to individuals. Many of the allottees may not have been Native American at all, but rather opportunistic settlers who saw a once-in-a-lifetime opportunity to own land. Adding to the confusion is the fact that many traditionalist Native Americans wanted nothing to do with Dawes or private landownership. In the case of the Muscogee, a leader named Chitto (Crazy Snake) Harjo rebelled against the entire enterprise, defying federal troops and some "mixed-blood" members of his nation.

Much of this complicated history is woefully misunderstood, even in eastern Oklahoma, where this history courses through everyday life. Even though I have Cherokee and Choctaw family members, while I was growing up I had no understanding of who, precisely, in our family was Native American and who was not.

My half brother's wife was Choctaw; did that make my brother Choctaw by marriage? Russell Cobb III's first wife was Cherokee, but were my cousins also Cherokee? They certainly didn't look like what popular culture deemed "Native." Some of them have blond hair and blue eyes. My grandmother proudly traced her family's history back to Indian Territory days in the town of Checotah. My grandmother's common law spouse was a famous Choctaw artist named Saint Clair Homer, and to him I owe my middle name. Homer was a supporter of the American Indian Movement in the 1970s. Given all these interconnections, I assumed I was part Choctaw for a long time. No one disabused me of this notion. But proximity is not the same as belonging. White Oklahomans—especially in the eastern half of the state—are unique in that they live and work on federally recognized Indian reservations, and not just those pertaining to the Five Tribes. There are thirty-nine sovereign Indigenous nations in the state. And yet whites outnumber tribal citizens by seven or eight to one. This peculiar arrangement leads to misunderstandings running from the mundane (Can Tulsa Police enforce a parking ticket on a tribal citizen on tribal land?) to the existential (What is race anyway? Who holds sovereignty over the riches of the earth?).

Dawes saw Indian Territory as the most promising place to bring about the end to what white settlers saw as the intractable "Indian problem." That is, the continued assertion by Indigenous people of their rights to govern themselves according to their own traditions, and to assert their treaty rights. By the standards of his day, Dawes was a liberal. He argued against the policies of people like Andrew Jackson, saying that his commission would treat Native Americans not as "savages" but as individual citizens, "not as an insoluble substance that the civilization of this country has been unable, hitherto, to digest, but to take him as an individual, the human being, and treat him as you find him, according to the necessities of his case."[4] As the commission turned Native Americans into private landowners, tribal citizens would "wear civilized clothes, cultivate the ground, live in houses, ride in Studebaker wagons, send children to school, drink whiskey [and] own property."[5]

In fact, the Dawes Commission ended up being a continuation of the Indian Wars by other means. Tribes' sovereignty over education, public safety, land management, and government was destroyed. Native American languages, spiritualities, and customs came under attack in boarding schools modeled on the Carlisle Indian Industrial School in Pennsylvania. Schools that had been run collaboratively by white missionaries and Native governments came under pressure to assimilate their students. There were eighty-three Indian boarding schools in Oklahoma, more than any other state. The fate of one such school, Tullahassee, is vital for understanding the story I am going to tell here. It is a complicated story that defies stereotypes and highlights the push and pull between federal Indian policy and tribal nations and individual citizens doing their best to survive in the face of what some call the "paper genocide" of the Dawes era and the birth of Oklahoma.

BLACK GOLD AND "DEAD INDIANS IN THE TITLE"

The discovery of oil in what would become northeastern Oklahoma, first at Red Fork in 1901, then at Glenn Pool in 1905, changed everything, not just in the region but in the global economy. Oklahoma was the nation's leading oil producer by 1907. The Dawes enrollees whose land was located over the petroleum-rich domes and anticlines should have become immensely wealthy, as they were entitled to subsurface royalties from oil and gas production. And indeed, a few did. Just south of Drumright, in Creek County, is the land of a Muscogee citizen, Jackson Barnett, called the "World's Richest Indian." Barnett built a Georgian Revival mansion in Beverly Hills in 1926 that became a must-see tourist attraction during the Golden Age of Hollywood. He had little interest in material possessions, but his wife, Anna Laura Lowe, an adventuress from Kansas City, persuaded him to build the mansion and acquire various automobiles. Jackson, evidently bored, spent his time wearing white gloves and directing traffic at the intersection of Rossmore Avenue and Wilshire Boulevard. A whitewashed version of Barnett's story may have been part of the source material for *The Beverly Hillbillies*. (Although the series creator placed the origins of the Clampett family in the Missouri Ozarks, Jed once stated that his family had been in America "before the Mayflower." Jed and Jackson sported similar facial hair and well-worn hats.)

Lucinda Pittman, another oil-rich Muscogee citizen, famously went to a Cadillac dealership in the town of Muskogee in 1925, was unimpressed by the cars on offer, and designed her own—complete with a blue racing stripe, red plush interior, silver cigar holders, and perfume bottles. A Muskogee newspaper described it as Pittman's "palace on wheels," a car whose luxury could not be rivaled by a millionaire's yacht or the private car of a railroad magnate. When the vehicle was delivered, Cadillac announced that Pittman's was the most expensive car they had ever produced.[6] And then there was Thomas Gilcrease, who used his oil money to amass one of the most prestigious collections of art about the American West, now housed at the Gilcrease Museum, one of Tulsa's major cultural institutions.

Even rich Muscogees like Barnett, Pittman, and Gilcrease, however, were used as pawns in a larger game involving the build-out of American oil infrastructure. Newspaper clippings of the era tell stories of fabulous estates reduced to ruin, of "rich Indians" disappearing under mysterious circumstances. They involved swindles, kidnappings, intimidation, and murder. The plunder of Osage mineral wealth through violence, long suppressed in the mainstream story of Oklahoma, is now familiar to everyone thanks to the 2023 film *Killers of the Flower Moon*. But that story did not occur in a vacuum. The Osage Nation borders the Muscogee Nation to the south and the Cherokee Nation to the east. The Mid-Continent oil field runs underneath them all, and all three converge on West Edison Street, near downtown Tulsa.

Muscogee allottees may have had wealth, but the power over their assets was increasingly consolidated in the hands of oil and gas companies, many of which still operate today. Later, Oklahoma oilmen like J. Paul Getty found oil reserves in Saudi Arabia that made the Cushing-Drumright Field seem like a warm-up match to the ultimate prize—mastery of the world's oil markets. As the Oklahoma oil fields dwindled in significance, the stories of the original allottees were forgotten.

The stories of these original owners have been thoroughly erased from the mainstream stories Oklahoma tells about itself. In Tulsa, in particular, allottees have little to no presence in the public memory, despite the now-common practice of Indigenous land acknowledgments. There is something unsettling about knowing that the land belonged to a particular person, to a specific family, that makes the history of dispossession much harder to ignore. I wanted to know specific details behind what seemed like stranger-than-fiction stories. I wanted to uncover the complexities of the lives of people I only knew as "dead Indians," inconvenient obstacles to real estate deals in eastern Oklahoma. In 2019, I set about trying to tell one story—just one story of one original landowner—that might reveal a larger truth.*

A BOY NAMED TOMMY

Angie Debo, working in the 1930s, was a laconic, studious woman with a small-town Oklahoma background and impeccable academic credentials (she earned an MA from the University of Chicago and a

---

* A note on the words "Muscogee," "Creek," and "Mvskoke." Europeans described groups of Indigenous people belonging to a confederacy of tribal towns in the Southeastern woodlands as Creek Indians, because their towns were built along creeks or rivers. The Creeks called (and still call) themselves Este Mvskokvlke, or simply Mvskoke, rendered into English as Muscogee. The word "Creek" continues to be used frequently and informally in Oklahoma. I use Muscogee to denote political affiliation, and Mvskoke for culture, language, and identity. The pronunciation for the town Muskogee, the nation Muscogee, and the language Mvskoke, is the same: muh-SKOH-gee.

PhD from the University of Oklahoma). She compiled a manuscript documenting how millions of acres allotted to tribal citizens quickly wound up as vast landholdings controlled by powerful Oklahoma men. The research led to threats against her life. But an Oxford-educated editor of the University of Oklahoma Press, Joseph Brandt, contracted with Debo to publish her work *And Still the Waters Run: The Betrayal of the Five Civilized Tribes.* Before the book could go to press, however, the president of the university, William Bizzell, realized that Debo's work could threaten not only the press but the whole university, as it depended on donations and political support from oilmen. Debo's book named names, some of whom were still living, like Senator Robert L. Owen, who Brandt thought might sue for libel. Debo could not understand; she had found his name on warranty deeds in county courthouses removing restrictions on allottees. It was right out there in the public. Either no one had noticed it, or they downplayed Owen's role in removing what were supposed to be guarantees against land swindling. Brandt fought for the publication of a watered-down version of the book, wherein Debo replaced many names with vague allusions to key players, but Debo refused to censor the names of Owen, and Charles Haskell, Oklahoma's first governor. President Bizzell thought the book was still too explosive. Brandt resigned from the University of Oklahoma Press and took over the editorship of Princeton University Press, which was happy to publish Debo's book in 1940.[7] This classic work was reissued in paperback in 2022.[8]

However, there were some people too powerful even for Debo to dare name. One was the Tulsa philanthropist Charles Page, who throughout the 1910s and '20s cultivated an image of himself as the state's most generous oilman. Debo barely mentioned Page at all, except to say that much of his wealth and philanthropy was derived from his victorious legal battles to possess the lands belonging to one Muscogee allottee, a boy named Tommy Atkins.[9] Page was a singular figure, even among the eccentric class of Oklahoma wildcatters. He directed all of his oil profits to a philanthropy called the Sand Springs Home, which funded an orphanage Page had built out in the wilderness west of Tulsa, a thick forest that once served as a boundary between the Osages and Muscogees. The orphans at the Sand Springs Home called the great philanthropist Daddy Page, and he often spoke about the children as if they were his own. He also provided homes for widows, who were housed in a sprawling community of cottages and given a daily supply of milk. The widows also had jobs at Page's industrial facilities—the cotton gin, the water bottling plant, the steel mill. In sum, Page created a place some called the Magic Empire: the town of Sand Springs, where the oilman's industries housed, fed, and employed thousands of Oklahomans.

I was curious about this boy, Tommy Atkins. It had been common practice among swindlers of the time to put child allottees into orphanages and then plunder their estates.[10] Was Tommy one of the Sand Springs orphans, or was he something else entirely?

Angie Debo reported the story of Tommy as Charles Page wanted it known for posterity. One of Page's orphans, Opal Bennefield Clark, published a biography of the man titled *A Fool's Enterprise* (1988).[11] As Clark told the story, Tommy Atkins had been a little Mvskoke boy allotted land in western Creek County. His mother, Minnie Atkins, had given birth to him in a barn behind a brothel in Leavenworth, Kansas, in 1885. Minnie left Tommy behind to follow her soldier boyfriend off to the Spanish-American War. She never came back for her son. Tommy grew up as an orphan near the federal penitentiary in Fort Leavenworth, fostered by Mollie Letcher, a Black brothel owner known as Granny.

When Tommy was a teenager, he disappeared during a flood. He was presumed dead, but not before the Dawes Commission put his name down on the Dawes Rolls. Minnie, who had settled down near Seattle, had assumed a new identity as a white woman from Texas. Tommy's enrollment worked its way through government bureaucracy until he was finally granted an allotment in 1903.

In 1912, ten years after Tommy's supposed death, a wildcatting Pennsylvania oilman named Tom Slick hit a gusher on white-owned land in western Creek County, only a few miles from Tommy's allotment. Slick's gusher brought forth light sweet crude, the most refinable and desirable petroleum on the market. And the timing could not have been better. By this time, it was clear that the automobile would be powered by gasoline in the future, not by steam or electricity. Even the British Navy was converting its fleet to petroleum-based fuel. The Southern Plains states of Kansas, Texas, and Oklahoma were the ultimate prize: at the time, the majority of the world's petroleum came out of this area—the Mid-Continent oil field—and, with the exception of tribal land in Oklahoma, most of it was in the hands of white Americans.

The area around Slick's gusher was likely to be oil-rich as well, but most of it was owned by "full-blood" Mvskoke allottees, a people whom Slick did not understand. They spoke no English, had little interest in paper money, and, perhaps most important, were subjected to a tangle of federal restrictions on land transactions that depended on Dawes Commission blood quantum determinations. Leases to drill on Muscogee land could be obtained, but only by those willing to take risks that their transactions might be voided by some federal agent. Tom Slick became known as "the king of the wildcatters," one of the richest men in the country. But he steered clear of lots whose ownership was unclear.

Charles Page was willing to take those risks. He believed that, of all the allottees whose land lay near Slick's gusher, one belonging to a dead Indian boy—Tommy Atkins—could be had with relatively the most ease. In Page's official version, the oilman then set off on a long clandestine trip to find Minnie Atkins, mother to Tommy, inheritor of his allotment. Page told the superintendent of the Sand Springs Home to deflect any questions about his absence. Page said he was going on a fishing vacation. Using skills acquired as a Pinkerton agent, Page combed the continent. He bought himself a ten-dollar Stetson, of which he was particularly proud. Page followed a tip to a mining camp in California. Pinkerton agents had few qualms about what we consider ethical standards in law enforcement today. Pinkertons lied, bribed (and took bribes), flipped sides for the right price, harassed and intimidated workers. They were also incredibly successful at finding their targets and solving crimes.

In California, he found the elusive Minnie Atkins cooking for cowboys and miners. Page told Minnie that her forgotten son, Tommy, was now going to make her rich beyond her wildest dreams. Minnie followed Page back to Oklahoma on a train. Minnie testified to Page's lawyers that she was the only living heir of Tommy Atkins, and then signed Tommy's oil lease over to Page's oil company, Gem Oil, which he ran with a Texas oilman named R. A. Josey. Page bought Minnie an eclectic, Mediterranean-style house with a wraparound porch, right across the street from Page's own mansion. There she lived happily ever after, a "rich Indian heiress" who made for good newspaper copy. It seemed like a rags-to-riches story straight out of Hollywood.

Even though Angie Debo had kind words for Page, she noted something quite peculiar about Page's involvement in cases involving missing Mvskoke children. In 1915, the federal government, with the support of the Muscogee Nation, had accused several oilmen of engaging in a fraud to create fictional Muscogee citizens whose land just happened to be sitting on oil deposits. Some of these cases involved missing persons and stranger-than-fiction appearances from beyond the grave. In one case, a Muscogee man named Barney Thlocco was assumed to have died from smallpox in Indian Territory in 1899, only to resurface as an ex–circus performer and Mexican revolutionary two decades later. He had not died at all, Thlocco claimed. He had run away to Mexico with a faction of Chitto Harjo's rebels. Now he wanted his land back. After some interrogation, it appeared that this Mexican Thlocco might have been an impersonator of the dead man. Debo alluded to the idea that Charles Page's Tommy Atkins might also have been one of these frauds: "It was doubtful if such a person had ever existed," she wrote in passing.[12]

In 1917, the Supreme Court took up the Thlocco case in *US v. Wildcat*. The court did not answer the question that truly lay at the heart of the matter—whether the man claiming to be Thlocco was a genuine Muscogee citizen from Oklahoma or a Mexican impersonating a Native American to get land. Instead, the court focused on the validity of the Dawes Rolls on which Thlocco's name was recorded. The Muscogee Nation argued that Thlocco had died before the important date of April 1, 1899—the cutoff date established by the Dawes Commission, after which deceased citizens could no longer be given allotments. They argued that Thlocco's entire allotment should be canceled and the wealth of the land returned to the tribe. In the end, the Supreme Court decided that reexamining Thlocco's case "would reopen so many questions and disturb so many titles that the Dawes Rolls should stand."

The Supreme Court, like the leaders of the petroleum industry, had no appetite to reexamine Dawes's work. The oil boom was transforming the world's economy—a few mistakes in some bureaucratic paperwork were inevitable, but not a reason to stand in the way of progress.

I found it disturbing that the court had brushed off the real question: Had Thlocco been cheated out of his land? Or, if he had died before the cutoff date, why had the Muscogee Nation not been able to recover the millions of dollars in royalties that had been redirected to the oilmen? I heard a Muscogee man muse on the question at an Oklahoma history conference in 2022.

"We could have been a mini Saudi Arabia!" he said as I talked about Atkins and Thlocco. That prospect raised another host of questions I don't think anyone was ready to answer.

I turned back to Debo's throwaway observation that Tommy Atkins was most likely a fiction. This seemed a little too far-fetched. I found a book on the work of the Dawes Commission that contained a footnote regarding Tommy Atkins. It only furthered the enigma. "Thomas Atkins was enrolled as Creek-by-Blood 7913," it said. "His case . . . contains hundreds of pages of testimony and exhibits."[13] Now it seemed that the case of Tommy Atkins, far from being the simple rags-to-riches story that Clark had put down in the Charles Page biography, had in fact been complicated and hotly contested.

Where were these testimonies and exhibits? It was hard to figure out. A Google search yielded little except a reference to several court cases involving Atkins and the Sand Springs Home. The cases had gone from the Creek County Court in Sapulpa all the way to the United States Supreme Court. They involved not only Minnie Atkins but also two other Atkins women. Tommy became known in the press as "the boy with three mothers": Minnie, Nancy, and Sally* Atkins all at various points claimed to be the one true mother of the missing millionaire boy. Each woman was backed by powerful oilmen and companies ready to claim this valuable allotment. The Tommy Atkins case had been treated like a footnote in history, when in reality it was a legal Pandora's box containing vital questions about landownership, racial identity, and oil wealth.

---

*The spelling "Sallie" is also used frequently in newspaper accounts and legal documents. Her legal name was Sarah Atkins, but that name almost never appears in the written record.

LOOKING FOR A PHANTOM CHILD

The "Tommy Atkins case" was in fact four separate court cases that came to trial. Each had plot twists and eccentric characters worthy of a noirish detective novel. Each one deserves its own chapter, and, indeed, receives one in this book. The first trial saw Nancy Atkins challenge a Sapulpa man named H. U. Bartlett over Tommy's heirship in Creek County Court in 1913. Nancy Atkins, the plaintiff, sued Bartlett, claiming that Bartlett's oil lease had been forged by an imposter of Nancy's sister, Minnie Atkins.

The second trial, also in the Creek County Court, began in 1914 and involved a second woman claiming to be Minnie Atkins, the woman who had signed Tommy Atkins's allotment over to Page's Gem Oil Company that same year. This caught the attention of the Department of Justice, which, together with the national attorney of the Muscogee Nation, sued Minnie and Page for fraud.

Thus began the trial of a third case (*United States v. Atkins et al., Equity 2131*) in 1915 on a much bigger stage—the United States District Court for the Eastern District of Oklahoma in Muskogee. At the time this trial was considered the most voluminous and expensive trial in Oklahoma history. It dragged on for three years and generated thousands of pages of trial transcripts and documents.

Just when the public thought it was all over, in 1919, a fourth trial began, shortly after the death of Minnie Atkins. A relative of Minnie's, a Black woman named Sally Atkins, came back from her refuge in Canada to sue the Sand Springs Home for illegally possessing her son Tommy's land in Creek County. This fourth case roiled the entire political foundations of Oklahoma, leading to claims of bribery, attempted assassinations, and the temporary imprisonment of a judge. By 1922, the Tommy Atkins case wound up in the US Supreme Court as *Page v. Atkins*. There were sideshows as well, as shadowy men came out of the woodwork to claim they were, in fact, the actual Tommy Atkins. My head continues to spin.

In 2020, I called Apollonia Piña, my research assistant and a Muscogee Nation citizen, to help me sort it out. We had met in 2018 while trying to figure out how a valuable piece of Tulsa real estate had been transferred from a famous allottee to a company that had created the subdivision where I grew up, Sunset Terrace.

Our working relationship had gotten off to a rocky start. Apollonia saw an article I published in the *Tulsa World* about this early-twentieth-century swindle. She sent me a Facebook message saying that the research would have landed better if it came from a Mvskoke perspective. I thought she was out to cancel me. To her surprise, I wrote back saying I agreed—the story should have an Indigenous point of view. I told her about Tommy Atkins. She seemed perplexed. At the time, Apollonia was working at a Tulsa public library branch and had connections at her tribe's Cultural and Historic Preservation Department. (She is now an emergency room nurse at a Creek County hospital, of all places.)

We eventually formed an unlikely research team that included a volunteer from the Maple Ridge Garden Club named Gina Covington and an Indigenous radio journalist named Allison Herrera. Gina turned the basement of her elegant home on "Black Gold Row" into an archive of forgotten Tulsa crimes. Allison thought the Tommy Atkins story would make an interesting podcast. As the list of characters climbed into the hundreds, Allison said the story was simply too complicated for radio. We scuttled the idea for the podcast, but I obsessively plowed through archives, hoping to solve the riddle of Tommy Atkins in this book.

Apollonia called her friend Violet, a lawyer and Cherokee citizen, with questions about guardianship and restrictions in early Oklahoma. Apollonia also called RaeLynn Butler, the head of Historic and Cultural Preservation at the Muscogee Nation's capital in Okmulgee. We also contacted a prominent oil and gas attorney of the Osage tribe who had connections to members of Congress in Washington. No one could really understand what we'd unearthed. I read the cases again and again, trying to make sense of what seemed preposterous: A fictional boy with three mothers helps to endow one of Oklahoma's most renowned philanthropies? I had to be misreading the story. After countless meetings and head-scratching sessions hunched over my laptop, the story developed some clarity.

Minnie, Nancy, and Sally Atkins had each claimed, under oath, to be the biological mother of Tommy Atkins. Moreover, a Muscogee freedman—a descendant of formerly enslaved people in the tribe—named Henry Carter claimed to be Tommy Atkins himself. They had all executed oil leases or property deeds to oil companies, but the controversy had led to a major federal investigation. The Muscogee Nation, the Bureau of Indian Affairs, and the Department of Justice countered that Tommy Atkins was "a lie, pure and simple"—the product of greedy oilmen's imaginations. At the center of that fraud, they alleged, was Charles Page.

Page and his business partners enlisted a US congressman, Scott Ferris; one of Tulsa's two daily newspapers; a former governor, Lee Cruce; and several prominent Muscogee leaders to support their claim that Tommy Atkins had existed, that the Minnie Atkins who had signed their lease to drill was his mother, and that their oil operations on Tommy's land were therefore legitimate. They caught the ear of President Woodrow Wilson, who in 1915 was briefed on the matter. The case disturbed the oil industry and federal politics and led to what appears to be a kidnapping of the Muscogee chief. Much of this was not revealed to the public and has never before been published.

After years of court battles, reversals, and mysterious deaths, the US Supreme Court heard *Page v. Atkins*, ultimately giving the land and its riches to Charles Page's Sand Springs Home in 1922.

I went to the National Archives and Records Administration in Washington, DC, to find the hundreds of pages of testimony and evidence referenced in a footnote of a book about the Dawes Commission.[14] I quickly realized that "hundreds" was a vast understatement. There were thousands upon thousands of records spanning several decades and many archives. Just the list of people named in affidavits numbered into the hundreds.

I wondered why the dozens of lawyers on the case did not simply locate Tommy's birth certificate. But even the circumstances of his birth were fraught with contradiction. According to Page, Minnie had stated that the boy had been born in a barn behind a brothel. But what Page did not mention is that Minnie had given another sworn statement saying that Tommy had been born in a hospital run by nuns in Leavenworth, and, curiously, a third in which she said there was never a Tommy in the first place.

As I continued to pore through the archives, RaeLynn Butler at the Muscogee Nation's Cultural and Historical Preservation Department sent some vital census records. The tribe is wary of white folks claiming some vague Native "heritage," so it has a clear system to determine who is and is not qualified for citizenship. Usually this is cut and dried: if a person has a direct blood ancestor on the Dawes Rolls, they are eligible for citizenship, regardless of their supposed blood quantum. Butler gave us a lot of documentation on Tommy: a tribal census, an enrollment card, and a map of his allotment. His enrollment card included his mother's name, Minnie Atkins, as well as a father listed only as "white man." The card also listed Minnie as belonging to Euchee Town, a unique group within the Muscogee Nation with its own language and traditions.

Butler handed us a copy of Minnie's Dawes enrollment document, with something odd on it: a red line through Minnie Atkins's name. Minnie had herself been stricken from the rolls. A thought occurred to me. Maybe she had been one of the many "pretendians" flooding into Indian Territory trying to get free land. Who was the nameless "white man" listed as Tommy's father? We were finding only more questions, none of which Butler could answer.

I went to Eli Grayson, a noted genealogist and Mvskoke activist for Black freedmen. Grayson often finds himself at odds with his own tribe over the question of tribal citizenship for freedmen. He usually has an answer to any dilemma involving old Creek Nation cases. I showed him what I'd found.

"You've stepped in some deep shit," Grayson said.

INTO "CROOK" COUNTY

In the winter of 2020, Apollonia and I went to see the Tommy Atkins allotment for ourselves. I rented a white Chrysler at Tulsa International Airport. The excursion would involve trespassing on land where human skeletons had been found at the bottom of oil tanks. The doyenne of oil industry history, Ruth Sheldon Knowles, called the routine killings of people during the boom times as "nothing remarkable."[15] It was a land of ghost towns and meth labs—Crook County, indeed. A geologist urged me to carry a pistol if I was out in the field, an insurance policy against outlaws and rattlesnakes.

Google Maps showed Mills's Sno Cone Stand as the only landmark indicating the boundary of Tommy's allotment. Apollonia spotted a metal sign, riddled with bullet holes, indicating an oil well called "Luther Manuel #1," operated by an oil company called Petco. It meant that we were on the allotment of one Luther Manuel—it was common practice to name oil wells after allottees, even after their descendants had long since sold off royalties. A white pickup truck was servicing an oil well nearby. As for the snow cone stand, it was abandoned.

Apollonia's great-grandparents had received land a little south of where we stood, at the fork of a gravel road and West Sixty-First Street in Oilton, Oklahoma. She'd never been to her family's allotment. The land had been chopped up and subdivided so many times that she was unsure who actually owned it. If there was oil out there, she'd never received a penny in royalties. That was a story I heard over and over from many people, a story that affirmed the reality that Dawes's master plan to assimilate Native Americans had led to an era of plunder and corruption, not civilization.

A steel gate blocked access to a gravel road next to the "Luther Manuel #1" sign. The creaky gate swung open easily, and I aimed the Chrysler up the road. Dark red mud splashed the car—the brownish red dirt a leftover from a layer of soil deposited here during Dust Bowl days. Apollonia looked at a scanned copy of a 1910 map of the Muscogee Nation on her phone. It was remarkable how this map, drawn out by hand in an era of tribal termination, still reflected the current landscape.

We found a rocky trail leading up the hill and followed it until Apollonia was satisfied that we had passed from the Luther Manuel to the Tommy Atkins allotment. It was one of those winter days in Oklahoma when everything feels brittle and dead, even though the temperature is mild. Sandy limestone outcroppings, juniper trees, and jagged hills gave the place an almost Mediterranean appearance, but the smell was unique to oil country. You can almost taste a sticky, tarlike substance in your mouth which, like the scented breezes of my Tulsa youth, had notes of a putrid sweetness.

A black horse-head-style pumpjack led us to the source of the smell. The pumpjack methodically hammered down its steel casing into the earth's crust, pulling up a viscous oil from some three thousand feet down. As the pumpjack drew back, we spotted brown crude, some of it trickling onto the ground. I touched my finger to the oil and then drew it close to my face. It had the look and consistency of a deep amber maple syrup—nothing like the coal-dark crude of the public imagination.

The area under our feet had once been endowed with one of the richest deposits of light sweet crude in the Western Hemisphere. What was left? A landscape littered with abandoned railway tracks, rusted derricks, and wide swaths of barren land. Companies like Petco were still drilling, but now the action was in fracking, and that had led to a new host of problems, including earthquakes and contaminated water. I grew up in Oklahoma never knowing what an earthquake felt like. On one recent visit, I was jolted awake around 3 a.m., feeling like I was lying on a trembling waterbed.

"This place feels haunted," I said to Apollonia, wiping the oil off my index finger. Apollonia had an affinity for ghost stories, but she also had a university degree in cross-cultural epistemologies and a dedication to empirical medicine as a nurse. Still, something seemed off to her, too.

"We need to get out of here," she said.

I pointed the Chrysler onwards through the Tommy Atkins allotment, hoping to see some sign that would pay homage to this figure at the center of the most litigated oil lease in Oklahoma history. Luther Manuel's identity might be almost lost to history, but pumpjacks still extracted oil from the earth in his name. Same for Tommy's neighbor to the west, Sarah Rector. But we saw no oil wells named after Tommy Atkins. The extant oil wells had only township and range coordinates, along with the Petco logo.

Apollonia shifted uncomfortably in her seat, quizzing me about what I would say if we were stopped by a Petco employee with a gun. I said I would tell the truth: we were researchers trying to get to the bottom of a cold case involving one of the nation's great oil fortunes. Apollonia laughed uncomfortably. I had long since left Oklahoma in pursuit of an education that, I had hoped, would take me far away from my home state. I studied comparative literature at the University of Texas at Austin and found a job as a professor at the University of Alberta, in Canada. I specialized in Latin American literature and culture, but now, after all these years, I was back on Oklahoma red dirt.

"So, you're just a professor from Canada out looking for a boy named Tommy who disappeared a hundred years ago?"

"Who could be threatened by that?" I countered.

"You'd be surprised," Apollonia said.

I hit a rut in the Oklahoma red mud and the Chrysler bottomed out. I threw it into reverse, but this only turned the rut into a muddy ditch. One back wheel lifted into the air as the front of the car sank further into the mud. There was intermittent cell service out here, and the only sign of life had been the white service pickup truck near the Luther Manuel #1. We had no business being back here, and now we were stuck. We needed to dislodge the car from the hole and get out before anyone from Petco found us. I raked gravel into the hole with my foot, which was now caked in red mud.

With the muddy ditch now covered in gravel, I slammed the Chrysler into reverse, and we were free. We found an abandoned road signposted "Old Highway 99" and passed a youngish white man with a beard in a white pickup truck. This was the same truck we'd seen before. I slowed down to read the lettering on the truck door: Petco Petroleum. The man made a motion for me to roll down my window, but Apollonia told me to step on the gas. She had been harassed and threatened before while exploring the Oklahoma backcountry. This land was, from her point of view, still part of the Muscogee reservation, and Apollonia felt it was her right as a tribal citizen to explore the land.

"Sovereignty!" she often retorted if someone questioned her presence on private land. But she didn't like the looks of the Petco man.

"I don't want to mess with this," Apollonia said, scrunching down in her seat.

I found a turnoff for Highway 99 and flew past Mills's Sno Cone stand. I didn't stop until we were back in Tulsa.

Apollonia was right to be suspicious of the man in the Petco truck. We later learned that oil field swindles in the area were still happening. In 2021, a Petco employee, David Owen West, was found stealing oil products in this area. West had run a scheme of billing his employer for bogus service operations. He'd also skimmed petroleum, reselling the oil to other companies and pocketing the money. West not only stole oil from dozens of wells around Oilton; he billed Petco for the transportation charge. In total West stole some $400,000 worth of oil and oil field equipment.[16] He pled guilty to wire fraud and mail fraud and as of 2024 was serving a twenty-year sentence in a federal penitentiary.

I talked about our trip down the Creek County back roads with an oil woman who pursues oil leases in the area. She always carries a gun on these excursions.

"Still Crook County," she said.

THE STATE OF MAGICAL THINKING

The natural resource curse has hit hardest in places with rich petroleum deposits. The discovery and exploitation of oil and gas reserves leads to a great windfall of wealth. One influential political science book labeled Venezuela "the magical state," with a heavy dose of irony and sustained criticism of the nation's dependency on such a fickle commodity.[17] No such irony accompanies the painting *The Magic of Petroleum* hanging in the Oklahoma state capitol. Oil is Oklahoma's primary mover and its lifeblood. But petro-states also experience higher average rates of violence, corruption, inequality, and poor health outcomes than other states. The problem has intrigued political scientists and economists for years: Why do places blessed with oil seem to be cursed with autocracy and war? People ask the question about Russia and Venezuela, but one could ask the same question of the state of Oklahoma, a place still awash in oil money but near the bottom in national rankings in health, well-being, and education. The most recent *U.S. News & World Report* ranking of education and health care put Oklahoma at forty-eighth out of fifty states. Yet Oklahoma's natural resources create billionaires. Case in point is the fracking billionaire Aubrey McClendon. McClendon, like Tom Slick and Charles Page before him, was an independent oilman who took risky bets to grow his company into a major natural gas producer, eventually rivaling ExxonMobil. In 2016, McClendon was indicted on federal conspiracy charges for artificially suppressing gas prices and rigging what were supposed to be competitive bids for land.[18]

McClendon smashed his Chevy Tahoe into an overpass in Oklahoma City the day after the indictment. The fracking king died almost instantly. Perhaps the resource curse filters down into individuals, like McClendon and several generations of Russell Cobbs. As the fourth and last in this line, I'm trying to lift this curse. Maybe the power and wealth derived from oil money led to a delusion of mastery that poisoned us psychologically, as well as societally. The reality of the climate crisis requires that we understand, for the first time since the discovery of oil in Oklahoma, that we will eventually have to transition to a life without oil.

I drove back to the Tommy Atkins allotment last summer. I needed to see, feel, and smell the place under the radiance of the Oklahoma sun in July. Mills's Sno Cone stand had been torn down, but the bullet-riddled oil sign from Petco was still there. Walking around Tommy's allotment in the hundred-plus-degree heat, I realized his story was not simply about a mysterious and possibly fictional kid, an oil fortune, and a Janus-faced oilman. It was a story about bloodlines, about identity, about our connection to the land and the future of energy. Our planet was on fire and yet my people—white Oklahomans, especially those working in oil and gas—still understood the combustion of carbon to be some sort of God-given miracle. When the price of oil declined in 2016, the governor of Oklahoma, Mary Fallin, called for an official statewide day of prayer for prices to rise. She left office in 2019 as one of the nation's most unpopular governors. Her successor, Kevin Stitt, tried to distance himself from Fallin, but he has upheld the tradition of the annual Oilfield Prayer Day.

Understanding the story of Tommy Atkins would help me understand how we got here in the first place. It was an infuriating story, but it was also one hell of a wild ride.

CHAPTER 1

GROWING UP IN THE TERRITORY
WITH MINNIE ATKINS

When Minnie Atkins was born on July 4, 1866, the lands of her tribe, the Muscogee, lay in ruins. A civil war within the Civil War had ravaged Indian Territory, causing more loss of life and property per capita than perhaps anywhere else, including Virginia. Her mother and father, Mary Jane Davis Atkins and Thomas Atkins, had already lived through the trauma of Removal on the Trail of Tears, what the Mvskoke called the *nene estemerkv*, the Road of Misery. Thomas's family came from the ancient Muscogee town of Coweta on the Chattahoochee River, on the border of present-day Alabama and Georgia.

Before Removal, Muscogee towns (*etvlwv*, pronounced DUL-wuh) were divided into white and red towns, white associated with peace, red associated with war. Coweta was a red town affiliated with the "Lower Creek" towns on the Chattahoochee River, where English traders intermarried with women connected to Muscogee leadership. "Upper Creek" towns, those farther away from the coasts and colonial influence, rejected the Lower Creek accommodation to European culture—especially Christianity and private property. The colonial powers of Spain, England, and, later, the United States, found ways to insert themselves into Muscogee affairs through intermarriage. A leader of the Lower Creeks, William McIntosh, was a prime example. His father was a Scottish émigré to the colonies who married a Mvskoke woman; the US Army appointed him as a general for his service in various Indian Wars.

McIntosh signed a treaty with the United States in 1825 that is still remembered as an act of treachery. The Second Treaty of Indian

Springs enriched McIntosh by ceding the Muscogees' title to their lands in Georgia, while carving out an exception for McIntosh to retain his own land and slaves. The treaty also provided for the removal of Muscogee people to Oklahoma.

Opothleyahola, the most respected Upper Creek leader, warned McIntosh against signing the treaty without the approval of the Creek National Council. "My friend," Opothleyahola said, "You are about to sell our country; I warn you of the danger."[1]

McIntosh had a deep familial connection to wealthy Georgia land-owners, including Governor George Troup, who was determined to remove Indigenous people from the state. McIntosh's rank of general was bestowed on him by the United States, not the Creek National Council, and many Muscogee warriors viewed him as a traitor. A Muscogee force known as the Law Menders descended on him, executing McIntosh and torching his house as retribution exacted for the ultimate treason. Although the federal government revoked McIntosh's 1825 treaty and signed a new one, the die was cast. Muscogee people were urged to "voluntarily" remove to Indian Territory or be hounded and terrorized by the waves of white settlers pouring into their lands.

McIntosh's son, Chilly McIntosh, made several trips between the Southeast and Indian Territory (Oklahoma). Several hundred Muscogees left Georgia during this voluntary phase. Thomas Atkins was born during this time, before Removal was forced at the point of a bayonet.

Thomas was born in Indian Springs in Georgia in 1828, but probably left his family's ancestral land as a baby. Lower Creeks took up homesteads along the Arkansas and Three Forks Rivers, and some lived alongside the Texas Road. The road was established by Americans rushing into Mexican-held Texas, where they sought to take up lands. It was also used by the Five Tribes as a sort of north–south highway, and later became the basis for the first railroad in Indian Territory, the Missouri, Kansas, and Texas.

It was here, along the Texas Road (now US Highway 69), near the town of Checotah, Oklahoma, that one of many coincidences in this story emerges. The Atkins family's homestead lies on, or adjacent to, Honey Springs, where the bloodiest battle of the Civil War in Indian Territory took place. Checotah is also where my great-great-grandfather,

William Hogan, decided to ignore the restrictions on white settlement in Indian Territory and started raising cattle. Easy access to the Texas Road was undoubtedly part of his decision to become an illegal immigrant. Many years later, Hogan's granddaughter would be crowned "Queen of McIntosh County" for her lifetime of service to Checotah Public Schools. William McIntosh might have been a traitor, but his family name designated home for my mother's family.

We had Thanksgiving dinners in my grandmother's modest ranch-style house, a throwing distance from the Texas Road. I remember asking my mom's aunts and uncles why, of all the places in the world, the Hogans chose Checotah to settle down and raise a family.

No one had a good answer for me.

AFTER A TRAIL OF BLOOD ON ICE

At the beginning of the Civil War, as states throughout the country declared their loyalty either to the Union or the Confederacy, the Five Tribes—occupying neutral territory in what was not yet the state of Oklahoma—were courted as allies by both sides. Some tribes sided with the South due to ties of kinship, while others stayed loyal to the Union. Both the Union and the Confederacy gave the tribes false promises of protection, and in the end both sides wrought unparalleled destruction on Indian Territory.

The Muscogee chief sided with the Confederacy and much of the tribe followed him, though a large faction tried to remain neutral. Foes of the Confederacy were forced to flee the Territory. They became known as Muscogee loyalists and they rallied around the leader Opothleyahola, the same man who had warned McIntosh against signing away land in Georgia. The loyalists had no way to get supplies. They fought three battles in Indian Territory on their way to Fort Row, Kansas, where President Abraham Lincoln promised a refuge from the suffering. Confederate forces hounded them. They faced starvation and were forced to eat their dogs and ponies. It is estimated that one third of the Union loyalists fleeing to Kansas died along the way. It was a little-known tragedy dubbed the Trail of Blood on Ice. And once there, they found that the promised supplies had not arrived.[2]

Before the war, Thomas Atkins's family had probably lived in a log cabin with ample livestock and a farm on Elk Creek, a short distance from the Texas Road in Indian Territory. Thomas had been captain of the Lighthorse, the Muscogee Nation's police force, for Coweta Town, an elected law enforcement position that gave him power to evict intruders from the States, confiscate whiskey (it was illegal to import liquor into Indian Territory), and, if need be, execute murderers. His farm and homestead were destroyed during the Battle of Honey Springs. In the aftermath of the Civil War, displaced Muscogee families like the Atkinses asked the victorious Union for federal aid to rebuild their communities, but Washington wanted land concessions in return. Thomas returned to his homestead with a new wife, Mary Jane Davis Atkins, the last in a line of several wives and the mother of Minnie.

As Minnie's life began, representatives from her nation were arguing over a new treaty with US officials in Fort Smith, Arkansas. The US government approached these negotiations with little generosity, as they held that the Muscogee Nation had betrayed its prior treaties with the Union by siding with the Confederacy during the war.

Despite the fact that many Muscogees had remained loyal to the Union, men like Thomas Atkins served as an example of the government's case for abrogating the old treaties. At the beginning of the war, Atkins had signed up with the Confederacy's First Regiment, the Creek Mounted Volunteers, reaching the rank of second lieutenant. He may have felt compelled to do so by his father-in-law, Benjamin Marshall, one of the wealthiest men in the Territory and an owner of more than a hundred enslaved people of African descent. Thomas had married Marshall's daughter, Millie, before the outbreak of the war.

Benjamin Marshall was one of the key figures who had allied the Muscogee Nation with the Confederacy. A Confederate general from Arkansas, Albert Pike, had courted friendship with Marshall, reminding him that Washington had betrayed his tribe many times and that the Union was not to be trusted. Pike convinced Muscogee, Cherokee, Choctaw, Chickasaw, and Seminole leaders that their sovereignty as tribes would be more respected by a loose Southern confederacy than by an expansionist federal government in Washington. Pike said that if Indian Territory ever joined the Confederate states, it would be as an Indian-government polity.

"A WILD SORT OF FELLOW": THOMAS ATKINS
BEFORE AND AFTER THE CIVIL WAR

Ben Marshall was part of a small mixed-blood aristocracy that ran cattle and had business connections to New Orleans, London, and beyond. Some members of this aristocracy sent its children to missionary schools, adopted Christianity, and spoke English. People like Marshall also served as landlords to poor white laborers willing to take a chance on life in Indian Territory. During the Civil War, this elite had stood to benefit from trading with neighboring Confederate states like Arkansas and Texas. Contemporaries of Ben Marshall wrote that he was so rich, there was not a bank in the region with the capacity to insure his deposits. He preferred gold or silver to cash, building a business on the export of rice, cotton, corn, and enslaved people to other states. As Marshall fled to the safety of Texas during the war, he had his slaves bury gold bars in coffee tins along the Texas Road. To this day, treasure seekers turn off US 69 to look for Marshall's lost loot.[3]

In 1863, at the First Battle of Cabin Creek, Thomas Atkins fought Union forces in Cherokee Nation lands, near the town of Vinita in northeastern Oklahoma. Confederate forces from Texas combined with Cherokee and Creek Confederate soldiers to fight the Union's First Kansas Colored Infantry, widely considered to be the first battle in which free Blacks engaged in combat with whites and Native Americans. Some of Marshall's slaves had fled to Kansas, joined the Union, and then fought against their former enslaver and his troops, including, most likely, Lieutenant Atkins.

The Confederate forces lost that battle, but they regrouped, attacked Union soldiers and Native Union loyalists at the Second Battle of Cabin Creek, and emerged victorious. Atkins traveled far and wide during the war, and he probably fought in Arkansas as well as Indian Territory. As the Union solidified its control of land, however, Thomas's regiment retreated into Mexico, and he may have remained there for some time, for Minnie Atkins's birthplace is recorded as the border town of El Paso, Texas.

Thomas Atkins, then, was an example of the federal government's case that the Five Tribes had been "in a state of actual hostility to the United States."[4] Thomas went back to his old job as captain of the Lighthorse in Coweta Town and served in that position from the

1860s until his death in 1877. The job required him to be constantly on the move. Presbyterian missionaries called on him to confiscate liquor. Cattle bosses pushing herds from Texas to Kansas City relied on Atkins to find stolen livestock. There were ex-Confederate outlaws who hid out in the hills of Indian Territory after robbing banks in the States. White and Black intruders tried to take up lands. Atkins's Lighthorse men could bring criminals to justice in Creek Nation courts, or they could deport them to Arkansas, where "Hanging" Judge Parker awaited them. There are no photos of Thomas Atkins, but his son Richard remembered him as a tall, hulking man shaped by a history of various wars and battles. In his time off, Captain Atkins charmed several different women in different parts of Indian Territory. He fathered at least seven children by four or five women. He was, in the words of Principal Chief Pleasant Porter, "a wild sort of fellow."[5]

Before the Civil War, the Lighthorse had been called upon to hunt down enslaved people who had escaped. After the war, some formerly enslaved people became Lighthorse officers themselves. The fluid nature of race in Muscogee society had long caught the attention of white Southerners, who in the 1840s had often remarked on the sight of Black people enslaved by the Muscogees who nonetheless had their own plots of crops and well-maintained cabins. The clear-cut lines between Black and white worlds that existed in Anglo America were often blurred in Indian Country. Many Muscogee slaveholders were themselves of mixed white, Native, and Black ancestry, the descendants of enslaved people who had intermarried or been adopted into the tribe. Some of the tribe's most prominent chiefs and warriors were, to Anglo-American eyes, clearly Black.

The topic of slavery was every bit as contentious in Indian Territory as it was in the States. Postbellum, in 1866, the question of what status to give newly freed Black people in Indian Territory was central to the future of the Territory itself. Tribal leaders were uncertain how to proceed. If they gave freedpeople the same rights as other tribal nation citizens, the Territory could become a magnet for the formerly enslaved in the Confederate states—called State Blacks—a prospect that terrified the mixed-blood aristocracies of the Five Tribes. Their primary fear was a wave of migration into the Territory by State Blacks who had no connections to tribal towns and no knowledge of tribal languages. Some of the Afro-Indigenous people in Indian Territory also looked with suspicion upon the newcomers, whom they labeled *watchina* ("Blacks from the States"). The mixed-blood planter class pushed to marginalize land claims by Black people.

In the end, the Muscogee Treaty of 1866 between the tribe and the federal government gave equal citizenship to the tribe's members who were formerly enslaved people. While Southern states imposed Black Codes that severely limited the freedoms of people of African ancestry, the Muscogee Nation adopted radically inclusive policies guaranteeing "an equal interest in the soil," meaning that enrolled freedpeople would, like Creeks by blood, be entitled to payments from the federal government. The formerly enslaved seemed to be on the road to true equality, but social and economic ties to the Old South made racism a stubborn problem. When the Dawes Commission arrived in Indian Territory, some thirty years after the end of the war, it would create two separate classifications for citizens of the Muscogee Nation: Indians-by-blood and freedmen.

The Atkins family was a microcosm of these racial, colonial, and tribal contradictions: Some members of the family had been enslaved themselves, while others had been Confederate soldiers. Some disavowed any African blood, while others happily intermarried with Black people. One branch of the family in Wagoner was headed by Dick Atkins, a Black man who claimed to be a son of Thomas Atkins. The racial mixtures, the complicated webs of tribal towns, Southern colonial conventions, and the legacy of slavery are not mere curiosities or footnotes to this story. They are at the heart of claims to land and wealth.

THE INTRUDERS: A NEW SOCIETY EMERGES IN INDIAN TERRITORY

As I was researching the story of the Atkins family, I realized I was wading into some deeply troubling truths. Eli Grayson was right—I had stepped into some deep shit. Since the rise of the Black Lives Matter movement, there has been a push, rightly, to remove Confederate monuments and debunk the heroic mythologies of Confederate soldiers and officers. A corresponding movement among Native Americans, Landback, has prioritized Indigenous histories and Indigenous views of US history. The Tommy Atkins story led me unwittingly into an awkward place where these two social justice movements collided in the historical record: where a slave-owning faction of an Indigenous nation found its lands being occupied by people who had suffered under slavery.

Minnie Atkins was the child of Thomas Atkins and his last wife, Mary Jane Davis. Davis's tribal town, her *etvlwv*, was Euchee Town. *Etvlwv* were the basic political and ceremonial units of Mvskoke society. The Muscogee Nation has always been a political arrangement that holds separate towns together for a greater collective good. Belonging to a *etvlwv* followed a person as they moved around; so, for example, Mary Jane Davis continued to belong to Euchee Town even though she lived far from the main population centers of Euchee people, near the town of Sapulpa. Because Muscogee tribal town identities proceed matrilineally, Davis passed down her Euchee identity to the three children she had with Thomas: Nancy, Lee, and Minnie.

Minnie grew up during a time in which an industrializing American economy—one based on railroads, coal, and private ownership of land—imposed itself on Muscogee society. In 1866 the US government forced a land concession to build two railroads through Indian Territory. Not until 1870, however, did the Missouri, Kansas, and Texas Railway Company start laying tracks.

The Atkins family watched as the MK&T—referred to as the Katy—started laying tracks close to their homestead on Elk Creek, bringing in more unauthorized white settlers from the States. The settlers were known in Indian Territory as "intruders" and were often treated as such by the Lighthorse. They could be fined or deported, but there were so many of them that the Lighthorse often relied on federal marshals—men like the famous Bass Reeves—to help out.

Even then, the settlers were undaunted. In nearby Oklahoma Territory, a group of settlers known as Boomers illegally formed a town on the site of present-day Oklahoma City in 1880. They were evicted by federal troops. A low-grade war dragged on between these Boomers and federal troops until 1885, when they were once again expelled.[6]

The coming of an east–west railway in 1886, the Santa Fe Railway, changed the calculation in Oklahoma Territory. The lawbreaking Boomers became legal pioneers in "unassigned lands" in the territory. Meanwhile, federal officials also wanted to open Indian Territory to mission schools and to legal, limited white settlement. In 1893, US government officials hinted that they might attempt to privatize the land in Indian Territory by allotting it to individual members of the tribes.

Allotment, most Muscogee leaders agreed, was a bridge too far. If land was commodified, whites would find a way to obtain it by hook or by crook. At the time, US citizens were still banned from owning land in Indian Territory. Still, many poor whites from the South took their chances, hoping that the federal government would one day grant them title to their homesteads, which were in most cases squats on Native land. Some of these settlers managed to get themselves adopted into one of the Five Tribes, either by intermarriage or by more ethically dubious means. Among this class of white settlers to filter into the Muscogee Nation were my maternal great-great-grandparents, who built a two-room house on the outskirts of Checotah, about a five-minute drive from the Atkinses' homestead. The Hogans had most likely sharecropped on land owned by a Muscogee allottee and bided their time until "surplus land" became available for sale.

CHAPTER 2

"INTO THE LIGHT BEFORE"

Minnie Atkins at Tullahassee and Carlisle

Out of the darkness behind us
Into the light before
Out from the long separation
In by the open door

—"COMRADES ALL,"
Carlisle Indian Industrial School song

Thomas Atkins and Mary Jane Davis Atkins died a year apart, in 1877 and 1878, most likely from smallpox or cholera. This left Minnie, Nancy, and Lee as orphans. Although the children had a large extended family through their father's previous marriages, their relationship with their half-siblings had a troubled backstory. The oldest half brother, Richard "Lump" Adkins—who said he got his nickname because "my mother used to call me a lump of sugar"—took after their father's way of life, roaming through Texas and Indian Territory as a cowboy and a lawman. Lump married a white woman from Texas, Sallie Ashworth. Their daughter, Katie, and her husband, Thomas Holden, became the legal guardians of Minnie, Nancy, and Lee.

When the Dawes Commission asked Lump why he spelled his name "Adkins" instead of "Atkins," he said he taught himself to spell it that way. He insisted on the D replacing the T. This choice was probably made to distinguish himself from another Richard—"Dick"—Atkins in the Muscogee Nation. The two Richards had the same father, Thomas Atkins. The Richards' mothers, however, were from entirely different social classes. Dick's mother was an enslaved woman born in Indian Territory and sold to a Missouri slaver shortly before the Civil War. Lump's mother was the daughter of Chief Benjamin Marshall, perhaps the richest man in Indian Territory. The prospect that Thomas Atkins had two sons named Richard, one with a slave master's daughter and the other with one of his slaves, was a scandalous theory even before oil money became the central concern of the Tommy Atkins affair.

The Dawes Commission originally rejected Dick's and his children's enrollment in the Muscogee Nation based, in part, on Lump's disavowal of his Black family. As we'll see, however, Dick was determined to establish his identity as a "Creek by blood," a bona fide citizen of the Muscogee Nation. A single ruling by the Dawes Commission was not going to stop him.

THE TULLAHASSEE MISSION SCHOOL EXPERIMENT

In any case, Thomas Holden chafed at the burden of raising teenagers from this curious family. In 1879, Holden succeeded in placing Minnie as a boarding student in the nearby Tullahassee Mission School. She was twelve or thirteen years old. Lee, having turned eighteen around the time of his mother's death, set out to become a lawman like his father. Indian Territory, plagued as it was by ex-Confederate raiders, bandits, bootleggers, cattle thieves, and civil strife, provided a lot of work for men like Lee. Nancy Atkins went through life with vision impairment, living in dire poverty. She was cast aside as "an incompetent" when her younger sister moved on to the Tullahassee Mission School.

Christian missionaries had begun to establish schools in Indian Territory shortly after Removal. The most prominent of these schools was the Tullahassee Mission School, a school for boys and girls built in 1848 and run with the support of the Muscogee National Council, the national government of the Muscogee people. Although Tullahassee is placed in the category of "Indian boarding school," it had a distinct history. To begin with, it was subject to the laws and customs of the Muscogee Nation, not to the whims of its white administrators.

The building was a handsome three-story brick building that could accommodate around eighty students, and the school was run by a South Carolina–born Presbyterian pastor named Robert Loughridge, who embraced bilingual Mvskoke-English education. Well-to-do Muscogee families, even those who opposed Christianity, sought to place their children in the school. The balance of power at the Tullahassee

Mission School was tipped toward Muscogee leaders, many of whom put restrictions on how Christianity was taught. Upper Creek leaders wanted a total ban on all preaching at the school, but Loughridge sought an accommodation that would allow for some Christian education, as well as Mvskoke language, games, and cultural teachings.

Around 1850, Loughridge hired a young seminarian from New York, William Schenck Robertson, to teach the boys. Robertson had earned a master's degree in theology and was full of idealistic notions of what Indigenous education should look like. Once in Indian Territory, the young teacher fell in love with a missionary's daughter, Ann Eliza Worcester, and took her to live at the Tullahassee Mission School as they continued to expand it. Their daughter, Alice Mary Robertson, was born in 1854. When she grew up, she would go on to run the school alongside her father.

Visitors at the time described the school as something of an idyll. The building was divided in half for boys and girls, with a wide staircase and "airy and commodious rooms on either side in each department." A visitor, Augustus Ward Loomis, commented that "the orchard, garden, workshop, tool-room, and stables are near; and the farm not far off." Down the road was "a frame building for a chapel, and a little distance from this, the Mission burying ground, over which many ancient oaks wave their branches in solemn cadence with the moaning winds." The cemetery, Loomis wrote, contained the remains of students as well as "some who once were missionaries in that field, but are now far away, [who] often return thither in imagination, for there is dust in that ground that is precious to them."[1]

Robertson and Loughridge divided the school day up into blocks of time for manual labor, theology, reading, and writing. Loughridge became an adept fundraiser for Indian education among liberals back East, while also placating many Muscogee leaders who saw him as the leading edge of another wave of white invaders. The issue of religion continued to be a source of strife. Traditionalist Creeks wanted Christianity removed from the curriculum, whereas progressives wanted proselytizing to take place. While many militaristic American men still sought the extermination of Native Americans, men like Loughridge used the language of Christian paternalism to encourage wealthy donors to support the mission of assimilation and evangelization.

ENTER MISS ALICE

Around the time that Minnie Atkins arrived at Tullahassee, Alice Robertson, then twenty-eight, was returning to the school after quitting her job as a clerk at the Bureau of Indian Affairs in Washington, DC. Robertson felt more at home among the wild turkeys and cornfields of Indian Territory than in the modern city. She was frustrated with the disconnect between Indian policy at the capital and the reality on the ground. When she returned to Tullahassee, she became a teacher and mentor to Minnie.

A photo at the time shows Minnie, the largest of six Muscogee girls, sitting in the middle of her classmates, her face locked in intense concentration. Minnie wears a tight dress and black bow tie, while three younger girls around her wear simple calico aprons. Sitting on the ground below Minnie is Robertson, her almost-white hair pulled back into a bun. Robertson gazes quizzically off to her left and rests her right elbow in Minnie's lap. Minnie's right hand appears to be curled up into a nervous fist while her left arm grazes Robertson's back. Robertson, though still in her twenties, already looks like an elderly matron. Atkins's full face and somewhat wary smile register as opposites to Robertson's bony and severe features.

Robertson was a walking contradiction. One of the most prominent public women in Oklahoma, she opposed women's right to vote. She was fluent in Mvskoke, but in 1881 she was recruited to be secretary for a new Indian boarding school in Carlisle, Pennsylvania, that punished the speaking of Indigenous languages. The Carlisle school was the brainchild of Captain Richard Henry Pratt, who served as the school's superintendent. Whereas at Tullahassee, Robertson had had to temper her missionary zeal with the Muscogees' policies against proselytizing, Pratt's school waged an all-out assault on Indigenous language, culture, and spirituality, using military discipline to forge Native youth into what he called "model citizens."[2] Pratt envisioned himself as a savior of Native Americans at a time when talk of Indigenous extinction was rampant. If some veterans of the Indian Wars saw their former foes as irredeemable savages to be destroyed, Pratt thought of himself as an educator who was saving the Indian from extermination. However, his school's insistence on punishing all expressions of Indigenous culture amounted to another front in a cultural genocide.

If this militaristic approach troubled Robertson, she did not admit it in any letters. She stated that she hoped to bring a cohort of Muscogee students to Carlisle. She lobbied her boss to take on at least twenty-five Muscogee students, but Pratt was more interested in educating "wild Indians" than students from the Five "Civilized" Tribes. Robertson's devotion to Mvskoke-English bilingualism at Tullahassee and the English-only approach she enforced at Carlisle are only understandable in the context of the ideology of "the true cult of womanhood," an anti-feminist movement of the time. As a woman devoted to upholding patriarchy, Robertson must have believed she had a duty to defer to Pratt.[3]

As Christmas of 1880 approached, the boys at Tullahassee cut down a tree and decorated it with presents sent from benefactors back East. The weather turned bitterly cold and all the stoves and fireplaces in the building were lit. A defect in the chimney led to a fire breaking out on the third floor during the night. Students could do little to stop the fire. They could only run up and down the stairs, trying to preserve vital items that would guard them against cold and hunger once the fire was over. Alice Robertson's father vowed to rebuild the school, but his efforts led him to exhaustion, and he died a year after the fire.[4]

Alice Robertson pressured Captain Pratt to accept some of Tullahassee's orphan students at Carlisle. Robertson believed that this group would become shining lights for Christian education among Native Americans. She also sincerely believed that they would show the rest of the nation that they were as bright and as capable as white Americans. Pratt initially resisted. Most of the Lower Creek children from Tullahassee already had exposure to English, Christianity, and American capitalist values. They would not dramatize the public relations narrative of assimilation and Americanization the way children from Plains tribes did. But eventually Pratt gave in.

"GOOD WHOLESOME CIVILIZED LIFE": MUSCOGEE STUDENTS ARRIVE

At the time that I ran across Minnie Atkins's name in the Carlisle archives, I knew only two things about the school. One was Captain Pratt's chilling motto for Indian education: "Kill the Indian in him, and save the man." The other was that Jim Thorpe, a famed Native

American athlete and one of the greatest Oklahomans of all time, had cut his teeth with the Carlisle School's sports teams. My grandmother from Checotah spoke reverentially about Thorpe when I was growing up. He was simply the greatest athlete to grace the earth, she said, and it was only the racism of the Olympic committee that took back Thorpe's gold medals in 1912 for having played professional baseball. In 1911 Thorpe had led Carlisle in one of the biggest football upsets of all time, when the Pop Warner–coached Carlisle Indians defeated the Harvard Crimson (then a major football powerhouse) in front of twenty-five thousand fans in Cambridge, Massachusetts. I figured, somewhat naively, that any school that produced an athlete like Thorpe could not have been all that bad. I would later learn that Thorpe represented one extreme end of the Carlisle experience—the Native American athlete as celebrity and national hero. He and his teammates were treated to comfortable accommodations, travel, and good food, and Thorpe defended Carlisle's mission his whole life. At the other extreme were forced student "outings" in which children were farmed out to do agricultural and other labor and which resulted in conditions of virtual slavery and abuse, followed by severe discipline and disease at school.

Then there was Minnie Atkins, one of Alice Robertson's pets. At first, Minnie seemed destined to embody Robertson's maternal, anti-feminist stances. "Miss Alice" taught Minnie to cook, clean, sew, and pray. Robertson described herself to a reporter as "the conservative woman who would cook a good meal rather than meddle with politics." Just as Robertson could not be contained by her own ideology, neither would her pupil settle down to a simple life of domesticity.

Robertson's cohort of Muscogee students stood in contrast to other pupils, who came from Plains tribes like the Kiowa, Comanche, and Cheyenne that were still resisting Christianity and capitalism, fighting the encroachment of white settlers throughout the West. Pratt drilled the children night and day in a schedule regulated by hourly bells. Ex-students recalled being haunted by the bells years later. Every edition of the school newspaper featured the voice of an editorial persona extolling the patriotic and Christian virtues of the school's administration. The persona was called The-Man-on-the-Bandstand, an anonymous but all-seeing entity who could detect any rule-breaking. The-Man-on-the-Bandstand watched students' every move, ready to report any lapse in discipline. Some who have researched the columns believe that they were written by none other than Richard Henry Pratt, although editorial duties might have been shared among school officials.

Carlisle's buildings and infrastructure had originally served the military and thus had very tight quarters. Disease ran rampant through the barracks, and the school was woefully ill-equipped to deal with illness. Rather than treat the students on campus, the school preferred to send sick students back to Indian Country, and many died during the trip. Other students ran away or died by suicide.

Minnie Atkins's tenure at the school began with a thorough physical examination. The school doctor struggled to categorize the Muscogee students racially. Some, like Minnie's friend Sarah Elizabeth Crowell, were categorized as white. Minnie was given a clean bill of health, but she and the other Muscogees were immediately hit by homesickness. Even such model students as Ben Marshall—Minnie's cousin, the grandson of Chief Marshall—wrote that they wept daily. "When we came there was many of us cried," Marshall wrote. "I won't be ashamed to tell that I cried because I [k]now I was not the only one that cried, but we are getting all right now and I hope we will feel better and go to work and make some body of ourselves."[5]

Robertson guarded the Muscogee girls from the abuses that occurred against some of the girls from Plains tribes. Robertson condemned the physical abuse and exploitation of Native children, but only in private. Even as horror stories—suicide, sexual and physical abuse—emerged into public view, Robertson stayed quiet on the subject, forging ahead with her own career.[6] She later cultivated a friendship with Theodore Roosevelt and became a nationally recognized figure known for her opposition to alcohol, women's suffrage, and Bolshevism. At Carlisle, she put immense pressure on Atkins to conform to the standards of a Victorian lady. Following the dress code at Carlisle, Atkins wore a button-down black dress with white cuffs at the wrist. The sleeves and collar were impossibly tight, as was the white scarf around her neck. Her black, wavy hair was plastered to her head. Atkins was part of a small group of Carlisle students who toured the country on a sort of propaganda campaign for Captain Pratt. Atkins wrote about a trip to Philadelphia for the *School News* in 1882. Nothing in her writing hints at the harsh conditions at Carlisle, but there is something stilted and forced as she writes about staying with two Philadelphia benefactors. Atkins wrote that the girls "were all treated well by the kind white people," who took them to a parade and a ride on a steamboat.

Atkins began to fall behind her Muscogee classmates academically around 1882 or 1883. She excelled, however, in cooking and dressmaking. Atkins sewed a shirt for Captain Pratt's son, who proudly wore it on a trip to Boston. She was sent on various "outings" to Pennsylvania families to work as a domestic servant. The outings had the objective of Americanizing the students, and Pratt vowed that the host families should treat them like members of their household. Work as a maid or cook would, in the thinking of the time, continue the assimilation process into Christianity, capitalism, and mainstream America. Pratt wrote that a Carlisle-sponsored outing "brings the Indian youth directly in contact with good wholesome civilized life and they absorb it rapidly and it absorbs them and they become a part of it."[7] It was all a part of a larger project of what Pratt called an intentional "treason to the tribe" and a faithfulness to the nation.

On these outings, Carlisle students worked for a nominal wage, and what money they did make was controlled by school officials. Reports emerged of school officials embezzling these funds, or students never being compensated for their labor.

On July 8, 1884, Minnie Atkins left Carlisle for good. Her skills as a dressmaker and a cook had caught the attention of a teacher named Mary Hyde, whose brother, George, was seeking a live-in housekeeper and cook. George Hyde was a wealthy banker in Leavenworth, Kansas, and Mary Hyde traveled with Minnie to take her to his home. Atkins never graduated from Carlisle, but few students ever did. In fact, graduation ceremonies were not held until 1890, and even then, most students were sent out to work before formal completion of school.[8] It is impossible to know what Minnie Atkins thought about quitting school to work in Kansas. Her mentor, Alice Robertson, approved. She viewed the mission of Carlisle as dovetailing with her other mission, that of supporting "the cult of true womanhood"—piety, purity, domesticity, and submissiveness in women and girls. As Minnie moved from Carlisle to Leavenworth, her tolerance for these "virtues" of womanhood would face an excruciating test.[9]

EXIT SARAH ELIZABETH CROWELL.
ENTER BETTIE RASPBERRY.

Some of Minnie's classmates from Carlisle found "the cult of true womanhood" to be another tool of oppression. These girls were eager to strike out on their own and forge their own identities in Indian Territory. A notable person in this regard was Sarah Elizabeth Crowell, from the tribal town of Hekachka. Crowell, known as Bettie, entered Carlisle with Minnie as part of the Muscogee cohort in 1881.

Bettie cut an interesting figure around Carlisle. At four feet eleven inches, she was the smallest of the Muscogee girls and one of the few whose race was listed as white. Her father was a white businessman from Muskogee, later arrested for stealing cattle. Bettie inherited his light skin and European features. Robertson praised Bettie as a student, and she excelled academically. She wrote for the Carlisle student newspaper and went on frequent outings designed to impress white benefactors.

According to one source, Bettie was part of the first couple to be formally married within the boundaries of Tulsa in 1886, when she exchanged vows with William J. Mann.[10] The wedding was a cause for celebration back at the Pennsylvania school. Carlisle officials sent silver spoons and a tablecloth to Indian Territory and celebrated the event in the Carlisle newspaper. Bettie's embrace of Robertson's values—purity, piety, and submissiveness—came to a definitive end in 1904 when she filed for divorce on the grounds of "extreme cruelty" by her husband. "Mann frequently drew a gun on her and threatened to shoot her if she failed to do as he desired," *The Oklahoman* reported in 1904. William Mann was later sued by a Native American for whom he served as a guardian.

Freed from the abuse of her husband, Bettie married again, to a man named Cyrus Raspberry who later became a leader of a group known around the state as the "Raspberry Gang." The Raspberrys were in and out of prison for charges ranging from forgery to larceny to bootlegging. Bettie Raspberry later became an important lynchpin in criminal conspiracies allowing oilmen access to restricted Indian lands. She was "well known in the courts for years," by the time she met Charles Page.[11]

Bettie's specialization was impersonation and forgery, but she once robbed a group of sixty Bulgarian laborers.[12] As someone who could walk and talk in two worlds, she dissimulated and lied for the right price. Guardians paid her to sign documents for other people. She was arrested many times, but her connections to the guardianship racket meant that she was let out early. It was in her capacity as a con artist for hire that she would once again encounter her Carlisle friend, Minnie Atkins, many years later.

Before we get to Bettie and Minnie's reunion, however, we first need to follow Minnie Atkins's move to Leavenworth in the summer of 1884, where the Tommy Atkins saga truly begins.

— CHAPTER 3 —

BECOMING A LADY

Minnie Lights Out for the West

George Hyde was the president of the German Bank of Leavenworth, Kansas, a town that had a high regard for itself when it welcomed Minnie Atkins in the summer of 1884. A city directory at the time boasted that "Leavenworth is the largest, most populous and wealthy city in the state." To the outside world, however, Leavenworth had a reputation as a frontier town with a seedy underworld of sex workers, adventurers, gamblers, and ex-cons. Town leaders like George Hyde wanted to change that image. The directory proclaimed it to be "one of the loveliest spots, both by nature and art, belonging to the United States in the west."

When Mary Hyde and Minnie Atkins arrived in Leavenworth, Minnie had recently turned eighteen. George Hyde wrote to Captain Pratt, "Minnie Atkins arrived safely yesterday and we are much pleased with her appearance. Will be pleased to report further after we are better acquainted."[1]

The Hydes provided Minnie with a bedroom next to the kitchen. The quarters were cramped, and Minnie soon found herself overwhelmed with domestic duties and a budding rivalry with the Hydes' oldest daughter, Cornelia (who was, by her own account, fully grown by the time Minnie moved in). Minnie chafed under the demands of Mrs. Hyde, who treated her not as a shining model of Indian education and pure womanly virtue but as a lowly servant, referring to her as a "buxom, untrained Indian."[2]

Almost immediately Minnie started looking around for another job. She had been taught by Miss Alice that, with the right education and manners, she would become a lady, worthy of property, citizenship, and the respect of white people. Her treatment at the hands of the

Hydes, then, must have registered as a disappointment. They gave her no space to meet with friends and insisted she come and go through the servants' entrance. On a day off, Minnie met another domestic servant who worked down the street: Sadie Ross, a Black Cherokee girl fifteen or sixteen years of age. Like Minnie's, Sadie's life had taken a twisted path from Indian Territory to Leavenworth. Sadie never held back in her judgment. She thought the Hydes treated Minnie poorly, so she invited Minnie to spend time at her house.

Sadie's boss allowed her a degree of freedom Minnie lacked. "I had a better house for her to come to," Ross later stated. "I had a better way for her to come to my place, because my place had a big yard and a big porch and we could talk there all we wanted to, it wasn't so convenient at the Hydes'."[3]

After a few weeks, Atkins mentioned a love interest, a soldier at Fort Leavenworth named Charles Peterkin. Peterkin was a twenty-seven-year-old white man originally from Barbados who had immigrated to Massachusetts as a child. In 1881, Peterkin enlisted in the Eighteenth Regiment of the US Army. He was deployed to Montana, where he first served as a clerk, then as a solider later reaching the rank of corporal. He was subsequently sent to Fort Clark, Texas, to counter what the army called "Indian depredations" from Mexico. In those years after the Civil War, Anglo settlers had established ranches in an area of southern Texas previously inhabited by the Comanches. Mexico, which hoped to retake lands they felt had been illegally seized in the Mexican-American War, offered sanctuary to displaced Comanches, Lipans, and Kickapoos, as well as a base from which to conduct raids to seize the Anglos' cattle, horses, and goods. The ranchers wrote angry letters to Washington and complained that the federal government was not protecting the southern border. They said they would take matters into their own hands if the army did not act.

The result was a series of skirmishes between the United States and the Lipan and Kickapoo peoples that dragged on until 1882. The African-Seminole scouts known as Buffalo Soldiers were an integral part of this conflict, and when Peterkin served with them, he most likely heard them speaking Mvskoke, the same language spoken by Minnie Atkins. It was after this conflict in Texas that Charles met Minnie.

Minnie quit the Hydes and on October 14, 1884, began a new job for a man named Herbert Grodevant. Grodevant held none of the pretensions about Leavenworth's "being one of the loveliest spots, both by nature and art" in the United States. He was a manager of a massive construction project around Fort Leavenworth that in 1875 became one of the nation's most infamous public institutions, the United States Disciplinary Barracks. The USDB, often referred to simply as Leavenworth, is to this day the only maximum-security military prison in the nation. Congress ordered its construction in 1873, but the biggest portion of it, The Castle, was part of Grodevant's work in the 1880s. Most of the labor for the heavy brick, mortar, stone, and steel construction was performed by the prisoners themselves.[4]

There was an old saying around Leavenworth: the routine of an inmate was nine hours a day of "pounding big rocks into little rocks." With little incentive for the inmates to complete the project, construction on The Castle went slowly.

Life with the Grodevants held none of the sophistication of the Hyde home, but Minnie Atkins seemed much more at peace with her new employer. No longer did Minnie have to have her hair coiffed to Victorian standards. Now she wore it in a traditional Indigenous style, in two long braids down her back. She wore loose-fitting and comfortable dresses and aprons, often with Indigenous design patterns. Gone were the days of impossibly tight sleeves and bodices. The roomy dresses led some people to suspect Minnie was pregnant shortly after leaving the Hydes.[5] Emily Ripley, a friend of the Grodevants, was pregnant at the same time. Called to testify about Minnie much later, Ripley broke down in tears. Her child had died in infancy, and the whole time in Fort Leavenworth had been very difficult for her. Ripley composed herself and recalled a woman she referred to as "Indian Minnie," a large woman with two long braids of black hair that she wore with simple servant's clothes. There was an odd exchange with lawyers about whether Minnie's belly was high or low. Minnie had inherited a large physical stature from her father, but thirty years after the birth of "Tommy," there was a lack of clarity about whether her size was attributable to pregnancy or not.

Whereas Mrs. Hyde had rarely set foot in the kitchen, Mrs. Grodevant often had meals there, inviting other women over to play cards and drink tea. Mrs. Grodevant also kept meticulous records, demonstrating that Minnie worked at their house from October 1884 until September 15, 1885, with one notable gap: two weeks during July 1885.

After Minnie left the Grodevants, she lived with Charles Peterkin for seven months at Fort Leavenworth. During this time, they became common law spouses. Minnie found work around town cooking, cleaning, and mending for various families. She worked for a man only identified as "a rich Jew" by all parties. By the end of 1885, it was clear to everyone that Minnie was pregnant, and Charles was assumed to be the father. As her due date approached, Minnie moved into the house of a midwife. Peterkin contacted a Catholic priest, Father Hall, hoping to have the child christened.

Minnie gave birth to a boy on July 31, 1886. This child was christened Robert Lee Peterkin by Father Hall, an homage to Minnie's brother, Lee. Charles surprised the priest by stating that he was not the father but that he intended to raise Robert Lee as his own son.

There was silence around the true father's identity. Minnie forever refused to say who the father was, as did the loquacious Sadie Ross James. I asked my research team—Apollonia, Gina, and Allison—about the weird gap in the biography. All of them suspected the same thing. For there to be such complete silence around the paternity of this child, he was probably the product of rape by a powerful white man whom other people were afraid to name. It seems entirely possible to me that the father was one of her well-to-do white employers.

MINNIE'S "INCESSANT TOIL"

Robert Lee Peterkin died on August 16, 1886, when he was less than three weeks old. A death certificate from the Leavenworth undertaker attested to his burial at Mount Muncie Cemetery in nearby Lansing, Kansas.[6] In 1888, Charles Peterkin was reassigned to Fort Logan, Colorado, and Minnie went with him. They were formally married that year and moved into a small house in a town next to the fort, which is now part of the Denver metro area.

Minnie cooked and cleaned for white families while Peterkin prepared for deployment, either farther west or possibly overseas. The following year they had a second child, a girl, whom they named Alice. One can only suspect that this was a tribute to Miss Alice, the closest thing to a mother figure Minnie had after her own mother's death. Tragically, Alice Mable Peterkin, like her older brother, Robert Lee, died in infancy. Unlike Minnie's other children, Alice was never forgotten. She was the first person buried at Fort Logan National Cemetery in 1890, and a photograph from years later shows an army band member playing taps beside Alice's grave.[7] A year after the death of Alice Mable, Charles Peterkin was deployed to Texas, most likely in response to a dispute along the Mexican border.

Minnie decided to stay in Fort Logan. In 1890, she gave birth to a boy who was named after Charles Peterkin but who adopted a different last name. This boy grew up to be known as Charley Harrison; a butcher from nearby Logantown named George Harrison (sometimes called George Harris) had become Minnie's boyfriend. It was said around Fort Logan that George was either part Native American or part Mexican. Together, the couple had a boy named Harvey Harrison, born in 1891. These children survived the perils of infancy and spent their early years at Fort Logan with their mother. Charley and Harvey were close in age, but quite different in physical appearance, and only learned later in life that they were from two different fathers. Charles Peterkin disappeared from Minnie's life after 1890, eventually moving back to his home state of Massachusetts.

In 1890, a "grass payment" was issued to all Muscogee citizens. The payments were derived from fees collected by the federal government for allowing US cattlemen to graze their livestock on lands of Native American nations as they moved toward railheads in the Midwest. Minnie, as a Muscogee citizen, was entitled to one of these payments. She intended to collect a payment for herself and her son Charley. (Harvey was not yet born.) That same year the federal government also agreed to pay Muscogee citizens "equalization payments" for the land that the US had seized from them after the Civil War. The feds issued a check for approximately $2 million to the Muscogee treasury, an amount based on an appraisal of the land that was less than its actual value. To disburse this money to its citizens in the form of "equalization payments," the Muscogee Nation called upon each of the forty-seven town kings to conduct a census of his town.

The English translation of the Mvskoke word *micco* or *mekko* was rendered as "king" or "chief," but neither of those titles quite captured the cultural context. The *micco* (town king) is not an absolute leader the way a king is, but he commanded respect from other members of a certain grounds, or tribal town. Universal respect for *miccos*, Apollonia told me, was a part of Mvskoke culture. *Miccos* were supposed to be recognized for their wisdom, compassion, and ability to achieve consensus without dispute. They were not elected but rather chosen by consensus.

The magical power of oil wealth, however, had little respect for traditional ways and challenged the benevolent hegemony of at least one important *micco*: Samuel W. Brown.[8] Brown essentially had veto power over who was listed as Euchee. The Euchee town king at the time was Noah Gregory. Gregory may have been recognized as the town king, but Brown considered himself to be the hereditary chief of the Euchee (or Yuchi) people. Brown put together a provisional list of the Euchees in a red notebook he carried around at all times.

Euchees speak a language unrelated to Mvskoke, and they have their own traditions. Some Euchees have sought an independent status as a federally recognized Indian tribe on their own. To make matters more complicated, some Euchees did not recognize Brown as hereditary chief. They doubted that Brown was who he said he was, believing that he was in fact the illegitimate child of the Texas colonist Sam Houston. The 1890 census was filled with errors at best and was downright corrupt at worst. Still, this list would determine who was entitled to an equalization payment.

Minnie Atkins and her siblings, born to a Euchee mother, were considered Euchees. At the time, Minnie's brother Lee was still in Checotah, so he was easy to account for. Lee wanted to become a deputy federal marshal, a lawman like his father. Minnie's sister Nancy had gone to live with her Black half-siblings in Wagoner. No one in the area was exactly sure what had happened to Minnie, however. Brown's secretary recorded her name as Mamie Atkins, along with a parenthetical remark that she had two children, Thomas and Mary. It is unclear where the names Thomas and Mary originated. Since Minnie could not be located to clear up matters, "Mamie" and the two names listed as her children were earmarked for payments of $29 apiece. In reality, Minnie had but one living child at the time, Charley.

The two payments amounted to close to two thousand dollars in 2024 money—not a fortune, but a potential relief from what Minnie called her life of "incessant toil" (small stakes indeed compared to the riches generated by Tommy's land).

We do know that there was some talk of a young Thomas Atkins floating around somewhere in the Muscogee Nation, a Thomas who had been born to either Nancy Atkins or to her sister-in-law, Sally Atkins. Thus, this 1890 census, compiled as if in a game of telephone, was then passed up the chain to the Muscogee National Council. The council determined to do its best to distribute per capita annuity payments to all verified citizens.

With Minnie gone from Indian Territory and her location unknown, it was unclear who would collect the $87 that had been allocated to her household. Muscogee officials decided that Lee Atkins could take the payment and send it to her. It is unclear if Lee ever tried to find his sister. By 1891, however, Minnie had heard about the equalization payments herself, and sought to claim hers and her children's. (By now Harvey had been born.) Minnie still had contact information for her old teacher, Alice Robertson, whose sister Augusta was now married to a Muscogee Nation judge named N. B. Moore.

By this time, Alice Robertson had attained almost celebrity status as one of the nation's preeminent upholders of "the cult of true woman-hood." She had departed from the Carlisle model of education to focus on a unique brand of maternalist education that she had developed. She was a walking paradox, a powerful public figure whose main message was to reinforce patriarchal ideas about a woman's place in society—in the home. She had transformed a girl's school in Muskogee originally called Minerva Home into Henry Kendall College, which would later move to Tulsa to become the University of Tulsa. "Give me a nation of great mothers," Robertson said, "and I care not who the husbands be."[9]

It was at the University of Tulsa that I discovered, in Robertson's archive, the only preserved handwritten letter from Minnie Atkins. Minnie wrote to Judge Moore, trying to get him to help her get her money back. On June 2, 1891, Minnie wrote to Robertson, appealing to her maternalism by noting that she was raising two baby boys on her own: "I support myself as I have always had to do by my labor and any assistance of this kind would not only be a great help to me but a partial relief from incessant toil."[10]

Minnie was also curious about what had happened to her parents' homestead on Elk Creek. She'd never received anything from their estate. She wrote: "I am fully aware that my parents left some property of what value I know not but I would like to know why I am excluded entirely from any benefit of it whatever if you can enlighten me on this point and tell me what to do I will be greatly indebted to you. I do not want you to say anything to Lee until you write me first and tell me where I stand. Yours Respect Minnie."[11]

The Minnie Atkins of this letter is a confident, capable writer who seems to understand that there is much more to her family's story than she has been told. Her words reveal a person suspicious of her patrons and determined to claim what is lawfully hers. It is unclear whether Robertson responded, but she did make sure the letter found its way into the hands of Judge N. B. Moore. Minnie, it became clear, would have to return to Indian Territory to clear up matters. She left Colorado behind and went back to the place of her youth.

Minnie's sister Nancy had not fared well in the years since Minnie had left for Carlisle. Nancy moved to the small town of Wagoner in 1889 when she was seventeen or eighteen. Wagoner was a railroad town on the Texas Road, close to the Cherokee Nation border. In 1891, she was arrested for stealing mail from her landlord. After a stint in prison, she was jailed again for drinking liquor—a crime in Indian Territory. Hers was a common tale. During this time, Native American and Black people in Indian Territory were frequently rounded up and imprisoned, often to enforce the payments of debts.

"A GRAVE INJUSTICE"

By the 1890s, whites had begun to outnumber Native Americans and Blacks in Indian Territory, but whites still had to work within a framework of Native sovereignty on a federal level. They did not do so willingly. White-run newspapers complained about their obligations to pay taxes to the Creek or Cherokee Nations. Such taxes were "a grave injustice," according to the editor of the *Muskogee Phoenix*. The editor admitted that many white settlers were becoming "embittered" by the fact that the tribal Lighthorse afforded them no protections, and they sought extralegal means to protect themselves.[12] Settlers used municipal police forces, Pinkerton agents, and railroad security agents as debt and contract enforcers to impose white supremacy in a society that had not—yet—recognized it as such. It is possible that Nancy Atkins found herself caught up in this rapidly changing world. By 1909 she had sold off her allotment.

Nancy spent a few years living in a tent behind a general store. At other times she lived among her Black half-siblings and cousins in Wagoner. Unlike old Thomas's other children, Nancy did not reject her Black family and was most likely living with her half sister, Chaney Trent, who had a homestead near Wagoner on the Verdigris River. Trent also helped maintain a family cemetery there called Knee-High Cemetery. The place is now a popular hunting and fishing spot that preserves no trace of the freedman cemetery.

Lee Atkins, meanwhile, retained much of their father Thomas's swagger. Lee had a reputation for settling conflicts with his fists, and he usually came out as the winner. In 1894 an Indian Territory judge in Fort Smith, Arkansas, appointed Lee as a deputy marshal. Fort Smith lay outside the boundaries of Indian Territory, but its courts oversaw federal business above the level of the tribes' jurisdiction. Federal deputies like Atkins had wide latitude to pursue and punish criminals in Indian Territory. Lee appeared to be following in his father's footsteps as a lawman with an intimidating reputation.

Despite Minnie's lack of trust in Lee, she went to join him in Checotah in 1894, her two young sons in tow. Minnie had accused Lee of stealing the grass payment but appears to have recovered it without any dispute. It may have been a simple misunderstanding based on the faulty information put down on the census by Sam Brown. Now that Minnie had some relief, she was pondering her next move.

Lee was called to a horse race outside town, in what may have been one of his first actions as a deputy marshal. Many people gambled on the horse races, and the event was fueled by illegal whiskey. One of the gambling bookmakers, Amos McIntosh, had some sort of personal conflict with Lee Atkins, and the two got into an argument. A fight broke out, and Deputy Marshal Lee Atkins decided to shut down the whole operation, angering McIntosh. McIntosh thought Lee should be in the business of arresting felons, not breaking up horse races. McIntosh told an associate that he aimed to kill Lee Atkins.

Later that evening, a relative of McIntosh's spotted Lee Atkins on the streets of Checotah. He warned Lee that Amos intended to shoot him. Lee brushed the warning off, saying he would settle the conflict in a fistfight without his badge. When Amos caught up with Lee in front of the Bumgarner Hotel, the two men swore at each other. They agreed to a brawl with no weapons, but then Lee called Amos a coward.

Amos drew a gun and shot Lee just above the ribs. Lee fell backwards. He shot again, this time penetrating the liver. Minnie caught word that her brother was bleeding out and rode on horseback into Checotah to help him. They got Lee to a hospital but there was nothing they could do. Minnie watched over him helplessly as he died the next morning. He was thirty-three years old.[13]

— CHAPTER 4 —

"MY NATION IS ABOUT TO DISAPPEAR"

Enrollment Begins

In 1895, with many names on the census still in dispute and the equalization payments still not remitted, Congress authorized the Muscogee town kings to compile another census. The federal government and the Muscogee Nation needed to resolve these disputed names before they could calculate the equalization payments.

In the five years since the first census, the number of tribal towns had shrunk from forty-seven to forty-four. The rapid and mostly illegal influx of white settlers into Indian Territory had disrupted the ancient tribal town structure, and as a result a few tribal towns had ceased to exist. They had "put down their fire," in the words of a Mvskoke elder: each tribal town had a sacred fire that had been carried on the Road of Misery from their traditional homelands to Oklahoma.

Once a tribal town was no longer viable to hold a ceremony, the fire was put out. It was a solemn affair, and one of the towns affected in that 1890-to-1895 interim was Cheyaha Town, which had accepted Dick Atkins as a citizen-by-blood in 1890. Cheyaha was known as a sister town of Coweta, where the name Thomas Atkins still held sway. In 1895, Dick Atkins and his children were stricken from the Creek rolls. All indications point to the family of the other Richard Adkins—the one born to Thomas and Millie Marshall—as orchestrators of the purge.

A Committee of Eighteen was appointed by the National Council to sort through names that had been contested. The process grew contentious, as some members moved to scratch names from certain towns, leading to other names being struck in response, all of this carried out with paper, pen, and scissors. Two hundred people were struck from the second census, leaving the payment at $14.40 per citizen, to be paid out in Okmulgee.

This time, Minnie was there in person to collect the money for herself and her children. George Harrison, the Fort Logan butcher, was out of her life. Before leaving Fort Logan, Minnie had begun to date a soldier named Harry Folk. Harry was ten years younger than Minnie and appears to have been a genuine, if somewhat naive, young man from a Pennsylvania farm who played in the Second Regiment Army Band. Harry was in no position to follow Minnie to Indian Territory. Harry's regiment was deployed to the Plains and had taken part in the Wounded Knee Massacre of 1890. It would soon be redeployed to Cuba during the Spanish-American War. Minnie and her boys stayed with her half sister and former guardian, Kate Holden, in Haskell, a town just southeast of Tulsa in the Muscogee Nation.

Minnie picked up four payments at Okmulgee, a total of $57.60. As she later told her friend Sadie James, she had only been entitled to three payments, but the census had listed four people in her household: herself, Charley, Harvey, and a person named Thomas. Thomas was a mistake, she said, but she took a payment for him anyway, figuring it referred to her dead father. As we'll remember from Minnie's letter to Judge Moore, she thought that her parents' homestead had been stolen from her and her siblings. While it is impossible to know exactly what Minnie Atkins was thinking when she accepted the extra payment, one can imagine her witnessing the widespread graft and legalized plunder then occurring and rationalizing the crime. Perhaps she thought of it as a small recompense for the loss of the family farm. While Minnie was taking the extra $14.40, white merchants "adopted" into the tribe were also collecting these per capita payments, and it seemed to be only a matter of time before noncitizens of the Five Tribes took over everything in Indian Territory. Just a few years later, in 1906, Creek principal chief Pleasant Porter told a journalist, "My Nation is about to disappear."[1]

MINNIE'S LIFE WITH HARRY

After collecting the payments, Minnie went back to Colorado, leaving her sons with Kate Holden, who had power of attorney over them. Minnie left no notes about where she was going, but she did promise to send financial support. Holden's husband did not want to take in the boys, and so he approached their aunt Nancy to be their primary caregiver. Nancy took the boys back to Wagoner, where they also lived among their Black Creek family.

Although we will never know exactly why Minnie left her children behind, the decision was most likely affected by the fact that she knew another war was on the horizon. Everyone working at Fort Logan was gearing up for a war with Spain—a war that would become known as the Spanish-American War.

In April 1898, Minnie's boyfriend, Private Folk, mustered for combat in Cuba, where he became part of the US occupying forces. Minnie was ready to travel with him, but it is unclear whether she in fact did accompany the regiment. Harry Folk was devoted to Minnie Atkins, at least at first. He knew nothing about her former life at Fort Leavenworth or her two sons in Indian Territory. As far as he knew, Minnie was a childless white woman from El Paso, Texas. Although we don't know whether Minnie went with him to Cuba, we do know that in 1900 she went with him to his next deployment, the Philippines, which Spain had ceded to the US at the end of the war. US troops occupied the archipelago and attempted to annex it; Minnie served as a cook for the army.

While Minnie and Harry were participating in the disastrous attempt to annex the Philippines, the United States was also attempting to terminate the sovereignty of the Five Tribes in Indian Territory. In 1898, the deceptively named Act for the Protection of the People of Indian Territory was passed, despite broad opposition from the Five Tribes. Signed into law by President William McKinley, the act abolished tribal governments and forced the allotment of land to the people that the Dawes Commission deemed to be citizens of a given tribe. The land left over would be deemed "surplus land" and opened for white ownership by people like my great-great-grandfather, William Hogan, who in 1905 bought a piece of this surplus land only a few miles from Thomas and Mary Jane Atkins's old homestead on Elk Creek.

One day my grandmother took me to the Checotah cemetery to see where the Hogans were buried. It was just a few feet from where many prominent Muscogees were also buried, and I asked her about them. Creek folks had been her friends, she said, but they had been treated "worse than dogs." I asked her what I had asked my great-aunts and great-uncles: Why this place?

At the time, in the early 1990s, Checotah was dying, the only growth in the town being the Walmart, where West Gentry Avenue intersected with the Texas Road. "I honestly have no idea," she said.

When I was a teenager, I wished William Hogan had picked any-place else in the entire world to settle but this humid, snake-infested hole in the Bible Belt. Between the Hogan family and the three generations of Russell Cobbs, I was rooted to Oklahoma, but it was a place I barely understood at all. I feel differently about it now. The knowledge that my grandmother, Dorothy Lee Hogan Songer, was buried in that same Checotah cemetery in 2001, about six miles down the MK&T railway line from Thomas Atkins's homestead on Elk Creek, fills me with a deep sense of obligation.

I need to set this story right.

"STRICKEN": THE FIRST ERASURE OF MINNIE ATKINS

Congress invested the Dawes Commission with the power and legal responsibility to determine who was—and who was not—an Indian in Indian Territory. The commission turned back to the censuses done by the Muscogee Nation in 1890 and 1895. When, in 1902, the Dawes Commission got to Tommy Atkins, listed as a member of Euchee Town, someone—most likely Augusta Robertson Moore, Alice Robertson's sister—made an observation: the only known Thomas Atkins connected to the Euchee was the Confederate officer and Lighthorse captain who had died many years before, the father of Minnie, Nancy, and Lee. Thomas had died in 1877, so what was he doing on an 1895 census?[2] A Dawes commissioner named T. B. Needles, looking back through the nation's records, noted that in 1895 Minnie Atkins had collected Thomas's $14.40 equalization payment. However, since no living Thomas Atkins was known to exist, on May 10, 1905, the principal chief of the Muscogee Nation returned the land patent granted to Thomas Atkins to the Dawes Commission. Legal passage of title from the Muscogee Nation to Thomas was held "pending further instructions." Cases like Thomas's, requiring investigation, were put in a special index called the Hold Up Book.

Muscogee Nation officials began to suspect that Minnie had made off with her deceased father's equalization payment on purpose. As both Muscogee Nation and federal officials sought Minnie Atkins for questioning, a theory arose. Perhaps the name Thomas Atkins had not been put on the census by mistake, but rather by Minnie herself in a deliberate and fraudulent attempt to collect an extra payment. If true, Minnie should be charged with wire fraud, a felony. However, every attempt to locate Minnie Atkins was coming up empty. The Dawes Commission sent letters to Fort Logan. The letters were returned unopened. Many people assumed she had died, a casualty of a smallpox epidemic that had claimed the lives of many Native Americans from 1898 to 1899. No one, it seems, knew that Minnie had been in the Philippines from 1900 to 1902.

With no leads as to her whereabouts, the Dawes Commission decided to make a provisional roll for Minnie Atkins as "Minnie Harris," after her boyfriend in Fort Logan (he was sometimes listed as George Harrison, and other times as George Harris). The roll listed her as a thirty-three-year-old citizen of Euchee Town. Minnie's Creek enrollment card is crossed out with a large penciled X. "No proof living," someone had annotated in 1899. Under her name was the word "stricken," underlined.

Although Minnie was assumed dead and consequently had been stricken from her tribe's rolls, Tommy Atkins continued to exist in Dawes's bureaucratic machinery. Tommy's enrollment in the Creek Nation worked its way through the Bureau of Indian Affairs, accruing official stamps from the Department of the Interior along the way from 1902 to 1905. Then it was held up by the Muscogee Nation. The principal chief sent it back to Washington, DC, pending further investigation.

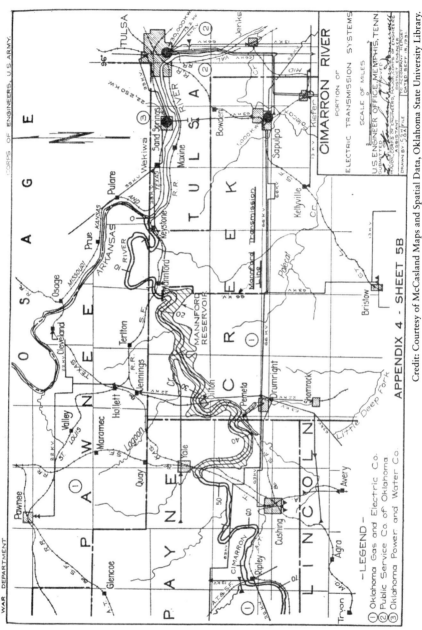

*Tommy Atkins's allotment lay between the wild oil field towns of Oilton
and Drumright in western Creek County. Nearby Tulsa was the financial
center of the state's oil boom, with the Osage Nation to the north
of town. Page's town, Sand Springs, is just to the west
of Tulsa and was connected via streetcar.*

CHAPTER 5

CHARLES PAGE,
THE "SECULAR SAINT" OF
MODERN-DAY TULSA

In modern-day Tulsa, Charles Page Boulevard parallels a former streetcar line connecting the downtown to its industrial appendage, Sand Springs. Every mile or so is a platform of crumbling concrete where passengers once boarded the Sand Springs Interurban Railway. After passenger service was decommissioned in the 1950s, the railway continued to carry freight for decades. The boulevard alongside the railway is called the Line in honor of its past glory as Tulsa's main streetcar line, and it has been in a period of long, slow decline for decades.

The miles of abandoned brick warehouses seem ideal for urban lofts or artists' spaces. Such revitalization, however, has proved elusive. Along the Line there is a retro-looking motel, the Holiday, that in another city might be a chic destination for hipsters. However, Tripadvisor reviews for the Holiday Motel are unanimously one-star. "Nothing but drugs, prostitutes, low lifes, cockroaches, bedbugs, and filth," writes one reviewer. "A nightmare."

My friend Lisa grew up near the Line. When we were in high school, Lisa would drive us to a convenience store on the Line to buy beer, as no one seemed to care about checking IDs on that benighted stretch of Charles Page Boulevard. We passed bars with motorcycles out front and boards over the windows. "Gun and knife bars," Lisa called them. Our group of friends dared each other to go in and buy a beer at one of these dives. No one ever took the dare.

In the early 2000s I became better acquainted with life on the Line when I went to report on a story about a group of workers from India laboring in a manufacturing plant in Sand Springs. They were skilled workers who welded and fitted pipelines for oil fields. They had been lured to the United States on temporary foreign-worker visas that matched workers to specific companies. A contractor found jobs for the Indian workers at the John Pickle Company, an oil parts manufacturer that ran a factory off Charles Page Boulevard, near the Line. However, the working conditions were egregious. Pickle deployed security agents to keep workers locked inside the plant in caged cells. The workers worked day and night with no possibility of leaving the plant, with pay as low as one dollar an hour. Pickle's agents confiscated the workers' passports. They were fed barely edible gruel. Armed guards hurled racist epithets at them. These skilled workers found themselves in conditions of virtual slavery, producing sections of oil pipelines that were shipped around the world, from Oklahoma to Kuwait.

At one point the workers attempted to escape but were rounded up by the guards, some of whom were off-duty cops. Finally, the workers caught the attention of a pastor named Mark Massey, who ran a small church nearby. Pickle let the men out for certain occasions, including church services. A few of them started attending Massey's church. Over a period of weeks, they told Massey about their working and living conditions. The pastor had two vacant rental houses in the neighborhood. He told them to escape. When they managed to do so, they found a key waiting for them under the doormat.

I read about the story in the local paper and decided to pitch it as a case of what can go wrong with our broken immigration system. What I did not understand then, and have only recently begun to understand, is that the episode of human trafficking at the John Pickle plant arose from a context of a paternalistic model of industrial capitalism with its roots in the Oil Capital heyday. John Pickle was a well-respected man in the Tulsa area, and he believed he knew what was best for his workers. He truly believed he had given the Indian workers good jobs, even though he had US workers doing the same job for $17 an hour. Pickle had taken the men fishing, to church, had even invited them over to his house for Christmas. A devout Christian and millionaire entrepreneur, he never really apologized to the fifty or so workers he had imprisoned in his plant (and to whom he was ordered to pay $1.24 million in 2006 for the crime of human trafficking).[1]

When he died in 2021, the *Tulsa World* ran an obituary for Pickle that celebrated his "mark on the world with . . . vision and drive."[2]

There was no mention of the workers he had imprisoned and abused, or the ruling against him.

Paternalism is the story of Sand Springs, and it is celebrated to this day in the town's place names and popular culture. When I was back in Tulsa in 2019, I caught a TV ad for BancFirst, a Sand Springs–based bank. The ad begins with an artistic rendering of a Muscogee village at dawn, but quickly transitions to a historic photo of a rotund white man surveying a growing city. "With the Territorial oil boom came an oilman with a dream to give back," the narrator intones.

The rotund white man is Charles Page. The narrator notes that Sand Springs was the product of Page's vision for an orphanage and a widows' village, funded from his own enterprises. His steel factory, railway, cotton gin, bottling plant, and many more industries all fed their profits into growing the Sand Springs Home. That "legacy of kindness," the narrator claimed, was also what BancFirst embodied. By all accounts, Pickle also thought of himself as a modern-day Charles Page: a benevolent, self-made businessman who had a personal touch with his workers. "Charles Page is a secular saint," Lisa told me. She had spent a few years at Charles Page High School before transferring to my private college-prep academy, Cascia Hall. She warned me that if I published anything negative about Page, there would be people in town who would take it personally.

"They will come after you," Lisa warned me. I brushed it off.

"THE INDUSTRIAL GIANT OF THE SOUTHWEST": BUILDING SAND SPRINGS

Throughout the nineteenth and twentieth centuries there were company towns all across the American West, resource extraction economies held together by one corporation. These were places like Segundo, Colorado, where most men's working and social lives were regulated by a company controlled by the Mellons and Rockefellers. But Sand Springs was something different: not a one-company town but a one-man town whose major industries, utilities, and train line were all directed by Charles Page. He made use of a loophole in the tax code: rather than own all these industries outright, Page put virtually all of his holdings—oil wells, industries, even downtown Tulsa buildings—in the name of the Sand Springs Home, which was classified as a charity. As such, it paid little to no taxes, even on its for-profit businesses. The home itself was an ever-expanding complex of residences and services for orphans and widows that is still in operation today on a bluff above the Arkansas River. Page liked to boast that all his profits went back into the home, but like much of Page's public face, the truth was much more complicated.

By 1969 the home's business operations caught the attention of the United States Congress. The Sand Springs Home was one of a few philanthropies around the nation operating for-profit business ventures that were exempt from taxes. Congress found that many wealthy individuals ran "private foundations" that had little social value, and mainly served as a way to dodge hefty tax bills. The Tax Reform Act of that year forced these philanthropies to divest themselves of their active business ventures. Officials from the home told Congress that they provided a safe place for hundreds of widows and orphans over the years, benefiting people who might otherwise have found themselves trapped in a cycle of poverty.[3] A scandal in late 1969 shattered the perception of the home as a safe haven for children, prompting the home's supervisor to flee the state. The unthinkable had occurred in the dormitory.*

By the early 1980s, however, the Oklahoma congressional delegation fought to restore tax breaks to the home. Senator David Boren helped carve out an amendment to this tax reform for the home in 1982, arguing that the business activities financed the charitable mission of housing and feeding orphans and widows.[4] (Senator Boren later served as the longtime president of the University of Oklahoma, but his legacy has been clouded by allegations of sexual misconduct that came to light in 2019.)[5]

One of Page's first risky ventures had been building the Sand Springs Interurban Railway in 1911. Page envisioned the railway connecting his town to the booming metropolis of Tulsa, the new Oil Capital of the World. Controlling Sand Springs would be his path to controlling Tulsa. And he who controlled Tulsa would also hold the key to the vast Mid-Continent oil field, stretching from Kansas to Louisiana.

One stop on the Sand Springs Railway took commuters to Commander Mills, then the largest cotton mill west of the Mississippi River.

---

* This scandal will be discussed in detail later.

The railway connected workers to a stop at the first steel factory in the Southwest, next to John Pickle's welding plant. Page also convinced a major company, Kerr Glass Manufacturing, to relocate its plant from Chicago to Sand Springs, enticing them with promises of low-wage workers and free land. Kerr Glass produced their iconic mason jars in Sand Springs until 1992. That plant, too, is now a shell of its former self, a testament to the decline of a town once called the "industrial giant of the Southwest."[6]

The Sand Springs Home for Widows and Orphans was built on a bluff above Charles Page Boulevard. Although the original building, a gracious four-story brick edifice with wraparound porches, was demolished in 2006, a more modest structure now houses the still-operational charity. Below that bluff is the Tullahassee Creek Indian Cemetery, a resting place for the town's displaced Muscogee inhabitants, located right in the middle of a strip mall parking lot. Many gravestones still stand there, hinting that the region has a much more complicated past than the one centered on a beneficent oilman and his industries. When I visit Tulsa, I go to the cemetery to pick up plastic bags. Much of the litter originates from the Dollar Tree across the way. A couple of years ago, appalled by all the trash I was finding, I asked an employee at the Dollar Tree who was maintaining the cemetery.

"The cemetery?" the clerk asked me.

"That one," I said, pointing to the plot of land in the middle of the parking lot.

"I never noticed that," the clerk said.

"See that rise in the parking lot?" I said. "There are bodies buried under there."

LOOKING FOR TOMMY IN SAND SPRINGS

At the end of Charles Page Boulevard, on a charming triangular park plaza downtown, stands the Sand Springs Cultural and Historical Museum, built in honor of Charles Page. The building is an Art Deco masterpiece constructed during the onset of the Great Depression by Chicago-based Lorado Taft Studios. Bronze chandeliers manufactured at Sand Springs's own Empire Chandelier factory adorn the inside. Bronze sconces are attached to walls made from highly polished pink Tennessee marble. Every window, every wall, exudes Art

Deco geometry and craftsmanship, much of it in bronze, marble, or terracotta. A permanent exhibit to the life and times of Charles Page serves as a testament to a singular philanthropist and the town he built.

When I first visited the museum in 2019, I found nothing about Tommy Atkins, on whom Page risked his fortune and that of the Sand Springs Home. Much of the exhibit covers the minutiae of Page's daily life—the stogies he smoked and the desk where he propped up his heels.

There's a poster describing Page's loyal German shepherd, Jim, a dog who could distinguish between the smells of virtuous and not-so-virtuous women. According to the poster, Jim listened in on all Page's business negotiations, and Page would ask him his opinion on people and business deals. Jim had his ways of communicating: a wag of the tail or the blink of an eye signaled approval. A "stare with an air of suspicion" indicated he did not approve. There was no word, however, on what Jim thought about Page's strangest and riskiest scheme: to convince the world that he had the only valid oil lease to the riches underneath the soil of the land of Tommy Atkins, a mysterious boy who some said had never existed.

I was on the verge of losing hope that the museum would contain any information about the elusive Tommy when I caught sight of a photograph dominated by a woman with her back turned to the camera. The woman's face is obscured in the photograph and her large frame is turned away from the viewer and toward a group of boys. The photograph has a ghostly texture, probably due to quick movements of the subjects, many of whose faces are blurred. A caption situates the photograph as having been taken at the dedication of the new home for orphans in Sand Springs on Christmas Day, 1918—the four-story brick building that was demolished in 2006. The faceless woman is identified as Minnie Atkins.

"Here she is!" I gasped, excited to see some recognition of the woman who went down in history as Tommy's mother. An employee overheard me prattling on to other visitors about the Atkins case and the wild story of the phantom child. The staff person approached to say that, contrary to the label's assertion, the museum is not entirely confident that the figure in the photograph is Minnie Atkins. Without a face, I could not positively identify her either. So many things seemed uncertain, including the central figure of the entire town: Charles Page.

CHAPTER 6

THE MAKING OF "DADDY" PAGE

The shape of Charles Page's early life is owed to his mother, Mary Ann Gottry, who was born in 1825 in the town of Haguenau, Alsace, a disputed area along the French-German border. When Gottry was born, Alsace was controlled by the French, but most of the population spoke German and had long identified with Germany. The town would be seized by invading German armies several times in the nineteenth and twentieth centuries.

The Gottry family feared their sons would be drafted into the French army. They sold their modest landholdings and booked passage to America in 1833 or 1834. They were not desperately poor like some immigrants, but life in New York City proved difficult for Mary Ann Gottry, an eight-year-old accustomed to a pastoral life of growing grapes and milking cows. Gottry's father forbade any language other than German to be spoken in the house.[1] In the early 1840s, Mary Ann met a terse but driven American man of Scottish and French descent, James Page. When Mary Ann and James became a couple, Gottry dropped her Catholicism and adopted Page's Presbyterianism.

James Page was a child of Scottish immigrants, but he identified first and foremost as a New Yorker. As a young man he embodied the imperial spirit of Manifest Destiny. An expansionist federal government had forced the Ojibwe and Potawatomi tribes to cede territory in 1829 from the lead-rich region of the southwestern Wisconsin Territory, where many Germans were resettling. When Page and Gottry met, Horace Greeley had yet to utter the phrase "Go west, young man," but Page had already caught the spirit of westward expansion. By 1844 the young couple had moved to the Wisconsin Territory, where they set up a home and had their first child, William. A biographical sketch of Charles Page's early life describes his mother as gentle and

compassionate, while James Page was "rather severe and puritanical."
Young Charles may have inherited his father's physical prowess, but
he clearly took after his mother in personality.[2] Charles helped her
bake bread, clean up the kitchen, and take care of the other children.

The Pages initially moved to Marquette County, Wisconsin, located
at the heart of the state's first economic boom, fueled by lead mining.
The discovery of Wisconsin lead presaged that of Oklahoma oil in
important ways. The rumors of instant riches led to chaotic patterns of
settlement, widespread fraud, and environmental destruction. Lead is,
of course, toxic, but in the 1800s, it was considered the "miracle metal"
and was used in myriad industries, from plumbing to typesetting and
printing to makeup to wine making. The Pages never made it rich
off lead mining, so they pushed on toward the Green Bay area—still
known in the 1840s as Indian lands—and settled in the town of Stevens Point in Portage County. James acquired a farm and worked as
a teamster, driving pack animals. James Page had little time for family
life. He plunged himself into work, acquiring more property, livestock,
and land in his efforts to prosper.

BACK TO THE TRAIL OF BLOOD ON ICE WITH THE PAGES

By 1860, on the eve of the Civil War, the Pages were prosperous, if
not wealthy, with nine children and at least $5,000 in savings. James
Page drove himself hard, determined to become a wealthy man. As
the 1860s progressed, he was diagnosed with cancer, and the cost of
treatment consumed his wealth. Page was a near-broke teamster when
he died in 1871. After James's death, not only did the housework and
child-rearing fall on Mary Ann's shoulders, but so did the financial
burden of running a household of nine children with no steady income.

The Pages' two eldest daughters picked up the burden for a while.
William had signed up with the Union Army at the beginning of the war
and he was assigned to the Third Wisconsin Cavalry Regiment, which
set out from Fort Leavenworth for Fort Row, Kansas, in 1862. Fort Row
was the terminus of the Trail of Blood on Ice, an absolute catastrophe for
Muscogees who rejected Confederate secessionists. William's regiment
was supposed to bring supplies and organize male survivors into Indian
Home Guard units that would retake Indian Territory for the Union. It
was part of a broader strategy to contain the Confederacy's influence

and expansion beyond Texas. An army surgeon described the scene that William Page witnessed on the Kansas border with Indian Territory. "It is impossible for me to depict the wretchedness of their condition. Their only protection from the snow upon which they lie is prairie grass and from the wind and weather scraps and rags stretched upon switches. Some of them had some personal clothing; most had but shreds and rags which did not conceal their nakedness, and I saw seven varying in age from three to fifteen years without one thread upon their bodies."[3]

Thus, in the early days of the war, one of the Page men from Wisconsin became intimately familiar with the affairs of Indian Territory. At this point, Opothleyahola was dead, as were one third to one fourth of all the refugees. Nevertheless, two Indian Home Guard units were organized for battle along with units of freed slaves and white Union enlisted men. Their first objective was to retake Fort Gibson, in the Cherokee Nation. William Page accompanied them as they moved southward through the Territory. By April 1863 they achieved their objective and seemed to have the Confederates in retreat. But these Confederates—including Lieutenant Thomas Atkins—were simply regrouping for "the Gettysburg of Indian Territory," the Battle of Honey Springs in July 1863.

In anticipation of this battle, William Page rode out of Fort Gibson with some scouts from the Indian Home Guards. Union General James Blunt expected an overwhelming attack by Confederate troops, perhaps as many as twenty thousand. That force would probably be coming from the south, up the Texas Road. Page rode with his wife, Fanny, who also served as a nurse, along with a few others, looking for signs of the coming invasion. They detected signs of forces approaching from the south. William and his company started back for the safety of Fort Gibson when shots rang out from the bushes.

William was hit by a rifle shot but managed to stay on his horse. He fired back and killed the man who had shot him. Fanny dressed William's wound. They galloped back to Fort Gibson, but William continued to bleed. He died on May 25, 1863. I cannot help but wonder if Thomas Atkins or one of the men under his command took the shot that felled William Page.

Many years later, an elderly Fanny Page would take her brother-in-law, Charles, to a gravesite in Fort Gibson, and recount the days the Page family first came to Indian Territory.[4]

"MOTHER, DON'T CRY"

After the deaths of William and then James Page, Mary Ann sought to protect her eleven-year-old son, Charles. She wanted him to stay in school, but the work of maintaining the house and farm while also looking after all the children proved too much for the widow to bear on her own. Charles dropped out of school and worked odd jobs like selling rabbit meat to people around Stevens Point, Wisconsin. Then the Panic of 1873 set in, caused by an overexpansion of railways and financial speculation. It led to bank closures, farm foreclosures, and plummeting real estate values. Whatever wealth remained from James Page's labor and savings now evaporated.

Desperate to generate income, Mary Ann rented out the rooms in the family house. She worked as a house cleaner, a nurse, a midwife. One of the boarders was the village schoolmarm, and part of the teacher's agreement with Mary Ann included providing reading lessons for Charles. One day, according to a retrospective of Page's life in the *Sand Springs Leader*, Charles caught sight of his mother struggling to straighten her back after scrubbing a load of laundry. Charles was coming in from the cold, carrying a load of firewood, when he saw Mary Ann silently crying over a steamy tub full of laundry. "Mother, don't cry," Charles said. "Wait until I get to be a man! I will take care of you and you won't have to work anymore, and I'll take care of all mothers and poor boys and girls, too." (A version of this story is also recounted by Opal Bennefield Clark.)[5]

Before his father died, Charles had envisioned himself as a great entrepreneur, a builder of cities. At age eight, Page was designing business ventures in the dirt outside the house. He built an entire miniature town, and some neighborhood kids kicked it down. Page was undaunted. "Some day I'll build a real town you can't tear down," Page said, according to Bennefield Clark.[6]

According to one tale, Page carved out whistles from wood and found a market for them. Rather than sell them for cash, Page traded the whistles for other goods. One day Page came home with a dog sled. When his mother pressed him to explain how he had purchased the dog sled with no money, Page spun a yarn about a series of "trades" involving his wooden whistles. This is one of those moments that has been recorded as Charles Page folklore, with several versions in print.

In one version, Page manages to trade his whistle for something of a slightly higher value, like a candle, then executes several more trades before finally landing his dog sled. There's another version in which he trades a whistle for a puppy, and then the puppy for the sled, which he hooked up to the family dog. Then, with dog and sled ready to ride, he went around town selling anything that could be sold.[7]

In any case, Mary Ann found the whole hustle to be a distraction from what her son should have been doing: learning to read and write. While other American impresarios of the coming Gilded Age were forming social networks in college fraternities or in the military, Charles Page was scrounging for money in odd jobs on the fringes of society. "I'm not a book boy," Charles reportedly told his mother.[8]

As a teenager Charles found some rabbit traps his father had used and taught himself how to use them. First, he trapped enough rabbits to dress and supply meat for his mother and siblings. Then, he dressed the extra rabbits and mushed his dog and sled around Stevens Point. The proceeds helped to feed the family. Charles also became Mary Ann's helper around the house, learning to bake biscuits and cook.[9]

Following in the footsteps of his teamster father, who had driven teams of pack animals, Charles learned how to work a double team of horses. He remained devoted to his mother, although she had her doubts about her ambitious son's ethical standards in business dealings. Page had an oversized physique, and it was clear that his physical strength would be backed by a corresponding ambition in business. By 1880 Charles had moved away from his mother's home and was working as a "call-out boy" and break man on Wisconsin railroads, letting passengers along the line know if trains were running on time or behind schedule.

Wisconsin's Indian lands were rapidly being co-opted by white settlers, and waves of German immigrants poured in to set up farms or work in lead mining. Their arrival came with a cost to the capitalist class. Many Germans understood and supported the trade unions that were organizing immigrant workers across Wisconsin and Minnesota, which the Gilded Age tycoons—John D. Rockefeller, Andrew Carnegie, Cornelius Vanderbilt—sought to suppress. Labor unrest hit the upper Midwest, and these tycoons deployed Pinkertons to gather information, infiltrate, and, if needed, provide muscle to suppress workers.

PAGE'S BRUSH WITH A GILDED FORTUNE

Although the Gilded Age is often called the Second Industrial Revolution, the vast accumulation of capital by robber barons came through the exploitation and financialization of land and capital, not through industrial innovation. Rockefeller vertically integrated the oil industry, controlling not just the end products, kerosene and gasoline, but also the land, the railways, refineries, and even the retail stores that sold them.

As a result, the gap between the working class and the captains of industry grew so wide that labor took direct action against railways, mines, and factories, from urban centers like St. Louis to company towns in Minnesota and Colorado.[10] Later in 1880, the twenty-year-old Page followed an iron ore boom in northern Minnesota, where he worked in police protection for a gilded-age tycoon named Charlemagne Tower. As the chief of police in the town, Page's main task would have been the repression of the labor movement. It's impossible to know exactly what his day-to-day life looked like, but historians of the era agree that the main function of the police in frontier towns (northern Wisconsin and Minnesota counted as "the frontier" in the 1880s) was to maintain social control over labor. Police were allowed to whip and beat men who were perceived as a threat to management. Although big cities like New York, Boston, and Philadelphia had publicly funded professional police departments at the time, smaller towns did not, and companies hired Pinkerton agents to do their bidding.

The hard labor required to mine lead, fell trees, and lay railroad tracks in Wisconsin and Minnesota led to demands for better working conditions. Scores of new unions organized the waves of immigrant workers in these states. As the region's newly industrializing economy emerged, clear lines were drawn between owners and managers on the one hand and laborers on the other. Workers wanted safer work conditions, prohibitions on child labor, and higher wages. But they were split on how to achieve their ends. Marxists led a general strike in St. Louis, and some radicals set fire to businesses. Owners and managers hired thugs, many of them Pinkerton agents, to inflict retaliatory attacks on workers.[11]

In 1877, a general strike in St. Louis led to a call-up of the US Army to subdue the workers. Railway employees walked off the job around the nation. Page himself was working for the Wisconsin Central Railway at the time. Page studied telegraphy on his own, learning a system of railway traffic control known as the block method of operations.[12] Page, though a laborer himself, had already cast his lot with the industrialists, not with the labor movement. When striking railway workers demanded food, one railway magnate, Tom Scott, president of the Pennsylvania Central Railroad, said, "Give [the strikers] a rifle diet for a few days and see how they like that kind of bread."[13] President Hayes sent out federal troops, but popular support was on the side of the striking workers, so ownership needed another way to deal with the paralyzing strike. They turned to private militias to put down an insurrection. Police forces at the time were likened to "wandering armies," and they had wide latitude to whip or beat people they perceived as criminals.[14] During labor unrest, police used tactics designed for the battlefield. Groups exchanged gunfire, from St. Louis to Pittsburgh. The strike was eventually broken, but in the process, labor unions had become better recognized and organized, especially the unions of railway workers.

Police were also seen as agents of social control and benevolence, leading houseless people to shelter or hungry people to soup kitchens. This is key to understanding the world of Charles Page. Police agents were like stern fathers, providing the carrot and the stick to ensure a rigid patriarchal system. In times of peace, police saw themselves as saviors.

CHARLES PAGE GOES WEST

In 1883, while working for the railway in Bay City, Michigan, Page met a woman named Lucy Rebecca Lavoice, an immigrant from Canada of French descent. Lavoice had had a son with a Quebecois lumberjack and fisherman, Guillaume Lavoice. In Bennefield Clark's telling, Lavoice was a widow, and Charles, predisposed to help women in this situation, took Lucy under his wing. Eventually, Lucy and her son, Willy, moved in with Page, who had been living in roadhouses as a boarder. In Clark's version, the couple married and Page adopted Willy before they headed out West to what would become Washington State sometime in the mid-1880s.[15]

Historical documents, however, tell a messier story. They show that when Page met Lucy in Michigan, Guillaume was very much alive. He had left his wife and child temporarily to take a job in the fishing industry in Lake Huron, Michigan. Tales of vast lakes and streams abounding in salmon then lured him to the emerald forests of western Washington. He settled on a piece of land near a salmon hatchery in the tiny town of Humptulips but found that the money was not in fishing but in the sawmills. Lavoice worked in the sawmills with the intention of bringing his wife and son out west.

Charles Page fit the profile of someone who, in a slightly different context, might have become involved in labor militancy. Due to his father's death, he had fallen from the capitalist class into the working class. His natural sympathies for widows and orphans suggest that he identified with the powerless in society. He was bullied by wealthier kids and did not seem to mind doing "women's work"—cooking and washing dishes. Moreover, many of his German and Scottish brethren found themselves marginalized by the English-descended power elite.

But in fact, Page saw labor unrest as an opportunity to surpass the modest financial achievements of his father by becoming a titan of industry himself. He must have identified with men like Charlemagne Tower, one of the first businessmen to exploit Minnesota's Mesabi Range, the site of rich iron deposits. The Pennsylvania coal-mining business had already made Tower a millionaire, and in 1875 he started buying lands in northern Minnesota. Tower moved from Pennsylvania to Minnesota in 1879 and began laying out plans for a city bearing his name, run by the Minnesota Iron Company.

It was in Tower, Minnesota, that Charles Page became the police chief in the early 1880s. Any attempt at labor organizing was dealt with by the immediate firing of the employee in question. Page, as the police chief of a company town, was charged with providing the muscle to make sure Minnesota Iron's operations continued without delays. Page may have picked up some business acumen from Tower, a man who cultivated a reputation as a philanthropist in his hometown of Philadelphia, but whose land claims were tainted by accusations of fraud. Minnesota law allowed "pre-emptors"—settlers who had arrived before a proper land survey had been done—to buy land cheap under a version of squatters' rights. In 1884, the *Minneapolis Star-Tribune* reported that Tower had filed false claims by fabricated pre-emptors to claim patents on land that the Minnesota Iron Company wanted to mine. This fraud would be repeated on a massive scale in Oklahoma, as lots in towns such as Tulsa and Muskogee were known to be claimed by bogus individuals serving as fronts for businessmen.

If the archetypal manager of the time viewed workers as replaceable cogs in a machine, Page, for all his antipathy toward the labor movement, understood the complexity of an individual's motivations. His attention to the human psyche made him an effective private investigator. Page was extraordinarily tenacious in tracking down wanted men and carrying out company orders. By the time he left Tower, he was working for Pinkerton's agency, which recruited Page to hunt down people the company's clients deemed threats. Page worked for Pinkerton's in the West during the better part of the 1880s, covering territory from Oregon to British Columbia. Although Pinkerton agents had been involved in a number of manhunts for famous outlaws and criminals, their bread-and-butter work was anti-labor surveillance and sabotage. They ran security for powerful people and engaged in extralegal espionage and repression, giving rise to all sorts of conspiracy theories. Presidents relied on Pinkerton agents for security, and they did covert intelligence work that later would be taken up by the FBI.

It is probable that Page was never a full-time employee of Pinkerton's, but that, like most agents, he worked for the corporation on the side while also running saloons and boardinghouses in the West. Page is listed on an 1887 Washington Territory census as a "saloonist" in Ellensburg, a frontier town on the Northern Pacific Railway, which connected the northwestern inland to Seattle. On at least one occasion around this time, Pinkerton's hired Page as a bounty hunter.[16]

In Charles Page lore, his time as a Pinkerton agent sharpened his sense of right and wrong, while also giving him insight into the mindset of criminals. At one point, according to Clark, Page tracked an alleged killer from the West Coast to Cincinnati, capturing the suspect and bringing him back West for trial. As the pair traded stories over a campfire one night, the man admitted that he had indeed committed murder. Page got credit for bringing the man to justice. In another story about Page, a heavyweight prizefighter showed up at a lumber camp where Page was, challenging men to a fight. Page reluctantly agreed, then maimed the man for life. It is impossible to verify these stories, but despite their questionable veracity, they have formed a mythic image of Page that still endures.

During Page's time among the rough elements of the Northwest frontier, he worked both sides of the law. In 1886, the Northern Pacific Railway reached Ellensburg, where Page ran his saloon. Western

Washington was now linked to the Midwest, leading to a new wave of land-hungry white settlers. Among his other jobs, Page worked as a colonization agent for the Northern Pacific. Colonization agents like Page functioned as a cross between real estate agent, salesman, and tourism promoter. Westward expansion was primarily driven by the railroads rather than by government, and the private nature of the business opened up the possibility for all manner of graft and swindles as railroads and their agents competed against one another.

In the early 1890s, Page made his first investment in real estate, near Tacoma, Washington. He worked out a deal with a sawmill to provide the company with raw wood to be milled into lumber, which he then used to build houses. The business appeared to be going well, and then Lucy got pregnant. The young couple was living about thirty miles outside Tacoma when Lucy went into early labor. They rode off on horseback in search of a doctor. Willy Page stayed behind in the protection of two men.

Charles and Lucy arrived at a hospital in Tacoma in time to save Lucy's life, but the baby was stillborn. Lucy was gravely ill from childbirth complications. The doctor said that she would not survive in the rough conditions far from any hospitals or doctors. The couple checked into a hotel, and Page pondered his next move. Page had a hand in many ventures: gold mining in British Columbia; silver mining in Colorado; saloons and hotels in Washington; railway expansion throughout the West. Page came from a big family and wanted children of his own. Lucy, however, appeared in no condition to bear any more children. Soon after, Lucy became sick with cancer, the same disease that had struck down James Page just when he appeared to be on the verge of achieving the American Dream.

Page sold his burgeoning home building business outside Tacoma and bought a hotel in town. The hotel business suited Page; he'd helped his mother run a rooming house after his father died. He took his profits from the Tacoma hotel and ventured out into the prune market. He thought he could leverage his wealth into cornering the whole business, but he knew very little about prunes, and lost a significant amount of money.

Meanwhile, Lucy was convalescing in Tacoma under the care of "Aunt" Fanny, the widow of his brother William, who had died in the Civil War. Page returned to Wisconsin in 1891 to care for his dying mother. He told Mary Ann Gottry that he would build a home for every widow or orphan in the nation so that no one would have to suffer as she had after the death of her husband. At Gottry's funeral, hundreds of children she had delivered turned out to honor her. Charles discovered among her belongings hundreds of tintype photographs of all the children she had helped.

He vowed to dedicate all his future profits to helping the widows and orphans of the world. This is the official narrative, anyway, and while it is undoubtedly true that he committed himself to this cause, he was also scheming a way to enrich himself. The hotel business had gone well, but the great American fortunes were being made in railways, in mining, and, as John D. Rockefeller was now demonstrating, in oil and gas. Great fortunes required total control of industry, from railways to minerals to energy. Page still believed he could master all of these things, given the right circumstances. And while Rockefeller had a public image as a soulless authoritarian with a cadaverous physique, Page imagined himself as his antithesis—the kindly father who could outmuscle a prizefighter if you poked him.

"DON'T YOU TITHE, MISTER?":
CHARLES PAGE AND THE DEPRESSION OF 1893

Over the next decade, Page mined for gold in the Okanagan Valley in Canada and in Idaho. He cut lumber in Washington. He built houses and did side work for the Pinkerton National Detective Agency. When the Panic of 1893 hit, Page was working as a colonization agent for Minnesota's Soo Line Railroad. The US economy was still on the gold standard, but reserves of actual gold were plummeting fast, as bank failures from Argentina to South Africa created a panic that spread to the United States. After the failure of the Erie and Western Railroad in July 1893, some banks suspended withdrawals of cash by depositors. Bank runs ensued, along with a massive drop in the stock market and a dramatic rise in unemployment. The panic turned into a depression, and Page's plan for a village designed to take care of widows and orphans seemed like a pipe dream.

In the post-1893 depression, Page sold his Tacoma hotel and headed south, running into another gold boom, this one in Cripple Creek, Colorado, in 1895. Whatever Page's early business successes had been in the Northwest, the depression following the Panic of 1893 led him to near destitution. The depression hit railways especially hard, and railways had long been the backbone of Page's economic activities. Page left Lucy in Colorado and went back to Canada, still in the futile pursuit of gold. During his travels in the late 1890s, he noticed a new industry in the West—oil drilling. He knew nothing about it, but heard people talk about petroleum as "black gold." Meanwhile, a new political movement, populism, caught fire in Colorado. The newly formed People's Party channeled widespread anger at robber baron capitalists and their monopolistic practices. Populists took power in Colorado in 1892 with a platform that favored organized labor, an increase in the minimum wage, and the breakup of large corporations.

Once again, one can easily imagine Charles Page pondering this divide between the haves and have-nots as the Gilded Age came to an end. At some point, near broke, he tried prospecting for gold either in the interior of British Columbia or in the Klondike. The economy still had not recovered from the depression after 1893. One day in the late 1890s he found himself almost penniless on a street corner in Victoria, British Columbia. As Clark tells it, Page had fifteen cents to his name. He was visiting some old partners to inquire about leases in gold-mining territory. Lucy Page was in Colorado Springs, her health declining. A cloudburst doused Charles with rain, and he scurried under an awning, where he bumped into a Salvation Army worker. The worker shook her tambourine in Page's face and told him to tithe to the poor. She explained that he should be donating a tenth of his income as a good Christian. Page was not a member of any particular church. He dug in his coat pockets and found his last fifteen cents.

"Don't you tithe, mister?" the worker said.

"I'll do better than one-tenth," Page replied and tossed his last fifteen cents into the Salvation Army jar.[17]

Now Page needed a loan to get back to the mountains and prospect for gold. A friend in Victoria asked Page if he knew how to handle oil leases. The new money was not in gold, the man said, but in "rock oil," the term widely used at the time to distinguish petroleum from oils obtained from whaling and other industries. Page had no idea how to handle a lease, but he was well versed in promoting land for speculation and in attracting people and money to places in the West. He got the loan he needed.

Oil and gas rights could be sold like land, but the real money was made in leases to extract minerals from under the surface. Unlike gold or lead, which were fugacious, oil and gas did not stay in one place but moved over time and in unpredictable ways. A defining aspect of US law—almost unique in the world—separates landownership into two strata: surface and subsoil (or mineral) ownership. In virtually every other country in the world, the subsoil is owned by the sovereign or a sovereign entity, usually a government. In the United States, a private individual may own rights to minerals to a given section of land and yet own nothing on the surface. That person can lease those minerals to another entity, such as an oil company, and collect royalties from the sale of oil (royalties are usually established at one-eighth interest). These minerals move in response to geological and human activity. Capturing the rights to these minerals was going to be complicated work.

Page heard stories of men collecting hundreds of dollars in commissions on oil lands. This was the work of a "lease hound," also known as a landman. The landman would go out into the field and draw up a lease, a contract with the landowner, to the minerals on the land. He would then contract with an oil company to do the drilling and extraction. This was obviously a complex business, one that the Rockefellers of the world negotiated through teams of lawyers and a network of businesses that could crush any competitor. But public sentiment, especially in the West, viewed Rockefeller and Standard Oil as greedy exploiters of the common man. Populists celebrated the notion of the independent oilman, the self-made individual. Although Charles Page had no political affinities for the pro-labor positions of the People's Party, his rough-and-ready image fit perfectly with the myth of the rugged individual.

Page was undaunted by the challenges. He went back to Colorado Springs to see if he could get into the rock oil game. He found some investors and drilled near Fort Collins, north of Denver, but hit only "dusters," dry wells. Then he went back to northern Michigan, where he had met Lucy and Willy. There were rumors of an oil field near Bay City. Here, too, he found only dusters. Page followed hunches from Michigan to Colorado, incurring debts and striking out.

Now a new century dawned, and Charles Page's only successes seemed to come from real estate speculation and saloons, not minerals. He helped develop a subdivision in Colorado Springs and moved into a modest cottage there on Corona Street. Willy Page is listed as living in the house in 1900, but soon thereafter he went to San Francisco to start a career in dentistry. Page's foray into the rock oil business seemed to bring him nothing but ruin, which was not surprising, since he had no training in geology or mineral leasing.

Lucy's health continued to be poor. She moved to Hot Springs, Arkansas, in hopes that the thermal waters there would help her recover. People believed the springs held a cure for everything from the "venereal peril"—syphilis—to diseases of the blood, malaria, and cholera. By the time Lucy arrived, this treatment of thermal springs as a cure for disease was established as mainstream, and even the US military used the baths at Hot Springs for rehabilitation. It was pseudoscience.

At the beginning of the twentieth century, then, Charles Page was a lone speculator with little to show for forty years of hustle. He was a classic American adventurer and entrepreneur, scheming and dreaming, precariously balanced between the American Dream and total destitution. There was no social safety net to prevent him from falling into ruin. He'd witnessed the ups and downs of an economy driven by rapid expansion into Indian Country. But now that country was fully settled by whites, and in its stead a new society based on real estate, petroleum, and resource control was emerging. There was no more frontier in America, so it was said.

There was, however, still one place mostly off-limits to ambitious white businessmen like Charles Page. There were rumors that this place, unlike Michigan and Colorado, held vast stores of petroleum. This was truly the last frontier on the continental United States—Indian Territory. The western part of Oklahoma, known as the Oklahoma Territory, had been opened up to settlement during land runs from 1889 to 1893.

The eastern half of this region, however, was still the property of the sovereign tribal nations known at the time as the Five Civilized Tribes. This land held no salmon in emerald lakes. There were no jagged mountains hiding veins of gold and silver. The soil was a reddish-brown color, good for cattle grazing but not much else. The "forests" were tangled with low blackjack, juniper, and post oaks. The water was muddy and sooty. In the summer, the territory was infernally hot and humid. In winter, ice storms and arctic weather blasted down the Great Plains from Canada. The Five Tribes had been initially exempted from the Dawes Severalty Act of 1887, the first grand experiment in allotment. As reservations were diminished or terminated in the rest of the nation after 1887, the Five Tribes managed to hold on to their governments and lands. Now, as the twentieth century dawned, white America wanted their lands too.

For a white adventure seeker in the early twentieth century, there was not much to recommend the place, with one major exception. An oil gusher had been discovered in 1901 at Red Fork, a town southwest of Tulsa. With newspaper headlines like "Geyser of Oil Spouts at Red Fork" and stories of crude erupting three hundred feet in the air, Red Fork caught people's attention. If Hot Springs in neighboring Arkansas held a sort of medicinal magic for people like Lucy Page, Oklahoma would be the source of financial magic—instantaneous wealth from petroleum.

Page had to see it for himself. In 1901, he caught a train on the Frisco Railway to Oklahoma City, a place that had been a tent city only a decade before. There he heard rumors about a boomtown about one hundred miles to the northeast, where amateur geologists armed with pseudoscientific divining rods and a winning smile could gain oil leases on Indian lands worth millions. These men could not own the land, as the federal government was in the process of deeding it to tribal citizens, but oilmen could get access to something more valuable than the land itself—its subsoil natural resources. Page's next stop would be Tulsa.

Meanwhile, the supposedly curative properties of the Arkansas springs failed to save Lucy from her failing health. She died in Hot Springs on May 30, 1905, and is buried there.

CHAPTER 7

OKLAHOMA JOINS THE DANCE

The First Oil Boom in Indian Territory

Up until his arrival in Oklahoma, Charles Page had fit the archetype of the pioneer in the American West: a mustachioed, cigar-chomping bear of a man who mingled with outlaws and desperados, prostitutes and robber barons, combining a youthful idealism with a bare-fisted approach to business. He had been a bounty hunter, a devoted son, a ruthless strikebreaker. Now he was also a grieving widower growing into middle age in a new kind of world.

A modern West was coming into view, powered not by horses but by internal combustion engines. Feuds were settled not with pistols but in courtrooms by lawyers who could telephone or telegraph virtually anyone in the world. In Indian Territory, newly platted cities offered cheap lots for business ventures of all kinds. Real estate speculation led to deals in which a Native American allottee would sell a lot to a speculator, who would then turn around and, after making some hastily constructed "improvements," flip the property to a newcomer for two or three times the price paid to the Native American. Dubious real estate investment deals, oil leases, and promises of mineral riches lured migrants into schemes. It was, in other words, a modern world not too different from our own.

Not everyone in this new West accepted the rules of the game. The Upper Creek traditionalists had not given up their struggle, and although they could not gain control of the Creek National Council, they rallied around Chitto (Crazy Snake) Harjo (also known by his English name, Wilson Jones).

Harjo viewed the Curtis Act of 1898 and the whole process of allotment as a betrayal of the old treaties, in particular, the treaty of 1832, which had guaranteed Indian Territory to the Five Tribes.

Although many, if not most, Muscogees agreed with him, it seemed futile to resist the full weight and power of the federal government. Nonetheless, Harjo persisted, and in 1901 he and his allies called a rally at a traditional ceremonial spot, Hickory Ground, south of the town of Henryetta. This rally turned into a rebellion against the pro-allotment factions in the Muscogee Nation. Harjo's leadership attracted additional allies from the Cherokees, Choctaws, Chickasaws, and Seminoles. Black freedmen also joined in. Harjo and his allies became known as the Snake Faction of the Muscogee Nation—a sort of government-in-exile whose main purpose was to uphold the treaty of 1832.

The Snake Faction created its own armed Lighthorse and forbade Native Americans to collaborate with the Dawes Commission. They publicly whipped tribal citizens who aided commissioners. They raided offices known to have allotment certificates and destroyed them. They sent President McKinley an ultimatum: end allotment, or they would go to war. Progressive Muscogees and US Indian agents (people employed by the federal government to handle Indian affairs) tried to explain to Harjo that the original 1832 treaty had since been superseded by other treaties. In response, Harjo and a delegation went to Washington, DC, in 1903 and produced the original 1832 treaty in a meeting with Theodore Roosevelt (McKinley had been assassinated). It stated that only an act of Congress could abrogate the treaty, and the treaties currently in force had not met this requirement.

Roosevelt shook hands with Harjo but promised nothing. Lobbyists in Washington told Harjo that they could help reinstate the old treaty for a fee. These lobbyists banked on Harjo's lack of English to sell him a bill of goods. By the time a group of US senators came to Tulsa in 1906 to investigate the chaos of allotment, Harjo had recognized the betrayal. He was again ready for war.[1]

The progress of allotment and the discovery of oil pushed the Snake Faction into a desperate position. Most citizens of the Five Tribes did not join the Snake Faction, and instead struggled to find a footing in an economy now based on leases, mineral rights, and private ownership. These were people like Minnie Atkins's old friend Bettie Mann, the former Carlisle student. Mann became one of the brokers in the system of land grafting that dominated early-twentieth-century Oklahoma. These brokers were often descended from mixed Creek,

Cherokee, and white families—people who were fluent in Mvskoke, English, tribal customs, Christianity, and American capitalism. Some of these people became known as the founding fathers of towns like Muskogee, Tulsa, and Okmulgee.

To Chitto Harjo and his followers, this class of people—the "mixed-blood aristocracy"—had become the epitome of everything wrong with the new order of things. Harjo's militia targeted these people—often associated with the Lower Creeks or progressives—with floggings and intimidation, bringing back the old divisions within the Muscogee Nation that had been forged before Removal.

Although Native Americans and Black freedpeople with allotments in Indian Territory quickly became outnumbered by white settlers in the first few years of the twentieth century, they still legally controlled most of the land. The Dawes Commission may have been a "paper genocide" for the long-term viability of Indigenous sovereignty, but the paper in question was extremely valuable. For a new class of white settler—one interested in the riches underneath the soil—the circumstances in Indian Territory posed high risk with potentially high reward.

At the time of the oil discovery at Red Fork in 1901, there was still a lot of land that had not yet been allotted by the Dawes Commission. Some self-taught geologists, known as "creekologists," believed that major oil deposits accumulated below river and creek beds. Their pseudoscientific beliefs led to real-world actions, including drilling into rivers like the Cimarron, while the tribe claimed riparian rights (ownership of the riverbanks) by law. Railroad companies transporting oil and other materials sprang up everywhere and wanted the local governments to force allottees to surrender part of their lands for tracks.

A notorious case occurred about half a block from my boyhood home, where in 1904 a ninety-year-old Muscogee citizen named Tuckabache tried to stop the Midland Valley Railroad from laying track through his hunting grounds. His guardian, Sam Davis, approved the easement despite the old man's protests. Tuckabache was so embittered by his fight against the railroad that he believed they would try to rob even his grave and his estate after his death. In his will, he ordered that salt be poured over his weapons. He was not completely wrong: in 1921, eleven years after his death, his family burial ground was relocated to Oaklawn Cemetery in order to make way for the subdivision of Sunset Terrace—where I grew up in absolute ignorance of any of this history. The history might have remained unknown to me had a realtor friend of my mother's not mentioned that my house had "a dead Indian in the title."

"A dead Indian," I came to learn, was an allusion to the contested nature of land transactions in eastern Oklahoma. The chain of ownership is often clouded by people with names like Emarthla, Tuckabache, Naharkey, and, yes, Tommy Atkins, whose lives and deaths haunt the seemingly placid order of things in Tulsa and Creek Counties. I thought middle-class homes for white folks built on ancient Indian burial grounds only happened in Hollywood movies. I had no idea that a not-so-ancient burial ground for Tuckabache and his family backed up to my boyhood home.

The fact that Tuckabache's family cemetery was dug up and relocated to the same place where human remains from the Tulsa Race Massacre of 1921 have been found only makes the story more chilling. The journalist Rebecca Nagle has found over 140 "quiet title" lawsuits in Tulsa County involving just one family of allottees, the Naharkey family.

The most recent was in 2016.

"A WHITE MAN'S COUNTRY"

The chaos of the allotment program brought other accusations of fraud. White Oklahomans accused Native Americans of getting in line twice for allotments. Native Americans accused whites of paying off corrupt census takers to get added to tribal rolls. Both groups sought to undermine African Americans and Black freedpeople by canceling tribal citizenship and imposing segregation. It was unclear who had jurisdiction over whom and who decided membership in different racial categories: who was an Indian, who was white, and who was Black and thus at the lowest rung of the new society. Anti-Black racism was an incontrovertible, implicit fact of life in the Indian Territory, but statehood, in 1907, brought forward explicit laws designed to make Oklahoma "a white man's country." The first order of business in the state Senate—Senate Bill 1—was the imposition of segregation in transportation in 1907.[2] Some Blacks sought to be reclassified as Indians by blood, and some Indians by blood refused to be labeled at all. Until 1907, Indian Territory was still technically in the hands of tribal governments, but everyone knew that statehood was inevitable. Tribal leaders made an attempt to create a Native-governed State of Sequoyah in 1905, but a majority of the residents in Oklahoma and Indian Territories favored a unified state of Oklahoma, although whether segregation would be reflected in the state's constitution continued to be a vexing issue. Ardent racists wanted to enshrine segregation in the state constitution, but they feared that President Roosevelt would veto statehood under those conditions.[3]

Amid all these political maneuverings around race, landmen combed through tribal documents, reports from Indian agents, and geological surveys, seeking to understand who owned what land, and how much they could charge for a lease to extract oil and gas from those landowners. They combed the scraggly wooded hills of Tulsa County in pursuit of the telltale signs of oil: natural gas leaks or "greasy" streams of water. They had a hunch that the hills with sharp western rock faces that gently sloped eastward held oil some 1,400 feet underneath the surface. These landmen were also known as wildcatters because they operated out in the woods, where wildcats were still undisturbed by modern encroachments. Geologists had competing theories about rock formations, water, and quicksand, while drillers themselves were convinced that the science of geology was bunk. They had their own tools of the trade, such as divining rods that would somehow point to the oil under the ground. These men were often convinced that God had anointed them with a power to divine where the oil was.[4]

In 1903, after hitting nothing but dusters, Charles Page finally struck his first well, albeit a shallow one, in the town of Chandler, southwest of Tulsa, in the northeast part of Oklahoma Territory, in Muscogee Nation lands. Now, with some capital in hand, Page moved to Tulsa, a nascent city staking its claim as the financial and transportation capital of the industry.

As Page consolidated his landholdings west of Tulsa, he looked outside of Red Fork to find more oil. Although the Red Fork gusher is remembered as the event that "brought Oklahoma to the dance" of the modern oil economy, in reality Red Fork had been a disaster for almost everyone. It turned out to be a relatively minor oil field, but that did not stop thousands of greedy speculators from arriving at this unincorporated town and setting up tents wherever they could find space. They overwhelmed the telegraph lines and the tiny railroad depot. They fought over land titles that they could not even legally own, since the property was located in restricted Muscogee Nation lands. Page secured a lease on the Emarthla allotment and got some drillers to test a well.

THE COLOR OF OIL

The Red Fork discovery shifted the calculus of everyone involved in allotment. Dr. J. C. W. Bland was a white physician married to a Mvskoke woman named Sue Bland. She had not yet filed with the Dawes Commission for her allotment when a pair of drillers backed by eastern investors showed up in a village near Tulsa hoping to strike oil. The investors held a bogus lease to hundreds of thousands of acres in the Muscogee Nation. The railway refused to let them unload their equipment, so Dr. Bland and an associate, Dr. Fred Clinton, stepped in to make a deal. They would provide the financial backing that these shady eastern investors could not, if they would drill at the base of Lookout Mountain, on what is the west side of Tulsa today. The drillers agreed, and the gamble paid off.

The team struck a gusher. A county judge gave Clinton power of attorney over Sue Bland, allowing Clinton to make legal decisions on her behalf. Clinton took a sample of the oil on a train to Muskogee where he met with a Dawes commissioner. Clinton and the commissioner filed an application for allotment in the name of Sue Bland right on top of the oil well.[5]

It is worth pondering the implications of this transaction. The discovery of oil on Indian land in Oklahoma is usually posited as a circumstance of dumb luck, giving rise to people like Jackson Barnett and Lucinda Pittman. The series of transactions at Red Fork complicate this narrative. Not only did white men know that there was oil around Tulsa before allotment; they conspired to put allotted land in the hands of Mvskoke people they believed they could control. They often used members of the mixed-blood aristocracy as brokers to transfer the land into white hands.

One of these brokers was Minnie's old Carlisle classmate, Bettie Mann, one of Alice Robertson's group of Muscogee girls who were supposed to translate the anti-feminist "cult of true womanhood" to a Native American context. Bettie was also the one "white" Muscogee girl and had already achieved some notoriety for being a party to the first marriages and divorces performed in the history of Tulsa. After suffering through an abusive marriage, Bettie became a fixture of the Tulsa underworld, doing dirty deeds for oilmen who did not want to be seen as involved in shady land deals.

Bettie was also the perfect guide for American businessmen who wanted to profit in Indian Territory: she spoke both Mvskoke and English, could pass as a white person, was competent in tribal and federal courts, and was familiar with both white culture and the tribal towns, clans, and culture of the Muscogee people. She could bend her ethical standards for a decent price and was willing to lie to a judge if that is what the business required. Bettie garnered a reputation as an outlaw with the Raspberry Gang, a group of Muscogees who specialized in oil lease forgeries. They would impersonate allottees for a fee, and the land could be leased or sold without the true owner ever suspecting anything until it was too late.

This mixed-blood aristocracy might have been able to negotiate this new "white man's country" of Oklahoma resource colonialism, and even thrive in it, but there were limits. When mixed-bloods attempted to assert control over their own lands and wealth, they found that their acceptance into the mainstream could be revoked at a moment's notice. (Native Americans were exempt from Jim Crow laws in Oklahoma.) Young men were shot, stabbed, or found mutilated on train tracks.

Natives were supposedly killed over a card game or a bottle of whiskey, but quick transfers of land titles after their deaths raise many questions. Women were kidnapped, raped, or shipped off to boarding schools while their lands were transferred to white owners or guardians who helped themselves establish fortunes that still anchor the cultural establishment of Tulsa. The conspiracy—there is no other word for it—against Muscogee allottees cast a wide net and was in no way limited to Charles Page. There is no comprehensive study (as there is in Osage County) that documents the crimes, but the names of people like Millie Naharkey, Lucinda Hickory, and Gabriel Emarthla are attracting the attention of descendants, amateur researchers, and a few professional historians.[6] Angie Debo may not have been able to name the names of the criminal masterminds in the 1930s and 1940s, but now their portraits are finally coming into focus.

RESISTING "THE ROAD TO DISAPPEARANCE"

All of this led Creek principal chief Pleasant Porter to ponder the curse that had come with the discovery of oil riches. Porter lamented the entire era as "the road to disappearance of his people." Following the Red Fork discovery in 1901, he wrote, "Had oil not been discovered, these parcels of land would not have been selected as homes by any person but would have remained as part of the residue of land which was to be used for equalizing the value of lots, and the discovery of oil should not remove them from that class of lands which had been contemplated to be set aside for that purpose."[7]

Porter believed that the proceeds of the sale of surplus land could have been redistributed as an equalization payment to Muscogee citizens. At the time, however, the Creek Nation was still struggling to account for all its citizens. Some did not want to be enrolled by the government and did everything they could to resist allotment—including, in the case of the Snake Faction, armed resistance.

In the midst of all this confusion, in 1901 a Dawes commissioner named Edward Merrick received an 1895 census of Euchee Town, verified by Town King Samuel W. Brown. Merrick's job was to figure out who on that census had still been living on April 1, 1899, using the census cards as a basis for his inquiry. The people who had died before that date would not have their enrollments forwarded on for allotment. A few Muscogee people had lived to be enrolled but then died before their allotment could be issued. In those cases, allotment land was passed to the deceased person's heirs.

Dawes commissioners were vested with powers by the US Congress to take oral testimonies under oath during the enrollment process. Despite their many errors, these testimonies are useful in reconstructing the networks of kinship and belonging that existed in Indian Territory on the eve of statehood. When citizens of these nations could not, or would not, go to Muskogee to give sworn testimony, a Dawes commissioner went out into the field, crossing rolling hills and prairies to find every single person and document them for posterity.[8]

There were some people listed on a census card who could not be tracked down, no matter how hard a commissioner worked. This was the case of Creek Indian #7913—the card belonging to Tommy Atkins. Neither mother nor father could be located to talk to the commission. The father was listed only as "white man." The mother, some suspected, was Minnie Atkins, but, as we've seen, she was presumed dead by her tribe.

There were five people with the name "Thomas Atkins" in the Muscogee Nation. Someone in the commission suggested that card 7913 was a duplicate and should be canceled. Merrick investigated the identities of the five living Thomas Atkinses. Two of them were a father and son from Artussee Town, which had no connection to Coweta or Euchee, the two towns associated with Tommy Atkins on card 7913. Those two could be quickly ruled out.

That left three more. One was from Coweta Town, documented as the son of Billy Atkins, born in 1884. Billy's father was the Lighthorse captain, Thomas Atkins, but his mother was Sullawatka (also known as Mo-we-lah-ke). Everyone knew Billy (Tooksie) Atkins, who was half brother to Minnie. Billy's Thomas was noted for his abilities in stick ball, a rough and tumble sport distantly related to lacrosse. This Thomas took an allotment six miles outside of Wagoner, and still lived there from the time of allotment until at least the 1920s. I cannot find evidence of his ever expressing any interest in making a claim on the land of 7913.

Now there were two Tommys left: Minnie's, and Dick and Sally's. Dick and Sally's Tommy had been identified by both the Muscogee National Council and the Dawes Commission as Black, while Minnie's Tommy was listed as one-half blood quantum. These two children could therefore not be duplicates, and so card 7913 must represent a separate person who needed to be enrolled. Merrick began the process.

On May 23, 1901, Merrick officially enrolled Tommy Atkins under the Dawes Commission. A year passed and no one came forward to claim Tommy's enrollment card or choose his allotment. Another year passed. Minnie had shipped off to the Philippines. Dick Atkins and his son Tommy had both died. Nancy, however, was still in Wagoner, spending time on Chaney Trent's land, taking care of her many half-siblings and working part-time as a laundress.

Then, on May 16, 1903, a document with the full force and power of the federal government of the United States of America behind it came into being. The document contained a patent in fee simple to two eighty-acre tracts of land on the very western edge of the Muscogee Nation to a boy named Thomas Atkins. Because no next of kin was available to select Tommy's land, the Dawes Commission had selected it for him. All the seemingly good land had been taken. The acting chair of the commission, Tams Bixby, picked some land in the cross timbers, a couple of miles from the muddy Cimarron River, where little of worth seemed to grow. It was close to the land of the Osage Nation, which had been in conflict with the Muscogees since Removal.

The mystery of Minnie's whereabouts remained. On August 24, 1904, in an attempt to get more information, Merrick called a cousin of Minnie's named Fred Bowers to appear before the commission in Muskogee.

Bowers still lived around the old Tullahassee Mission School, where Minnie had been a student before it burned down. The place had been reborn as an all-Black Oklahoma town. Bowers said his only interest in the Atkins case was to see that Minnie, if she was alive, received her rightful allotment. But Bowers was another middleman involved in land transfers to wealthy white men. He worked as a guardian to Muscogee allottees and stood to make some money by selling her land.

The problem was that Bowers had lost track of Minnie and had only scant information to share. He knew she had married but did not know the name of her husband. He had heard that she'd gone to California. Since she left, another relative had received a letter from her. The letter asked "something about her father," Bowers said. "I will see them about it and get more evidence."[9]

Next the commission brought forth Sam Brown, second cousin to Minnie, the hereditary chief and onetime town king of the Euchee, who had overseen the 1895 census that had registered Tommy as Minnie's son. Nearly ten years had passed since that census, and Brown had also lost track of Minnie. "I don't know if she is living or dead," Brown said.

He hinted that Minnie had taken more than her fair share of the 1895 annuity payments from the government and that after that she had "left the country"—meaning the Muscogee Nation. For years the Dawes Commission continued to investigate Minnie's whereabouts and to come up empty. Finally, in 1907, as Oklahoma statehood was imminent, the Dawes Commission decided to issue a ruling on Minnie. By that time the values of the land allotments had soared as a result of the oil boom. Commissioner Bixby sat down to write his ruling. His statement is worth quoting at length:

> It appears from the records in the possession of this office that on April 24, 1901, the name of Minnie Harris [this last name taken from George Harris] was listed for enrolment by the commission to the Five Civilized Tribes on Creek Indian card field number 3718; the name of said person appearing upon the 1890 authenticated tribal roll of Euchee Town, which listing was done in order to preserve whatever rights said person might have as a citizen of the Creek Nation. This office has, th[r]ough field parties operating in the Creek Nation and by interviews and this office of prominent Creek Indians of extensive acquaintance, made every effort to ascertain the whereabouts of said person but no further information has been obtained. It is considered that this person is not entitled to enrolment either because she died prior to April 1, 1899, or because of non-residence or because she has been enrolled under some other name. *I am therefore of the opinion that the application for the enrolment of Minnie Harris as a citizen of the Creek Nation should be dismissed and it is so ordered* [emphasis mine].[10]

As Bixby wrote this definitive judgment on her citizenship, Minnie was living with her husband, Harry Folk, at Fort Lawton in Seattle, prepping meals for soldiers. She had no idea that the shadowy figure of Tommy Atkins would soon reenter the scene. The stakes would be considerably higher than the $14.40 she had collected in his name in 1895.

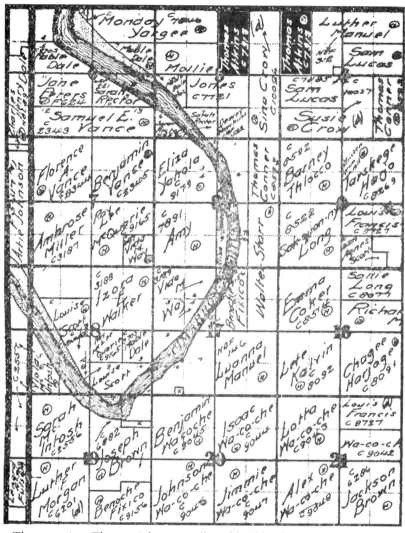

The mysterious Thomas Atkins was allotted land by the Dawes Commission in a corner of the Muscogee Nation—later, Creek County—thought to be of little value. Tommy's allotment sat on top of a rich oil field discovered in 1912.

— CHAPTER 8 —

EMARTHLA OF THE SNAKE FACTION

Chitto Harjo's rebellion against allotment had failed, but his Snake Faction refused to give up the struggle, even as statehood approached. Anti-allotment forces had contemplated yet another removal, this time to Mexico or even Bolivia. A few Muscogees left for northern Mexico, where Indigenous people had a long history of resistance and self-determination in the face of Spanish colonization. Nevertheless, Harjo concluded that Indian Territory was the Muscogees' "last and best resting place. We see no great unoccupied West toward the Setting Sun as in old times to which the Indian may be pushed."[1]

The Snake Faction launched their first rebellion in 1901 near Eufaula, Oklahoma. It was short-lived and largely symbolic—Harjo was captured by federal authorities, as were over two hundred men and boys who'd rebelled with him. The incident did attract a lot of media attention around the world—many easterners were sympathetic to his claim that the white man had betrayed his original treaty. Harjo's rebellion sparked a mix of fear and excitement around the nation. The *St. Louis Post-Dispatch* predicted a bloody war with the Snake Faction, but readers in Los Angeles read an account of a man whose people "held land in common and roamed the forests in nomadic fashion."[2]

The relatively nonviolent uprising also lent sympathy to Harjo's plea deal for a short sentence; it was this media attention that led to the meeting with President Roosevelt in 1903. In 1906 Harjo made a remarkable speech in the Seaman Building in downtown Tulsa. He addressed a group of US senators whom he had invited to come to the Territory to witness firsthand the plunder of Indian lands and wealth. Senators from as far away as Connecticut were there. Harjo spoke in Muscogee as his interpreter, David Hodge, translated into English.

Harjo's story began in 1492, when Indigenous people first encountered Columbus. From that point forward, Harjo said, Indigenous people had sought to uphold solemn treaties to share the land with the newcomers. Harjo said that Europeans and Indigenous people were "all one blood; we have the same god and live on the same land." Harjo mentioned the broken treaty of 1832, which had promised Indian Territory to his tribe for eternity. Instead, his "white brothers" had confiscated Native lands.

The latest treachery was allotment. "I think my lands are all cut up," Harjo said. "I have never asked that to be done, but I understand it had been done. My treaty said this would never be done. All that I am asking you, Honorable Senators, is that ancient agreements and treaties wherein you promised to take care of me and my people, be fulfilled."[3]

The speech was a sensation in the national press, further solidifying an image of Harjo as a romantic embodiment of the noble savage. The *Houston Post* published an elegiac article about the "old chieftain" with a "rebellious spirit," whose tribe now, inevitably, faced the "final dissolution."[4]

The elegies and laments from big cities did nothing to stop the invasion of whites looking to claim a piece of the black gold bonanza. In fact, sensationalist headlines about Harjo led to a narrative of a "war in Oklahoma" between Harjo, who now supposedly had an army of hundreds of Black and Native followers, and white police officers accompanied by a posse. The *New York Times* reported, falsely, that six whites had been killed by a new uprising. Governor Charles Haskell called out the militia. Indian Agent Fred Cook reported back to Washington that white settlers were agitated about Harjo's newfound Black supporters, and rumors of a Black armed revolt were spreading all across eastern Oklahoma. The historian Daniel Littlefield, who spent a career researching the relationship between people of African descent and the Mvskoke, concluded that this "war in Oklahoma" was actually a racial panic on the part of whites, who were alarmed to see so many armed Black and Native men in one place.[5]

The entire episode began over stolen barbecue. A white man was smoking some meat in his smokehouse. He had left the smokehouse, then returned to find his slab of meat gone. He accused Harjo's men of stealing it, but they forced him to retreat by showing them their rifles. Harjo was adamant that no one in his group stole the man's barbecue.

Haskell's militia and a white posse escalated the situation, leading to a shoot-out at Harjo's cabin in Henryetta that left him wounded.

What happened after that is the stuff of legend. Most likely he retreated deep into the lush Kiamichi Mountains in southeastern Oklahoma and died there in 1911 at the home of a Choctaw citizen named Daniel Bob. But there are several other stories in circulation. Some say he recuperated and moved to Mexico. Another theory is that he died in the shoot-out, but his followers burned his body so that he would never be recognized. One of the first textbooks on Oklahoma history, published in 1916, claimed that Crazy Snake was living out his last years in a village in Bolivia.[6]

Although the press at the time portrayed Harjo and his followers as terrorists or criminals, historians like Littlefield understand the struggle as one over land and resources under a Jim Crow regime of racial capitalism. The alliance between Black people and Muscogee traditionalists was uneasy at best, and downright hostile at worst. Harjo himself did not favor full rights and citizenship for Black Muscogees.[7] Nevertheless, Harjo's followers, Black people, and even some white socialists saw an opportunity to build solidarity around the notion of shared land, racial equality, and a fair distribution of food and livestock. Their revolt inspired another insurrection during World War I, the Green Corn Rebellion, which was decidedly anti-war and socialist in its ideology.[8]

In the aftermath of the "Smoked Meat Rebellion," over two hundred people were arrested, the majority of whom were of African descent. The Snake Faction and their allies faced charges ranging from murder to horse stealing to possessing liquor. Almost all of these charges were dropped. Federal agents wanted to make sure Harjo surrendered on the assurance that he would be given a fair trial. Agent Dana Kelsey found that much more violence and damage had been caused by white marauders than by Harjo's followers. Once the sensationalism around the event had died down, it was clear that the Smoked Meat Rebellion had been portrayed falsely in the media. I cannot find any evidence that there were any felony convictions against "the Snakes," as they were called. Almost all the Snakes returned home, even though many of their homes had been torched by white gangs.[9] Among those arrested and able to return home was a man known only as Emarthla.

There were many Emarthlas in the Muscogee Nation, but the others had taken first names or titles to specify which one they were. The Emarthla arrested during the Smoked Meat Rebellion had never given Dawes commissioners a first name, and he rejected the widespread practice of taking an alternative Christian name. On his final enrollment on the Creek rolls, there is an Emarthla from Lochapoka town whose single name is put in quotation marks, a reflection of a bureaucrat's frustration with the paucity of information. (Native Americans who did not come forward to enroll themselves were enrolled by the commissioners themselves based on secondhand testimony.) It is impossible to know if this is the same Emarthla listed as part of the Crazy Snake Faction, but, like Chitto Harjo, the man from Lochapoka town was certainly opposed to allotment.

On April 26, 1901, the commission persuaded Emarthla to give some information about himself. He told Commissioner Bixby that he lived in a cabin along the bottomlands between Turkey Mountain and the Arkansas River, just west of Tulsa and north of Red Fork. He had about 4 acres under cultivation and hunted game and fished in the river. He and his son, Gabriel, had built a fence as an "improvement," probably to keep out intruders. Emarthla's homestead was only about three miles from the village of Red Fork. After the 1901 gusher at Red Fork, the town had been overwhelmed by thousands of adventurers hoping to get a piece of the black gold rush. Emarthla must have felt like he was under assault. Unable to read or speak English, Emarthla signed an X on his application for an allotment that included his 4 acres. The rest of his 160 acres were dispersed around the region. (A good portion of this land is off Charles Page Boulevard in West Tulsa, bordering on Sand Springs.)

Emarthla's lack of English language proficiency was enough for a county judge to declare him incompetent to manage his own affairs. Consequently, like most "full-bloods," he and his son were made wards of a court-appointed guardian. These guardians played their wards like cards at a poker table—acquiring or discarding them for pure financial gain. Emarthla probably had little idea that his land was a commodity to be bought and sold, although he was aware of the threat the newcomers posed.

In 1905, Charles Page, who was expanding his drilling territory, acquired a lease to drill several wells on Emarthla's land. By the end of the year, Page's Victor Oil Company was producing 350 barrels a day—not a gusher like Red Fork or Glenn Pool but modestly successful. Three wells became significant producers that year, and Page rejected an offer of $65,000 ($2.2 million in 2024 dollars) to sell his lease to a bigger oil company. The Emarthla lease solidified Page as a significant player in the industry. In 1907, after statehood, Page saw a chance not just to lease the land to drill but to own it. The main obstacle was the federal restrictions placed on Oklahoma Indians.

A county judge had appointed a man named Samuel C. Davis as the guardian of Emarthla and his son. Davis was a mixed-blood Mvskoke who worked with his wife, a white woman named Ethel Davis, to broker land deals. The Davises helped Charles Page and other oilmen circumnavigate restrictions on the sale of land from tribal citizens with more than one-half blood quantum. On June 2, 1910, Emarthla died of unknown causes. Five days later, on June 7, 1910, Ethel Davis paid Gabriel $300 for a warranty deed that gave the Davises a portion of his father's land. "Dead Indian" titles were suspect. The federal government forbade full-bloods like Emarthla from selling their land, but with the man now dead, did the restrictions still hold force? The warranty deed protected the Davises against future claims of damages or of an unclear chain of title. Charles Page now negotiated with Ethel and Sam Davis for full ownership of this land.

A month after he sold part of his inheritance to Ethel Davis, Gabriel went with his friend Mooney Wilson to a poker game in Tulsa. Gabriel flashed a wad of cash to a witness on his way back home to Turkey Mountain. Wilson and Gabriel were walking along the MK&T Railway tracks west of downtown Tulsa when they were ambushed and shot. Their bodies were dragged onto the track shortly before a westbound train hit them at 1:30 a.m. It was a gruesome scene—several newspapers reported that their bodies were mutilated, their limbs severed. The police investigation centered on the theory that a petty criminal had robbed the pair, as they were left with only two cents on their dismembered bodies and signs that someone had emptied their pockets. A railroad agent for the MK&T initially said that they had been drunk and vomiting on the tracks when they were hit by the train. The *Tulsa Tribune* seemed to support this account, but other reports indicated that they were murdered first and later dragged onto the tracks to make it look like an accident. A few weeks later, a notice appeared in the newspapers announcing the settlement of the Emarthla estate. The administrator was Samuel C. Davis.

The Davises would have surely known that as "full bloods," the Emarthla men were under federal restrictions that did not allow them to sell their land. Indeed, many years later it became apparent that there was a cloud on the title to these allotments. In 1960, in an effort to clear the title, the Sand Springs Home (which ended up owning much of the land in question) sued the heirs of the Emarthlas to be finally rid of this ghost that haunted real estate transactions in Tulsa County.[10]

The judge in charge of Emarthla's probate was N. J. Gubser, who was later revealed to be in debt to Charles Page. Page had lent Gubser $4,000 in a real estate deal involving Robert Pittman Jr. This Pittman was the son of Lucinda Pittman, the owner of the fancy Cadillac, the "palace on wheels." Page—as we'll see—had a long record of meddling with county judges, lending them money in exchange for favors or real estate. For a while, the practice seems to have gone unremarked upon. Judge Gubser did not even try to deny that Page had given him money.

Two Tulsa lawyers (R. L. Davidson and W. I. Williams) fought to have Robert Pittman's guardianship moved to Colorado, away from the network of Oklahoma grafters. Even by the standards of Tulsa, this case "was something appalling," Davidson and Williams wrote to the Creek national attorney, R. C. Allen. "You can readily see the great impropriety of Judge Gubser . . . becoming indebted to Mr. Page, who has a great deal of business in this court in the way of having deeds and leases from full-blood Indians approved."[11]

Tulsa County Judge Gubser and Creek County Judge McDougal allowed guardians to "borrow" money from their Indian wards. These guardians made investments in real estate and oil drilling, effectively using the wards as banks. Unlike banks, however, the Native American allottees rarely reaped a profit from the arrangement.

With the Emarthla lands under his control, Page set his sights on a small Muscogee village called Adams. Page eyed the land not so much for the oil but for his lofty dream of creating a village for orphans and widows. It was here he would fulfill his promise to his mother, to provide food and shelter to those who could not afford it.

To make the plan work he needed not just one allotment but a vast swath of land with room for a working farm, houses, recreation, a workshop, and eventually a zoo and amusement park. With the money he made in Glenn Pool, he turned to Sam Adams, a son of a well-known Muscogee warrior, Lieutenant Thomas Adams, who had served in the Civil War with the Creek faction that supported the Confederacy. Sam Adams was interested in selling his inherited allotment but was concerned about a burial place called Tullahassee Creek Indian Cemetery, near the village of Adams. As of 1908 the cemetery contained the graves of dozens of Muscogee people. There were many more to come. Adams, only twenty-four years old in 1908, would be one of many Muscogees—including Gabriel Emarthla—who died suspicious deaths between 1910 and 1913 and were buried in this cemetery.

Sam Adams also had an offer from another white man, Huddleston, who wanted to build a schoolhouse on his inherited allotment. According to Opal Clark, Charles Page took Adams to the Tulsa County courthouse to complete the sale of the land. The court clerk found that Adams had already sold his land to Huddleston. Huddleston and Page had apparently both been trying to persuade Adams to sell his allotment to them. The clerk said,

> "Sam, you can't keep changing your mind. . . . You declare Mr. Page's claim illegal, then you say it's legal. Make up your mind, Sam. Who are you selling this land to?"
>
> "Mr. Page," said Mr. Adams.
>
> "Now Sam, this property isn't yours anymore. Do you understand?" said the clerk. Sam nodded. "You can't sell it anymore."[12]

A couple of years later, in 1911, Adams died at the age of twenty-seven. His guardian was Ethel Davis. Davis, meanwhile, procured other deeds from dead Muscogee minors, including one from fourteen-year-old, Lucinda Hickory. A present-day relative of Lucinda's, Tatiana Duncan, grew up hearing oral histories about the suspicious death of Lucinda but was taken aback to learn that Davis obtained the deed the same day Lucinda died.

Mary Fuswa Evans, of the Emarthla family, watched the number of graves in the Tullahassee cemetery in Sand Springs grow as her cousins, aunts, and uncles died early deaths. Evans was concerned that Page's plans for Sand Springs would put the cemetery in jeopardy. She asked "Uncle Charlie" if he would sell it back so that she could protect it.

Page reportedly said to Evans, "I will not sell you the land but I will see that it is always taken care of."

Mary Fuswa Evans believed him.

THE DEATH OF A GUARDIAN

The rash of early deaths of Muscogee people whose affairs were controlled by Samuel C. Davis and Ethel Davis subsided after 1916. On December 18, 1916, Sam was visiting his lover, Daisy Carter, in Joplin, Missouri. In his pocket he carried a telegram advising that his divorce decree from Ethel was to be granted the following day.

Daisy and Sam went to a theater performance in downtown Joplin and had returned home when they heard someone violently break into the house. Assuming it was a burglar, Davis grabbed a pistol and ran downstairs. The electric lights did not turn on, so Sam struck a match to light a candle. As the match flared, the intruder shot Sam. As Sam lay dying, the assassin fled on foot, but not before Daisy caught a glimpse of him and an accomplice.

Samuel C. Davis was dead before the divorce was issued. The administrator of his estate was Ethel Davis, who blamed "that hussy" Daisy Carter for the whole tragedy. Ethel admitted trailing Sam to Joplin several times and convincing the police there to arrest him on adultery charges. Sam was arrested, but as part of the divorce settlement, charges were dropped. The Joplin press covered the affair breathlessly, as this "half-breed" oilman and his young lover, seen all over town, had been attacked by a pair of strangers. The oilman was dead. Suspicion in Joplin fell on Ethel.

The Tulsa press, then as ever, was sensitive that the murder might reflect poorly on the leading men and women of Tulsa, given the Davises, key roles in transferring land from allottees to oilmen. Charles Page had relied on the couple to act as administrators and guardians for landowners, but they were related, either through blood or marriage, to many other powerful players, including Dr. J. C. W. Bland (a founding father of Tulsa's oil industry) and then mayor John Simmons.

While the most logical explanation points to a hit on Sam ordered by Ethel, the *Tulsa World* speculated on a bizarre twist. According to

Ethel, the divorce telegram was a fake court decree that Sam presented to Daisy Carter. Sam Davis had gone to Joplin to finally break up with Daisy, but his spurned lover realized that the decree was bogus. Daisy, in a fit of jealousy upon discovering that Sam would not leave Ethel, murdered him. The *World* painted Ethel Davis as a grieving widow and Sam as a victim of Daisy Carter.[13]

Daisy was never held as a suspect by Joplin police, but the case remained active for law enforcement as well as for Daisy. Agents followed a lead out to California, where a Joplin man named Lester Henderson was arrested for highway robbery in 1921. After Sam's murder, Daisy had married a Texas oilman, but their relationship was troubled by the unsolved killing. Daisy never quite got over the Tulsa man. Her husband was reportedly jealous of the dead lover and ordered Daisy to never speak of Sam Davis. The news about Henderson's arrest rekindled a desire in Daisy to solve Sam's murder.

A California sheriff intercepted a letter Henderson sent to a Joplin friend from San Quentin State Prison. In it, Henderson recounted details of a killing which were remarkably similar to the murder of Sam Davis. While police never took seriously Ethel's theory that Daisy killed Sam, a dark cloud of suspicion hung over Daisy's head. She wanted to see Henderson prosecuted.

In 1921, the *Joplin Globe* seemed confident that this new angle would lead to the resolution of a sensational crime involving the Tulsa oilman. But the case was dropped and, in 1924, Lester Henderson escaped from prison.[14] Ethel Davis lived out her days in a mansion in Maple Ridge, occasionally gracing the society pages of the local newspapers. In 1946, her collection of over seven hundred pieces of hand-painted china was sold at auction. Ethel Davis died, having spent the last thirty years of her life without anyone in Tulsa printing a word about the murder of her husband.

The passing of Sam Davis in 1916 meant that Charles Page needed a new middleman, someone to deal with the messy affairs of restricted Indians and their land. He found that person in former Indian agent Frank Long, who would become a central figure in the Tommy Atkins case. Long was not Native American, but he seemed to know every influential character in what had been Indian Territory. Long understood that even if the Five Tribes were "on the road to disappearance," Indigenous people themselves were still quite present.

— CHAPTER 9 —

BARTLETT'S QUITCLAIM

The Run on Tommy's Land Begins

On a moody October day in 2022, I drove on old Route 66 from downtown Tulsa to the town of Sapulpa, the seat of Creek County. The county's records are housed in the courthouse there. I wanted to look up H. U. Bartlett, the Sapulpa oilman who seems to have been the first in the oil business to try to locate Minnie Atkins, in 1912.

The Bartlett name was one of the first to appear in the tract book in the Sapulpa courthouse, where all Creek County land transaction records are kept behind a counter staffed by a helpful woman in the clerk's office. The clerk told me I could look at the tract book; photocopies would be one dollar per page. No photography was permitted. I stood at a table with an unwieldy book the size of a modest tombstone at my fingertips. I had to locate Tommy's land by section, township, and range, using the Public Land Survey System. This system, whose roots are in the first era of American expansionism after the Revolution, was used by the federal government to divide up land for colonization and record the divisions. This system was vital to westward expansion as it provided clear demarcations for public and private lands and kept track of land holdings via geographic survey markers rather than features of the natural landscape.

I pinpointed Tommy's land. He had been issued land patents to two eighty-acre sections in the southwestern quarter of Section 4, Township 11, Range 7, in Creek County. These were known as lots 2 and 4.

The land was perilously close to the Osages, who had a difficult relationship with their new neighbors after Removal. The first grantor in the tract book was the Muscogee Nation, to Thomas Atkins, grantee. This came into force as soon as Oklahoma became a state in 1907.

For the first five years after statehood, the tract book recorded no transactions on the land. Then, on October 2, 1912, Bartlett filed a quitclaim deed, signed by Minnie Atkins, transferring the property to him. A quitclaim is a fast, but often precarious, way of transferring property from one entity to another—it transfers the seller's interest to the buyer with no warranty. Bartlett then began soliciting bids to lease the mineral rights to what was now his land. He leased the rights for one of the lots to Gypsy Oil Company, a subsidiary of Gulf Oil Company.

Gulf Oil was a major player. As the name suggests, Gulf specialized in oil pipelines to the Gulf Coast of Texas. Its major investor was Andrew Mellon, one of the richest men in the nation. Gypsy, a Gulf subsidiary, built pipelines from Oklahoma to the Gulf Coast refineries. On the other lot of Tommy's land, Bartlett signed a quitclaim deed that transferred ownership to Robert Oglesby, who then leased the minerals to McMan Oil Company. This seemingly worthless land was suddenly a focal point of oil exploration.

I stood there in the courthouse wondering how Minnie Atkins could have signed a quitclaim deed to Bartlett in 1912—a time at which everyone, even her closest relatives, believed she was either dead or completely cut off from her Oklahoma roots. Bartlett and then Oglesby had taken a risk buying the land from Atkins using quitclaim deeds: if some sort of cloud on the title emerged, there would be no financial protection for them.

Sure enough, a cloud appeared, in the form of Nancy Atkins. In 1913 Nancy sought to prove that the allottee, Tommy Atkins, had been not her sister Minnie's son but her own. She asserted that the quitclaim that Bartlett had received from Minnie in 1912 was a fraud.

How could this have happened? Had Bartlett been duped by a woman claiming to be Minnie? Or had he sought out a viable woman to play the role for him? We know that the Cushing oil strikes made headlines when they began in 1913. On January 2, 1913, the *Oklahoma State Register* reported "thrilling scenes where poor men are making fortunes in a day," overcrowding towns in Creek County with armies of "hobos, millionaires, plungers, gamblers, and women with rough cheeks."[1]

We also know that the news caught the attention of a new class of people known as grafters in Wagoner. The graft employed by these men—skirting or ignoring federal law in acquiring Indian lands—was a badge of honor for some of them. They did not consider the label "grafter" as an insult. Nancy had been working as a laundress in Wagoner when she heard the news that her sister Minnie had somehow emerged from the grave—or from complete obscurity—to claim one of the allotments found to be rich in oil.

We will never know if it was Nancy or her guardian, Micco T. Harjo, who decided to come forward, but in any case, Nancy claimed that the real Tommy Atkins was the product of an unwanted pregnancy that she'd carried to term in 1890. That pregnancy had been a subject of shame for Nancy, but she was willing to give details and name witnesses who could testify to the child's birth.

To prove Nancy's case, her team relied on witnesses in Wagoner who placed Nancy walking around town with a young boy named Tommy at the time of allotment. A resident named Andrew Jackson testified that he'd nearly run over a small child in the 1890s and had seen Nancy Atkins emerge to pick the child up. He asked her, "Is this your child?"

Nancy had responded to Jackson by calling the child "my boy."

Another Wagoner resident, Henry Anderson, a foreman for a railway company, testified that in either 1901 or 1902 he'd found one of his workers, Ellis Harris, digging a hole behind the house of one Elnora Williams. The woman in question had been Nancy's midwife and she testified that Nancy had given birth to a child around that time. Henry Anderson asked Harris what he was doing. Harris showed him a little box. In that box, Harris said, were the remains of Nancy Atkins's baby. He was burying the infant for Nancy, who was gravely ill following the birth. Anderson opened the box for himself and saw the dead infant. A third Wagoner resident, John Ford, remembered seeing Nancy pregnant behind the Davis and Jones Mercantile Store in 1899.

Nancy's lawyers also tracked down the woman who had impersonated Minnie and signed Bartlett's lease. Her legal name was, in fact, Minnie Atkins, but she was completely unrelated to the Minnie of Muscogee citizenship. It came out that this Minnie had been found and then lured into fraudulently signing the lease by the notorious Bettie Mann—the well-connected crook who did the dirty work of grafting oilmen. Prosecutors asserted that Bettie Mann had set up the fake Minnie, and Mann was convicted of forgery in Tulsa County as a result.

The question then arose as to the fate and whereabouts of the real Tommy and his mother. Even as Nancy seemed to build a case that she, not Minnie, was the mother of a Tommy, Page suspected that the real Minnie had to be out there, somewhere. If she was alive, whoever could find her and get her to sign over her land would instantly gain a fortune. A nationwide search began.

A former treasurer of the Muscogee Nation, Ellis Childers, knew all the characters involved in the case. He had gone to school first at Tullahassee, then at Carlisle, and had also served in the National Council's House of Warriors. White men knew and respected Childers. He had been around for that 1895 census and payment. He also said he remembered Tommy, and testified that he believed Tommy to belong to Nancy Atkins of Wagoner. As we've seen, the witnesses Nancy produced all had vivid stories, albeit conflicting ones—some remembered Nancy's child as a young Black boy; others, as a mixed-race girl. Some remembered the child dying in infancy in 1890, while others swore they saw him playing in the street in 1901. Despite these contradictions, in February 1914, a Creek County judge ruled in Nancy's favor, granting her the allotment and throwing out Bartlett's oil lease.

A state newspaper proclaimed "Valuable Oil Lease Settled."[2]

It was anything but.

— CHAPTER 10 —

"ALL CROOKS AT TULSA"

Minnie Atkins and the Receivership Hearing

Almost as soon as Nancy Atkins won her lawsuit in Creek County Court, an oil company affiliated with her began drilling on Tommy's allotment. A few months later, however, Charles Page and his business partner, R. A. Josey, emerged with another oil lease to the same land. By the spring of 1915, Gem Oil Co. was producing around fifteen thousand barrels of oil a day on Tommy's land. Their lease, like Bartlett's original deal with Gypsy, was signed by a Minnie Atkins.[1]

Page and Josey insisted they had the *real* Minnie Atkins this time. She was alive, well, and overjoyed to learn about her late son's fortune. She leased the oil rights to Tommy's land to Page and Josey, and had given a deposition to one of the most prestigious law firms in the state, Rice and Lyons. Page, who made it a habit of lending money to Tulsa and Creek County judges, thought his case was unassailable. At first, it was. Tulsa newspapers reported that Gem Oil had won the day; indeed, they began drilling and profiting immediately. The *Tulsa World* gave no indication that the newspaper would one day become Page's chief antagonist. "Tommy Atkins Actually Was, Witnesses Say," ran one headline. The *World* reported that a reverend from a church had been brought in to court to deliver a sermon on the good works of Charles Page.[2] Not only had Page stepped in to solve the case of the boy with two mothers, but he declared that the profits would go toward the construction of a new building for orphans.

This new Minnie testified convincingly about having given birth to Tommy at Fort Leavenworth in 1886, the product of a short relationship she'd had with a white man. On the strength of her testimony, the court ruled that the allotment legally belonged to this Minnie Atkins.

Her lease to Page and Josey was legitimate, and the revenue could flow to the Gem Oil Co.[3]

At this point via his strategic loans Page had secured leverage over the men tasked with regulating guardians and oil leases: county judges. Tulsa County Judge N. J. Gubser was one such person, as we've seen. Given the influence of the corrupt network of judges, guardians, and oilmen, some allottees tried to flee the state. Robert Pittman's family, for example, tried to have the child's estate moved to Colorado. This was a common strategy among allottees—move the entire estate out of the pit of vipers that was the Oklahoma grafter network. Corrupt probate courts plundered estates. Moving out of state was one way to escape this system. Judge Gubser tried to hold up the move, declaring that Pittman could not remove the guardian. Judge Gubser did not recuse himself when Pittman's father asked the judge to remove his son's guardian, even though the man was financially obligated to a network of grafters, including Page. Judge Gubser's colleague in Creek County, Judge Josiah Davis, was even more brazen, absconding with over $6,000 from a Muscogee minor's estate.[4]

The national attorney for the Creek Nation, H. L. Mott, had called attention to widespread corruption in Oklahoma courts and had initiated a number of lawsuits in an attempt to fight back. Although Mott was eventually driven out of office in 1914, his replacement, R. C. Allen, continued the work of fighting corruption and agreed to collaborate with the attorney general of the United States to cancel all oil leases on the Tommy Atkins lands. Allen and officials from the Department of Justice had been following the developments in Creek County, especially the increasingly convoluted story of Tommy Atkins.

In 1915, the federal government, along with the Muscogee Nation, moved to cancel the patent to Tommy's allotment, asserting that Tommy had never existed. Before the allotment could be canceled, however, the court needed to do something about the vast amount of riches flowing out of the land. It could not simply halt oil production. That was out of the question. Oil had become vital to the development of the national economy, to say nothing of the local economy, and would soon be the primary mover of America's war machine. President Woodrow Wilson was advocating for a network of highways for automobiles, which would facilitate an economic boom and help provide for national defense. The federal government never wanted to stop the flow of oil but did want to contest who controlled it. While the whole mess was sorted out, Allen and the US attorneys on the case thought the most logical solution was to appoint a court-designated receiver who could oversee the operations.

Judge Ralph E. Campbell moved to appoint a receiver for the Gem Oil Company's drilling operations on the Tommy Atkins lands. Receiverships are typical in fraud cases in which a corporation has been sued and a judge believes there is a chance that the owner will destroy or waste assets. Judge Campbell understood that Page and Josey might drain off or waste the oil on Tommy's property if it looked like they were going to lose the case.

Page and Josey appealed the receivership and fought it with everything they had. They had a lot to hide. Unbeknownst to Judge Campbell (though surely he suspected it), the two oilmen had started a secret operation to extract oil from Tommy's allotment but store it outside his land in steel tanks. This both artificially raised the price of oil by creating an impression of scarcity and also prevented government officials from realistically estimating the true volume of what was being drilled.

To avoid discovery, Page and Josey used the receivership hearing—which should have been a short legal procedure—to present as much evidence as they could muster, just to keep temporary control of the operations while the larger question of Tommy's existence was sorted out. This led to a drawn-out hearing in which Page and Josey's appeal had to be resolved before the federal trial could begin in earnest.

When the receivership hearing began, Minnie didn't want to testify, but "Page wouldn't have it any other way," she told a confidant.

Minnie contemplated backing out altogether, but Page assured her the end was in sight and promised her $5,000. The receivership hearing was excruciating for Minnie. Page's lawyers, who were supposed to be acting in Minnie's defense, instead chose to drag her reputation through the mud in the service of establishing an all-important fact: Tommy Atkins existed but had been abandoned by his mother. She had been so ashamed of Tommy that she left him behind and denied his very existence for years.

C. B. Stuart, Page's lead attorney, said that Minnie, as a young woman, had fallen into "evil ways" while working in the Hydes' household in Leavenworth, and he insinuated that she had engaged in sex work while living there. However, in his statements he often confused Minnie's name for that of Lily White, a well-known prostitute in the town. Court transcripts show that Stuart mistakenly referred to Lily White as "Minnie White."

Cornelia Hyde was called to testify. She said that, while Minnie had worked for the Hydes, a soldier hung around the back door of the house, hoping to catch the attention of the "voluptuous, unrestrained Indian girl."[5] Later, in the spring of 1885, Hyde spotted Minnie in front of a Leavenworth brothel owned by Granny Letcher. Thirty years had passed, but Hyde was confident of the dates and the fact that Minnie was "in a pregnant condition."[6]

Even if Cornelia was to be believed, there was a chronology problem. Minnie's first statements held that Tommy was born in 1886. Now a credible witness had the birth occurring earlier, most likely in 1885. R. C. Allen, Creek national attorney, further questioned how Cornelia was able to identify Minnie at all, given that Granny Letcher's place was in a "disreputable" part of town, and the well-to-do Cornelia would not have wanted to be seen on Choctaw Street.

There was also another Indigenous woman in Leavenworth, known as "Indian Mary," who worked in the sex trade. People often confused the two women, and Page's lawyers seemed to invite their conflation. Allen wondered if the woman spotted outside the brothel might have been Mary, not Minnie. A handful of locals who hung around Granny Letcher's place remembered Indian Mary as a young mother often seen carrying around her son, Tommy York. Indian Mary had been found murdered in a ditch with her throat slashed in 1883, before Minnie Atkins had even arrived at Leavenworth. It was entirely possible that in the ensuing thirty years, Cornelia Hyde conflated memories of two Native women into one, making Tommy York the son of Minnie Atkins. Minnie's old friend, Sadie Ross—later known as Sadie James—appeared in the courtroom as well. James said that Minnie had been quiet, frustrated, someone who ached to be respected by genteel Christian society even if she often found herself marginalized by it. Whereas the Hydes described Atkins as a vain, flirtatious young woman who perfumed herself for soldiers, James said her friend wore a "plain dress and an apron," and had but one love interest, Private Peterkin.

The contradictory statements of the witnesses seemed to frustrate the lawyers on both sides, who filled up the hundreds of pages of testimonies with objections based on hearsay, incompetence, argumentation, and irrelevance. The supposed pregnancy of Minnie during that crucial period during the spring and summer of 1885 was also hotly contested.

"HE WAS A VERY OBEDIENT CHILD": RECOLLECTIONS OF TOMMY IN LEAVENWORTH

One key witness in the case was George Crilley, an elderly white livery driver who claimed to have known Minnie Atkins quite well while she was in Leavenworth. Crilley operated a stable on Seneca Street, across from Granny Letcher's place. He was often hired to drive people around town or into the fort itself. Crilley not only saw Minnie pregnant at Granny Letcher's; he claimed to have known her baby. Crilley said that Minnie left the child with Granny Letcher to follow Private Peterkin to Colorado in 1888, and he, Crilley, grew fond of the child. Crilley gave Tommy a nickname, Commodore. Crilley said that the child "played in my carriages and would take both hands and lean over the dashboard and pretended that he was whipping the horses."

Crilley loved Commodore. "I knew him so well, he was a very obedient child," Crilley said. "He would stand up between my limbs and I remember often taking his hat off when he was three or four years old and rubbing his head and saying, Commodore that will give me luck. I used to call him that, and he would walk up to me and take his hat off and hold his head over for me to rub his head; he seemed to think that was part of the business."[7]

Crilley was pressed by both sides to identify the child's race. Had this Commodore been white, Black, Native, or some combination? Crilley struggled with the question. At first, he said Tommy "wasn't what you would call dark; he was a kinder [sic] light, a real light child." Crilley then reconsidered, "He had some dark features to a certain extent about him; dark appearance."

Tommy's perceived race was of utmost importance. It was not simply a matter of prurient curiosity to know if the father was Black, white, or Native. Minnie was contending that Tommy was white, and so the George Crilleys of the world were needed to confirm the child was not Black. Crilley was asked if it was common practice to rub the head of a Black child for good luck. He seemed confused.

Mollie "Granny" Letcher herself was a widow, a Black woman who had been born into slavery in Tennessee. While the Leavenworth aristocracy may have seen her house as a destination for immoral acts, other people viewed Mollie Letcher as a generous woman deserving of her nickname. Apparently everyone—the judge included—knew her as Granny. One of Letcher's boarders, Martha Miller, said that Granny "kept people's children that . . . didn't have any home and wanted to work out." Miller had left her own child in Granny Letcher's care because, she said, she trusted her.

Once again, however, the issue turned on race. Almost all of the children under the care of Granny Letcher were known to be Black or mixed-race. If Tommy's father was an unknown white man and Tommy had been born from a tryst, then the boy would have been one of very few non-Black children, if not the only one, around Letcher's house. Crilley's testimony—that the child had been light with some dark features—fit with a possible parentage that included an Indigenous mother and a white father, but this child in question had essentially vanished in the 1890s. Crilley's testimony also shifted over time.

The timing of Tommy's birth was another delicate question. The birthdates of Minnie's first two children, Robert Lee and Alice Mable, were incontrovertibly established as 1886 and 1888. These children, unlike their phantom brother, Tommy, had verifiably lived and died, with the birth certificates, witnesses, and burial sites to prove it. The only way Minnie could have also given birth to a Tommy who had been a child in the late 1880s, as Crilley and other witnesses asserted, was if he'd been born before both Robert Lee and Alice. The window for Tommy to have been born was thus quite narrow: between May and September 1885. Minnie was not pregnant when she left Carlisle in July 1884, but she had become pregnant with Robert in September 1885.

Cornelia Hyde's statements therefore carried a lot of weight. She had seen Minnie pregnant during the spring of 1885, hanging around Granny Letcher's. There was also a witness named Mattie Cobb—deemed a "reputable white woman" by Page's fixer, Frank Long—who claimed that Minnie had waited on her when she was pregnant with a daughter born on April 20, 1885. Cobb's daughter later played with Tommy Atkins. Given that Cobb's pregnancy overlapped some with Minnie's, Judge Campbell seemed eager to hear more details. Cobb said Minnie would have given birth around the end of May 1885.

She remembered him as an infant. Tommy, she said, was mixed Black and Indigenous but "favored the Indians," with "light brown" skin, "high cheeks, black eyes, and black hair." Page's team had established a timeline and witnesses. But the race of the child vexed everyone—especially Minnie, who was adamant that her child was not Black.

Given the chronology, it was entirely plausible that Minnie had yet another child before Robert Lee, with yet another man. Considering that Minnie was proven to have arrived in Leavenworth on July 11, 1884, and that Robert Lee was born on July 1, 1886, there was a narrow window for the conception of Tommy Atkins, probably a couple of months into her residence at the Hydes'.

If, as Cornelia Hyde's testimony implied, this child had been born at Granny Letcher's, then there was a distinct possibility—a probability—that the father was Black. From Minnie's perspective, such a scenario went against everything Miss Alice had prepared her for: becoming a literate, respectable lady who could enjoy the rights and privileges of white society. Those same rights and privileges had been snatched away from Black people during the early days of Oklahoma statehood in 1907. Miss Alice collected racist images of Black children for her photograph collection. (I found an image in her archive of a Black boy, his clothes in tatters, carrying a basket of eggs and proclaiming: "I dun foun' dat nest!") Now Page wanted her missing child to be Black? Everything was going wrong, even as she contemplated the real possibility of becoming rich. And, as her legal team went on to probe the possibility that Tommy's father might have been a Black soldier or even a relative of Sadie James, it was getting worse. Minnie Atkins was horrified.

AGENT DLABAL AND THE INVENTION OF THE DICTOGRAPH

One day, after some grueling depositions by attorneys in a law office, Minnie was approached by a tall, attractive white woman who said she was originally from Czechoslovakia. She gave her name as Albina Dlabal. Dlabal gained Minnie's confidence by doing some tailoring work for her, offering to pick up and drop off garments for alteration. Minnie had grown suspicious of strangers, but she opened up to Dlabal.

Dlabal listened to Minnie's stories without interruption or judgment, which probably came as a relief. Minnie complained about the onslaught of lawyers, reporters, and investigators, who grilled her constantly about youthful indiscretions to bolster whatever narrative of Tommy Atkins suited them best.

"To face thousands of people in the Court Room was nothing easy with all those smart lawyers from both sides getting a crack at you," Minnie said.

"I was never in a court room," Dlabal responded.

"O, God," Minnie said, "you don't know what it means."

"Tommy Atkins was a n*****, was he?" Dlabal asked.

"No, but they had a n***** boy that they called Tommy Garrett, and they wanted him to get the land, not me. No n*****s for me!" she said to Dlabal.

Minnie Atkins refused to tell anyone Tommy's father's name. "That is something the world will never know," she said to Dlabal.

Minnie felt a mixture of shame and rage when she talked about her treatment in the courtroom. Everyone, she said, was a liar, especially those with ties to Tulsa. "They were all crooks at Tulsa," Minnie told her friend. "They all lied and made [me] swear to lies. It never pays to do anything crooked; once you've done wrong and lied about it, then it was pretty hard to do right things."

Minnie told Dlabal she was growing frustrated with her husband. Harry had been devoted to Minnie, but the prospect of riches had changed him. He grew reckless with money and suspicious that Minnie was intending to back out of Page's case. Minnie had misgivings not so much about Page but about Frank Long, who seemed to be willing to stoop to anything. She also resented her attorney, E. C. Hanford.

Harry damaged their car, an Oakland Six, by putting oil on the wheels. Minnie also said that Harry needled her for not following orders to stay home and stay quiet. He said she had gotten "too independent and smart since [I] learned to drive the car." She admitted to flirting with the electrician, which also drove Harry crazy. Minnie suggested to Dlabal that they go out with some of the handsome men while Harry was away. In another one of their talks, Minnie told Dlabal that Harry had threatened her. Dlabal recalled that Minnie had told her that Harry "was going to put a muzzle on her. Someday he would take her out in the machine alone, and drive her at sixty miles an hour and give her something to holler about."

Minnie had no idea that "Albina Dlabal" was an alias for a government-contracted special investigator, most likely from the infamous union-busting Pinkerton detective agency. Dlabal had been sent by the government to obtain Minnie's honest account of Tommy's identity. She'd secretly planted a dictograph in Minnie's house—a new technology.

By 1913 the inventor of the dictograph, Kelly Turner, had devised a way to have speech picked up by a microphone and recorded remotely onto a vinyl disc. Turner told the *New York Times* that "mere whispers" could be picked up and remotely recorded.[8] The technology quickly became a part of many major criminal investigations and union-busting activities. Dlabal's recordings were transcribed and then sent to the US attorney's office, which included the transcriptions in its exhibits for the trial. Today, such recordings would be considered a violation of a person's Fourth Amendment rights against unreasonable searches and seizures. In the 1910s, it did not seem to occur to anyone that secretly recording speech might be a violation of that protection.[9]

In the courtroom and in depositions, Minnie's statements about Tommy were maddeningly fluid and contradictory. She initially stated that she'd had a total of four children, one of whom, Thomas, had been born at the Sisters Hospital in Leavenworth in 1886. But the sisters who ran the hospital could find no evidence of Tommy's birth there. All evidence suggested that the infant had been Robert Lee Peterkin, not Tommy Atkins.

Minnie then changed her story again, saying that she had given birth to Tommy in a barn behind Granny Letcher's place. Letcher had died before the trial occurred, so this version could not be verified. Minnie was the only living person who had witnessed Tommy's birth, but she told at least four different versions of the story. The pressure on Minnie to tell one clear, coherent story about a child whom she had either repressed all memories of or invented out of whole cloth took its toll on her mental health. She grew fearful about everyone around her, even her own surviving children, Charley and Harvey. She was kept inside Page's home for four days while the legal team discussed her testimony. She confessed to Dlabal that she had grown suspicious of everyone around her, except for Dlabal.

The shifting details of Minnie's accounts of Tommy were a major front upon which the government attacked her credibility. To keep up the pressure on her, R. C. Allen and the Department of Justice assembled a chart, "The Conflicting Stories of Minnie Atkins." The chart was organized like a spreadsheet, showing how Minnie's story changed depending on whether she was being interviewed by Page's attorneys, the government, or a spy such as Albina Dlabal. The prosecution submitted this chart to Judge Campbell as an exhibit, suggesting that Minnie was being manipulated by forces beyond her control.[10]

Finally, sometime in 1915, Minnie settled on one story. It was a painful story, which in the social context of the time made her look like a lascivious woman with loose morals, the opposite of the restrained lady Alice Mary Robertson had wanted her to be.

Minnie swore that this new story was the honest truth. As she revealed the details in the federal courthouse in Muskogee, she answered questions in short, staccato phrases. She now said her first son had been not Robert Lee Peterkin but a boy named Tommy, born at a "bawdy house" run by Granny Letcher when Minnie was only eighteen years old.

Minnie was asked about Tommy's father, but she refused to answer. No one pushed her on this question, as it was irrelevant to Tommy's citizenship in the Muscogee Nation. One of Page's lawyers, Ben Rice, asked Minnie why she had not told the truth about Tommy's birthplace to begin with. "Well," Minnie said, "I just simply said it because I didn't want to tell where he was born."

"Why didn't you want to tell?" Rice said.

"Well, I just didn't want to because—" Minnie said.

"Because Granny was a negro?" Rice said.

"No, but she didn't run a very good house, and I didn't want everybody to know my business."

Ultimately, the testimony was persuasive enough that Gem Oil was allowed to continue managing its own operations with the caveat that they post a bond worth nearly $1 million.

It took Page almost everything he had to post that bond.

— CHAPTER 11 —

MINNIE ATKINS IN SEATTLE

How had Charles Page found Minnie Atkins in the first place? Opal Clark's biography tells of an expedition through the West using his detective skills, outwitting rival oilmen until he found her in a mining camp in California. The reality was even wilder than what Opal Clark recorded, but it had little to do with Page himself. The mission to find Minnie was mostly carried out by Sadie James and Bettie Mann, who were played against each other by Frank Long.

Sometime in the spring of 1914, as Page and Bartlett fought Nancy's rich Arkansas backer, J. A. Ferguson, in Creek County Court, Long was at work on another angle. At Page's behest, Long contacted Captain McNab, Harry Folk's commanding officer at Fort Lawton, in Seattle. Long had known to contact McNab thanks to a tip from Sadie James.

James had managed the unthinkable. She had impersonated a federal Indian agent, navigated a racist, sexist society, and penetrated the security of a military base thousands of miles from her home. There she had located a person, Minnie Atkins, who even the almighty Dawes Commission believed was dead. James was in no position to negotiate with Captain McNab about Minnie's husband, his subordinate, Sergeant Harry Folk, to persuade Minnie to get involved in the case, but Frank Long was.

Long told Captain McNab that Sergeant Folk's wife stood to become a multimillionaire. Page hired a Seattle attorney, E. C. Hanford, to come and meet Minnie and Harry at the army base; present at the meeting would be Long and Captain McNab.

Hanford and Long promised Minnie a $4,000 preliminary fee for the Tommy Atkins oil lease. Page's standard procedure in such deals was to obtain leases for oil and gas drilling, not actual deeds to the land. But this case was proving to be so vexing that he wanted

Hanford and Long to eventually get the land itself from Minnie. The title to the allotment could be obtained, as it was inherited land from a half-blood tribal citizen. That meant that federal restrictions were probably not in play.

Minnie seemed hesitant to sell her land outright. In fact, she felt hesitant about the whole operation. Her suspicious nature told her there might be more at stake than what Hanford and Long were presenting. She was right to be suspicious. A US probate attorney for Indian Affairs named Frank Montgomery had been tasked by the secretary of the interior to be on the lookout for fraud among Indian estates. As part of that assignment, he had been watching the hunt for Minnie Atkins through his own agents. He, like Long, had also traveled from Oklahoma to Seattle, where he hired a Pinkerton agent of his own named Robertson to follow the movements of Bettie Mann and Sadie James. Before Long and Hanford had a chance to work out the details of the story they wanted Minnie to tell, Montgomery had also showed up at Fort Lawton.

Montgomery obtained a telegram that Hanford had sent to the registrar of deeds of Creek County, showing that Minnie had transferred her royalty interest and possibly her title to Charles Page. Why did this woman, believed to be dead but living a quiet life as a cook on an army base, suddenly have such riches to give away? Montgomery suspected Minnie was not an honest dealer, but he was not sure if she was willingly playing along in this scheme, or if she was being forced to lie.

Montgomery wanted to give Minnie a chance to come clean in case she was a pawn in a bigger scheme. If what she signed turned out to be untrue, she would be guilty of wire fraud and possibly conspiracy as well. Montgomery, perhaps naively, thought it best if all the interested parties met on the army base to discuss what was known and decide on the proper course of action.

"A LIE, PURE AND SIMPLE": MINNIE CONFESSES, THEN RETRACTS HER CONFESSION

Captain McNab, Montgomery, Long, Hanford, and Minnie Atkins all gathered in a stately home on Fort Lawton's Officers' Row. Minnie sat on a sofa and became very quiet as she listened to Montgomery.

He summarized the situation. The telegram to the Creek County clerk had aroused suspicion among federal agents like him, who were on the lookout for swindles involving Indian lands. The land in question had already been involved in a prosecution for a forgery—the oil lease given to Bartlett and signed by the fake Minnie Atkins. There were multiple oilmen on this land with various real estate instruments, all claiming their right to drill there. But the very existence of the allottee—Tommy Atkins—was in doubt. If Minnie could make a simple statement of the truth, it might be possible to avoid legal complications.

Hanford and Long whispered back and forth to each other, pacing in and out of the room and standing near a fireplace. Minnie had questions for Montgomery. Before she would talk to him about anything, she wanted a guarantee of immunity from prosecution. This was a problem.

If, as Montgomery suspected, Minnie had lied about the 1895 payment to Tommy, it would set a bad precedent to grant her immunity. He told Minnie he "was in no place" to grant immunity. It was also unclear whether Montgomery, as a probate attorney, even had the power to grant someone immunity. He stalled for time, hoping he could get to a telegraph office or telephone exchange and secure an immunity deal from someone in the Department of the Interior.

Meanwhile, Hanford told Minnie that if she gave Montgomery, a government attorney, a false statement, she would be liable for a charge of perjury, a felony punishable by up to ten years in prison.

Minnie sat still on the sofa as the men buzzed around her. For twenty minutes Minnie went back and forth in her mind, contemplating her options. To Long and Hanford's complete surprise, Minnie suddenly started talking about Thomas Atkins.

Here was the truth: She was not the boy's mother. But, yes, she had withdrawn a $14.40 payment in his name. The payment had already been made up. Someone needed to collect it. The only Thomas Atkins she knew of was her father, who had died well before 1895. Minnie said she had given birth to three children: Alice Peterkin, who was dead, and Charley and Harvey Harrison, who were alive. She omitted any mention of Robert Lee Peterkin, the boy whose father was a mystery.

Silence filled the room. "There was absolutely nothing said by anyone in the room except Minnie Atkins," Montgomery later said.[1]

Now that Minnie had admitted to false testimony and to taking a payment under false pretenses, she asked again about immunity. Montgomery said he would ask Washington to grant her immunity—if she would make the statement in writing. McNab, Montgomery, Hanford, and Minnie Atkins came to an agreement, which Montgomery later described in court. "If I succeeded in procuring immunity, Captain McNab was to deliver me this written confession. If I did not secure immunity for her that Captain McNab was to burn it."[2]

They went upstairs to McNab's private office. Hanford wrote down what Minnie had said and then handed her the document for her signature. As Minnie read the statement, Hanford reminded her about the possibility of prosecution if it contained lies.

She listened, and then, without a word, signed her name. She left the document with McNab. Minnie took Frank Montgomery back to the Folks' house, where she made lunch. "She was pleasant and hospitable," Montgomery said.

After lunch, Montgomery and Minnie went into Seattle. Minnie knew that Page had by now wired her the $4,000 preliminary fee she had been promised, and she wanted to withdraw it from the National Bank of Commerce immediately. It was common practice at the time for grafters to swindle Native Americans by reversing such transactions and leaving no paper trail. She told Montgomery that the $4,000 was to be hers, "win or lose."

Montgomery was also in a hurry. He composed a telegram to the commissioner of Indian Affairs, Cato Sells, updating him on Minnie's confession and her request for immunity:

Sells, Commissioner, Washington DC.
December 17, 1914.

Minnie Atkins today confessed to me in presence of Captain
McNab and Hanford she never had child Tommy Atkins.
That Thomas Atkins for which she drew grass money was her
father. I promised her would attempt to secure immunity from
prosecution for perjury and conspiracy. Immunity will have
to come from Oklahoma State authorities. Recommend that
effort be made. I directed that agent Ligon, County Attorney

*Creek County and secure necessary action. Minnie's confession
corroborated by affidavits in my possession. Necessary to work
quickly and quietly as Oklahoma and Kansas parties appear to
be seriously involved.*

Montgomery.[3]

As Minnie and Montgomery made their way back to the latter's
hotel, Montgomery approached a shadowy man who had been tailing
all the parties involved. This was Agent Robertson, the Pinkerton man
ostensibly in the employ of the government. Montgomery was working
with Robertson, but he suspected that the Pinkerton agent's loyalties
were not entirely transparent: he worried that he might be working
both sides and leaking information to Bartlett in Sapulpa. At the time,
the nascent Bureau of Investigation—forerunner to the FBI—did not
have the capacity to compete with the Pinkerton agents. The creation
of the modern FBI in the 1920s would soon do away with the need
to work with the Pinkertons, but for now, Montgomery had to keep
Minnie close and the Pinkerton agent closer.

Montgomery dropped his briefcase. Robertson picked it up, and
as he handed it back to Montgomery, the attorney whispered to him
that everything was going according to plan. This may have been a
ruse to keep Robertson at bay.[4]

The next morning, Montgomery met Harry Folk at the train station
next to the Vancouver Barracks. They headed to the fort, where Minnie
was supposed to sign a new statement, with Montgomery's promise of
immunity. Montgomery was eager to wrap up the case. As a probate
attorney who dealt in Native American estates in Oklahoma, he was
over his head in case work. Now that Montgomery had Minnie's confession, he could get back to work in Oklahoma. Charles Page was at
the center of other investigations in Montgomery's portfolio, including
one case in which Page appeared to have bribed Judge Gubser to allow
one of his affiliates to become the guardian for Robert Pittman Jr., the
son of Lucinda Pittman, the famous Muscogee woman who convinced
Cadillac to make her a special car.

Folk and Montgomery went back to Captain McNab's quarters
and waited for Minnie to meet them. However, McNab had some bad

news for the government attorney: Minnie Atkins had retracted her previous day's statement about not having a son named Tommy Atkins. Montgomery was stunned. Harry let loose with a stream of emotional backstory: His wife had been unable to sleep the previous night. She had spent much of the night sobbing with her head on the diningroom table. Folk accused Montgomery of pressuring his wife into a story that was not true. She had agreed to the immunity deal, yes, because she had committed a fraud in 1895 during the grass money payments. But that fraud had been minor compared to the millions at stake in Tommy's estate. And who could really blame Minnie for taking that extra payment? She had just lost a daughter in infancy. Furthermore, everyone had been on the take during the Dawes Commission. Minnie's crime had been minor considering all the white men who lied to get themselves land or guardianships of wealthy estates.

Montgomery had no time for all these rationalizations. He needed to find the written confession and hold her to it. Harry said that Minnie was now afraid that he would desert her after finding out about her lost children. Given the drama and emotion of the prior day, Folk said, Minnie's statement should never have been accepted by anyone in the government.

As Harry spoke, Montgomery began to suspect that Hanford was behind the retraction. Minnie came in and appeared nervous and jittery. The statement that Minnie had signed and given to Captain McNab was gone, never to be seen again. The only evidence Montgomery had of Minnie's initial statement was the telegram he had sent to Commissioner Sells the previous day. Now the group at the fort—Harry, Minnie, McNab, and Hanford—all seemed to agree that the "confession" had been forced by Montgomery the previous day.

Montgomery tried to hide his disappointment in Minnie and his growing anger at Hanford. He resolved to take the issue up with Hanford. He would use the Pinkerton agent, Robertson, and Sadie James to get Hanford into a hotel room in Seattle and see what he had been up to. Montgomery felt that he could get Hanford to admit that he had pressured Minnie into retracting her confession. Then, Minnie herself would come back around and admit that she had been forced to lie.

Montgomery believed that Page and Josey also had a hand in the retraction. Montgomery testified in *U.S. v. Atkins et al.* that Minnie had shown him a damning letter from Page. In it, the Sand Springs oilman pressured her to stick with the story he'd given her—and also implied that he could have her replaced with another woman who would be happy to lie to create a Tommy Atkins for $5,000 (approximately $150,000 in 2024 dollars). Montgomery had a backup plan as well, he wrote. Frank Long had found a man in Leavenworth claiming to be the true Tommy. Witnesses in Leavenworth, including a leading Black attorney named Dennis Jones, were prepared to verify the man's claim. He had connections around Granny Letcher's place and a convincing yarn that Minnie had given birth to him after an affair with a Black man. Page said that this Tommy was ready to sell his land to him for $10,000.

The implication was clear: Minnie was expendable. There were other mothers of Tommy Atkins, and, indeed, plenty of Tommy Atkinses as well. They were willing to play Page's game for a better price.

"Minnie seemed surprised that Page and Josey would undertake to defeat the claim they had advanced for her," Montgomery wrote in his notes on the case. Minnie had made the mistake of thinking that Page wanted to help her. After all, he was known as Daddy Page, father to the orphans of the world, helper of unfortunate women like her.

Montgomery felt confident that Long and Page were behind Minnie's changing stories, and he concluded in a report to R. C. Allen that the encounter with such a wild scheme had affected him personally. "While it may be that my enthusiasm to get to the true facts of this case might perhaps warp my judgement," Montgomery wrote to Allen, "yet at the same time having come in personal contact with the moving actors in this drama, I must admit that the case looks like a conspiracy to defraud the Creek Nation of this property and that the story of the birth of Tommy Atkins is a lie pure and simple, founded upon perjury."[5]

— CHAPTER 12 —

"UTTERLY UNWORTHY OF YOUR CONFIDENCE"

The Campaign Against R. C. Allen

Richard Clyde Allen would be no one's idea of a white savior. He was born in 1882, a Southerner from North Carolina with a tall slope of red hair and a reputation for pomposity. Allen fit the mold of the old Dixie elite. He came from a family that journeyed on grand tours of Europe and sent their children to private colleges like Wake Forest, where Allen completed his law degree. Rather than settle into a life in the southern aristocracy, however, Allen went to Indian Territory in the early 1900s to start a law practice. He went from Muskogee to the small town of Coweta, where he started a firm specializing in real estate transactions involving Native American minors. His Coweta Realty Company followed a similar trajectory of other real estate firms, acquiring titles of dubious legality to allottees' lands.

For the first few years of his practice, Allen appeared to be following the track of a second-tier grafter, engaging in what E. B. Linnen, a Bureau of Indian Affairs special investigator, called a "common practice" by dealing in "full-blood inherited titles." As it was unclear in the eyes of the law whether inherited deeds from full-bloods could be sold free from any restrictions, Allen and his ilk were aware that they were taking a risk by acquiring inherited full-blood titles. It was entirely possible that they could close a transaction only to have a probate court rule that the title was still restricted from sale.

Allen and his associates might make a reasonably good offer for a title, but they would only pay out a small portion of their offer at closing. The rest of the money would be held in an escrow account in a bank until a court cleared the title of encumbrances such as liens or restrictions. This was supposed to happen in probate courts, which were notoriously corrupt. People like Allen would make any possible excuse not to pay the balance of the transaction. Linnen said that Allen "was of the opinion that the titles would eventually be good and if so, at the price they were paying for the lands, he would be benefited financially."

However, many of the titles were not good. Many are still clouded to this day. When the chain of ownership was unclear, Allen found himself on the hook for large sums of money, which he could not always come up with. He would then find himself hit by lawsuits from Muscogee landowners demanding the rest of the payment. He had dozens of pending lawsuits against him for this very reason.

Despite his questionable finances, in 1910 Allen decided to run for district judge of Muskogee County, borrowing heavily from local businessmen to fund his campaign.

Allen's campaign slogan, "No negroes on juries," left no doubt as to his view on race. He sought his votes from what some euphemistically called "the liberal element" of Muskogee. The term had nothing to do with political ideology and everything to do with tolerance for bootlegging, gambling, and prostitution. One self-described bootlegger named Frank Walkup said, sure, Allen wanted their vote, but so did every single Muskogee politician. Candidates like Allen would rail against the bootleggers while campaigning; once elected, they would settle into an agreement with them based on tolerance and the occasional payment of a fine.

Allen won the election, though there were accusations that his supporters had dumped the ballots with votes for Allen's opponent in the Verdigris River. However, once in office Allen shocked his bootlegger supporters by following through on his campaign denunciations, refusing to grant pardons to notorious bootleggers and saloon keepers. They felt betrayed by a man they assumed would conduct business as usual.

Around the same time, the national attorney for the Muscogee Nation, a white man named H. L. Mott, was earning the enmity of powerful Oklahoma oilmen by exposing town lot frauds. As the Muscogee Nation's national attorney, Mott was charged with protecting the well-being of the Nation's citizens, including protection from fraud.

Town lot fraud was a complicated swindle: the lots in cities like Muskogee and Tulsa had been created by the federal government in the late 1890s in expectation of growth after statehood. These lots would be the basis for urban development—sites for homes and businesses. The federal government intended for these lots to be purchased at auction by new settlers. However, many of the lots were already occupied by people authorized by the Muscogee Nation to reside in the Territory. The government offered those people the opportunity to buy the property at one half the appraised value. The residents could then either make improvements and continue to live there or sell the property on the open market and be guaranteed a handsome return.

Mott investigated some of the transactions in Muskogee and found that in dozens of cases the occupants of the land were "dummies"— people who either did not live on the lots or did not exist at all. Grafters would forge quitclaim deeds and other real estate instruments in the names of these dummies, leading to huge profits that were funneled up to a handful of powerful men. Those cases suggested even bigger frauds in the booming city of Tulsa. Before long it appeared that a statewide conspiracy existed not only to acquire lots through dummies but to then artificially spike the value of the lots before their sale. In 1909 a grand jury was impaneled by Judge Ralph E. Campbell (the same judge in the Tommy Atkins case) to investigate who was behind the conspiracy. The indictments that followed included the Democratic governor of Oklahoma, Charles Haskell, along with several respected businessmen in the eastern part of the state. These revelations shocked the nation, leading to headlines in papers like the one in the *Fort Worth Record and Register*: "U.S. Grand Jury Indicts Haskell of Oklahoma for Town Lot Frauds," the Texas newspaper reported in 1909.

Mott argued on behalf of the Muscogee Nation that all fraudulent dummy lots should have their titles returned to the tribe. The lots would be "surplus lands." The tribe could then sell them, develop them, or simply hold on to the land. Mott was revealing Democrats like Haskell to be a national embarrassment. Mott began to receive death threats. Governor Haskell fought to remove Mott from office.

Candidates for the position of national attorney for the Muscogee Nation could be nominated by the principal chief, but it was ultimately at the discretion of the secretary of the interior and the president of the United States as to whether to allow the chief's nominee to be able to serve the tribe.

Three Oklahoma congressmen went to meet with President Woodrow Wilson and attempted to convince him to fire Mott. President

Wilson was reluctant to do so. Mott's investigation had raised serious questions about the legitimacy of the white settlement of Oklahoma. If many of the town lots were frauds, forgeries, or claims filed by nonexistent people, what about the allotments? At a time when a major oil boom was on in Oklahoma, all the clouds in the titles could lead to major disruptions. Wilson did not want that. The Mid-Continent oil field was now indispensable to the American economy. But Wilson was disturbed by the reports he read. Wilson's secretary of the interior, Franklin Lane, decided to allow Mott's appointment as national attorney of the Muscogee Nation to expire in 1914. Mott was not exactly fired, but he was not rehired and was thus forced to leave his investigation of Haskell and others unfinished.

The men behind Mott's departure now mobilized to find a more malleable replacement. Their choice: Judge R. C. Allen, who as a grafter with debts to other grafters was believed to fit the bill. Allen, like them, was a southern Democrat who believed in white supremacy. He had engaged in certain questionable business practices himself, and it seemed logical that Allen would not cast any stones at town lot owners or guardians of Indian estates, lest he himself be investigated.

INVESTIGATING THE DUBIOUS REPUTATION OF R. C. ALLEN

When it came to Allen's unscrupulous land deals, one case continued to be talked about. In 1909, before he was elected judge, Allen had made a deal with a young Black man named Cecil McKinley. McKinley had been in Wagoner with his friend Jacob Nelson, who had lost a leg and needed help getting around while he served on a jury in the district court. While McKinley waited for Nelson in town, an unknown man approached him with a proposition.

The man knew that McKinley was fond of a fifteen-year-old Muscogee freedperson named Martha Verner, but her parents believed she was too young to entertain marriage suitors. However, her father, Ben Verner, had recently been sent to jail. That removed one obstacle. The stranger said he knew Allen, who could arrange a marriage license between him and Martha. There was just one catch: after the marriage, McKinley would have to sell a substantial portion of Verner's allotment to Allen.

Allén's proposal interested McKinley, but he, too, felt that Verner was too young for him to marry. The Wagoner man took McKinley to meet Allen, who convinced him to go along with their plan and marry Verner. Martha, as an underage Black and Native American girl, had little legal agency. These matters would be decided for her. The group went back to McKinley's house in Wagoner.

Allen hired a carriage to escort the couple to Coweta for the wedding ceremony and then to his private practice. McKinley was supposed to sell eighty acres of Verner's land to Allen for $1,000. Allen paid him $150 up front, and then gave him a promissory note for $700. Allen told McKinley that he would receive the last $150 from Verner's guardian, J. H. Thigpen.

McKinley's friend, Nelson, also received a $25 payment from Allen. Nelson's part in the scheme had been to quash any doubts McKinley had about the hasty land transaction. Martha Verner—now Martha McKinley—kept copies of all these transactions. Months, then years, went by, and neither Cecil nor Martha McKinley received the outstanding payments for the land. The guardian, Thigpen, proved to be no help either. In 1915, Martha, no longer a minor, claimed that she had never seen a cent from Allen. She also sued her husband Cecil for divorce.

In 1915, after Allen had been national attorney for one year, the Bureau of Indian Affairs (BIA) appointed Edward B. Linnen to investigate Allen's fitness to serve in that role. Someone in the Interior Department was under the impression that Allen was extremely unpopular among the Muscogees and that they wanted him fired. Complaints had been sent to the secretary of the interior about Allen's shady past. Other letters came in accusing Allen of misusing Muscogee funds for travel to the Pan-American Exposition in San Francisco in 1901. Allen's swindle of Martha Verner and Cecil McKinley was reported as well.

Linnen noted that Allen's Coweta Realty Company "invariably paid a small sum of money, ranging from $10.00 up," for a deed. "The balance of the alleged purchase price was set out in a contract signed by the grantee in favor of the grantor."[1] The recorded contract was often a sham contract, with the real value of the property stated in a ledger book not available to the grantor. Even when the real value was made available, it could often be misrepresented to non-English-speaking Mvskoke people. The practice was so common that grafters often boasted about their swindling skills in public. Linnen wrote that although R. C. Allen was clearly a part of the grafting set, he was in no way unique. By 1915, investigations into the plunder of tribal estates were starting to turn up in Congress, in federal courts, and across newspapers. One Oklahoma congressman sought to curtail the few powers the Muscogee Nation still had at its disposal. Linnen took his job of investigating wrongdoing among Indian estates very seriously, and it appeared that Allen's practices were unethical. But the true origins of the investigation with which Linnen had been charged were more complicated than he himself understood. Ostensibly the investigation had been demanded by Muscogee citizens, but the evidence suggests that the only people who truly opposed Allen were a handful of well-placed businessmen who worked as translators, landmen, or agents of the Gem Oil Company.

When Linnen publicly reported McKinley's story of being defrauded by Allen, Allen denied everything, claiming that Verner and McKinley had already married by the time he became interested in the eighty acres. But this assertion was contradicted not only by all the interested parties but also by the date on the marriage contract itself. Linnen questioned Allen directly about his involvement in grafting. "The only excuse offered by Mr. Allen for purchasing lands of this kind was that it was common practice, and he personally was of the opinion that the titles would eventually be good," Linnen wrote.[2]

Allen's defense, in other words, was that everyone was doing it— even the governor of Oklahoma. Linnen had had little exposure to the Oklahoma ways of doing things. His understanding was simply that the fox should not be appointed to protect the henhouse.

Continuing his investigation, Linnen met with tribal officials, along with county and state politicians, and asked them about Allen. "I find that R. C. Allen's political standing with his own party and with party leaders in Tulsa, Wagoner, and Muskogee Counties, and with the state organizations, to be very poor," he wrote.[3]

One of the men he spoke with was Charles Page, who told Linnen that "he did not regard Allen as being a competent attorney or honorable man."

GETTING ALLEN'S SCALP

Linnen had every reason to trust Page. The oilman had saved a Tulsa orphanage, the Cross and Anchor, from bankruptcy. He built business and directed a philanthropy, constructing a colony for widows and orphans, which was nationally recognized as a work of pure charity. While Linnen conducted his investigation, newspapers reported that Page was paying, at personal expense, to send dozens of his "adopted" children to the World's Fair in San Francisco. The *San Francisco Bulletin* heralded the children's arrival. Page "spends every Sunday afternoon with them at the home and it is a fight almost as to who will get to sit upon 'Daddy' Page's knee," a reporter noted.[4] Everyone seemed to believe that Page had actually adopted the children. He had not.

Page had financial reasons to undermine Allen, as did his business partner, Josey. After Judge Campbell appointed a receiver to handle the operations in the Tommy Atkins oil field in 1915, Josey hung around the lobby of the Hotel Tulsa to complain about Allen to anyone who would listen. Josey told Nat Ligon, a probate attorney from Creek County, that when Allen had first come on as national attorney for the Muscogee Nation, he had had a high opinion of the man, but that was to change.

Several weeks before the receivership hearing, Josey went to Allen and offered to show him the Gem Oil Company's entire hand. Josey would reveal to Allen exactly how and why Minnie had changed her story so many times. Sam Brown would vouch for Tommy Atkins being the person on the 1895 census. Josey, a Texas oilman, thought that Allen, a proper Southern gentleman, would see that the Gem Oil Company was not the enemy. The enemy was the meddling federal government who thought it knew what was best for Indians.[5]

But Allen balked. He was, by all accounts, a heavy drinker subject to bouts of rage. Page and Josey had crossed him, and now he took it personally. He refused to reciprocate. Furthermore, he told Josey that he had been duped by Page, who aimed to take full control of Gem Oil. The idea that Josey had been a naive player in the Atkins lease affair angered him and insulted his intelligence. Now Josey let his opinions be known in public. He called Allen a "damnfool and a foreflusher." Ligon said that in the Hotel Tulsa lobby, Josey vowed "to get [Allen's] goat . . . and proposed to play him at his own game, and make it a personal matter of the Atkins fight." Josey's remarks about Allen "were frequently punctuated with profanity."[6]

Page, who was often more restrained than his partner in public, told the federal government's attorneys that he "was going to get Allen's scalp." Page blamed Allen for airing the philanthropist's dirty laundry in the courtroom. And given what Sadie James would say later, the laundry would be stained forever.[7]

Allen grew frustrated that Linnen, as an agent of the federal government, was investigating him. In his mind the true criminals were Page and Josey. Allen boasted around Muskogee that "he would put said R. A. Josey and Charles Page in the penitentiary." These powerful oilmen "were crooks, thieves," he told his associates. At one point, he got so drunk in Muskogee, he had to be carried home by his friends. The whole way home, he ranted about Page and Josey. A Muskogee resident named Morris Brown often drank with Allen and said that the Tommy Atkins affair "drove [Allen] to drink."[8]

As Linnen's investigation wore on, numerous businessmen, politicians, and ministers came forward to tell him that Page and Josey had mounted a well-financed campaign to smear Allen's reputation. W. D. Hume of Muskogee was one such supporter of Allen. Hume wrote to Linnen in 1915, asserting that most of the charges against Allen were "pure, unadulterated bunk," levied by grafters who feared he would prosecute them. Hume's letter cited Charles Page as one of the key masterminds behind the anti-Allen campaign. "I can tell you that it is the big oil men like Charles Page of Tulsa, and other[s] interested like him, who are fighting so strenuously in the Tommie Atkins case to help him hold his Millions, and one certain guardian Wm. P. Morton of Okmulgee who fears that he must soon disgourge defrauded money."

Linnen collected scores of letters and statements that the real problem lay not with Allen but elsewhere. At some point he realized that his entire investigation of Allen was a result of Page and Josey's smear campaign.

Linnen's attention shifted to the two oilmen. He believed they might have been responsible for a conspiracy he'd heard rumors about—a plot to pay Muscogee citizens to sign a petition demanding Allen's termination. In 1915 Linnen began taking depositions on that matter, looking into Page and Josey's interference with Muscogee politics. Josey tried to stop this new turn. He wrote Secretary of the Interior Franklin Lane a

Minnie Atkins poses for an official school portrait at Carlisle Indian Industrial School in 1883.

Chitto Harjo led two rebellions against allotment. This photo was taken in 1903 as he prepared to travel to Washington, DC, to meet with President Theodore Roosevelt.

A statue in bronze of Charles Page by the sculptor Lorado Taft stands in downtown Sand Springs, Oklahoma. The monument to Page includes figures of orphan children looking up at Page.

Alice Robertson was born at the Tullahassee Mission in 1854. A mentor and teacher to Minnie Atkins, Robertson achieved national fame as an anti-feminist while also becoming only the second woman elected to the US Congress.

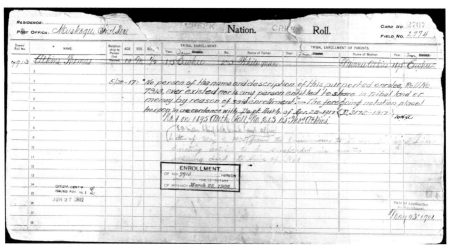

"No person of the name [Tommy Atkins] ever existed" was annotated by a Dawes commissioner on Tommy's enrollment card. Nevertheless, he was allotted land.

Tullahassee Creek Indian Cemetery sits in a strip center parking lot in Sand Springs, Oklahoma.

Thomas Atkins's Certificate of Selection for his two eighty-acre allotments in near Oilton, Oklahoma.

Muscogee girls entering Carlisle in January 1881. Minnie Atkins is first on right. Elizabeth Crowell (aka Bettie Mann) is third from right. Mary Alice Robertson is in the front row behind two students.

The Sand Springs Railway line still parallels Charles Page Boulevard connecting Tulsa and Sand Springs. Locals still call it "the Line," although the track is rarely used.

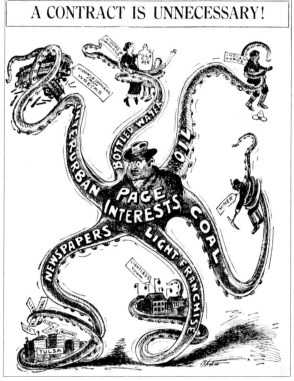

A *Tulsa World* cartoon from 1919 depicts Charles Page as an octopus controlling Tulsa's industries with "lies" and "blackmail."

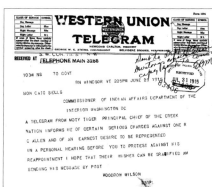

Woodrow Wilson sounded the alarm about Creek attorney R. C. Allen based on Page and Josey's campaign against him.

"World's Champion Santa," Charles Page. Contrary to press reports and lore, Page never adopted children from the Sand Springs Home.

Nathaniel Atkins, older brother of Thomas Atkins, followed the trials in Oklahoma and beyond. He continued to believe that the Tommy in question was his brother and that his family had been defrauded.

The graves of Tuckabache and other Lockapocha people were removed to make way for Tulsa's Sunset Terrace subdivision. The remains were taken to Oaklawn Cemetery in 1921.

SADIE CONFESSES PAGE RELATIONS

Negress Tells of Clandestine Visits to Dark Office and of Frameup.

COMPLETE DISCLOSURE MADE

Admits Knowing All the While That Tommy Atkins Never Existed.

MUSKOGEE, June 9.—Altho the existence of Tommy Atkins is the basis of the great legal drama now coming to a close here, interest centers in two of the principal actors—Charles Page and Sadie James. Page is the Tulsa millionaire who holds a lease

Principals in Tommy Atkins Case

SADIE JAMES   CHAS. PAGE

"Sadie Confesses Page Relations." A *Tulsa World* story hinted at a scandalous testimony given by the roadhouse owner in the federal trial against Charles Page and Minnie Atkins.

Rusting machinery of oil field equipment near the Tommy Atkins allotment in Creek County, Oklahoma, in 2023.

A mural celebrating Tulsa's oil history greets arriving passengers at Tulsa International Airport.

The house of Minnie Atkins Folk still stands on Main Street in Sand Springs.

Destructive oil field fires were a common occurrence in the Cushing-Drumright field. This one likely erupted from a lightning strike in near Drumright.

Apollonia Piña and the author inspect a stuck rental car on the Tommy Atkins allotment as her son, José, squeals with delight.

rambling letter that smeared Allen's reputation. He closed the letter by stating that Allen was "utterly unworthy of your [Lane's] confidence."

Josey was not the only person to appeal directly to Secretary Lane. Muscogee citizens supportive of Allen, some from the House of Kings and House of Warriors, urged Lane to look deeper into the situation. Bunnie McCorsa, a member of the House of Warriors, sent a telegram to Lane in 1915, writing that the people fighting Allen's reappointment "were paid to do so."[9]

Not only were people being paid to sign a petition; they were also being lied to about its nature. McCorsa and other Muscogees fluent in both Mvskoke and English realized that the English translations of the petition were deceptive. "I know many Indians who signed complaints against Allen for money who had no real grievance against him. I urge his [re]appointment."[10]

The petition was widely circulated in Oklahoma newspapers and was presented to Secretary Lane. It called Lane's attention to the McKinley affair and reminded Lane that there were still lawsuits pending against Allen or the Coweta Realty Company in Oklahoma courts. Although it didn't mention the ongoing litigation around the Tommy Atkins case, a letter from the Indian Rights Association (IRA) left no doubt that Allen's presiding over the case figured prominently in the campaign against him. The IRA was a highly influential group of mostly white people who, much like Henry Dawes, sought to assimilate Native Americans into the American mainstream. They saw themselves as protectors of Indians, and called out abuses in places like Oklahoma, but their noble intentions contained more than a hint of paternalism, and their inability to understand the reality of life in Indian Country was on full display when they endorsed the persecution of R. C. Allen.

The association's Washington agent, Samuel Brosius, wrote to Secretary Lane on July 9, 1915, to address the question of Allen's involvement in the Tommy Atkins case. From Brosius's letter, it is clear that someone had convinced him that Allen would not rule in favor of returning the land to the tribe, as petitioned in the lawsuit, but rather would sell it on the open market and pocket the proceeds:

In the celebrated Tommy Atkins case in which Mr. Allen seeks to set aside a fictitious Creek allotment which is now very valuable by reason of its rich deposits of oil, etc. it is understood that Mr. Allen, if not actually favoring, has acquiesced in the contest being prosecuted by a non-citizen Creek Indian, who seeks to secure this allotment by showing it was improperly allotted to Atkins. If the allotment to Atkins is cancelled and a non-citizen is declared entitled to the property, the Creek tribe of Indians will apparently not profit thereby, since the property goes to an outsider. This we submit indicates that the energy seemingly displayed by Mr. Allen in the case, and the large amount of money belonging to the Creek Indians which has been expended by him in the matter, will not benefit the Creek tribe in the least, these being the Indians whose interests he is employed to protect.

Brosius had been misinformed about Allen's case. While it is possible that Allen might have the chance to profit from an allotment returned to the tribe, he was not a citizen. The Muscogee Nation would be under no obligation to sell the land to Allen, or even give him a chance to buy it. A victory for the Muscogee Nation would have amounted to a cash windfall for the citizens and another piece of public land reclaimed by the tribe. Perhaps Allen thought he would have an inside track on acquiring a canceled allotment, but there were no guarantees. Had Brosius been misinformed by Page and Josey?

A few Muscogee leaders did genuinely oppose Allen. Sam Brown Jr., son of the elder Sam Brown, led the attack. Brown met with twenty-two of these figures in May 1915 to discuss removing Allen. They did not want to meet at the capital in Okmulgee and decided to have the proceeding conducted only in the Mvskoke language. Principal Chief Moty Tiger was not invited. Although Chief Tiger came from a traditionalist background and spoke little English, he was no Chitto Harjo—he was not in favor of a rebellion against allotment. He also seemed to be happy with Allen's work.

About a month after the meeting, on June 28, 1915, a taxi driver in Okmulgee, H. M. Draper, was contacted by a local attorney, Alex Johnson. Johnson instructed Draper to drive Johnson and an associate to Chief Tiger's house, about eight miles south of Okmulgee. Johnson told Draper to avoid all main roads. To make sure Draper kept quiet about the whole thing, Johnson offered him twenty-five dollars for the trip (around $750 in 2024 dollars). When they arrived at Chief Tiger's house, Johnson and his companion brought Chief Tiger to the car, and they then drove to Muskogee, whence Chief Tiger was put on a train to Washington, DC, escorted by Sam Brown Jr. Draper overheard one of the men say to Tiger "that his Boss wanted him [Tiger]."

The boss in question could have been any number of people—President Wilson, Secretary Lane, or someone in the Page-Josey contingent. Wilson knew that very valuable oil land was at stake in Oklahoma, and when he was made aware of the campaign against Allen, he sent a telegram to Cato Sells, now commissioner of Indian Affairs. In the telegram, dated June 28, 1915, President Wilson said he had been told about "serious charges against one R. C. Allen and of an earnest desire to be represented in a personal hearing before you to protest against his reappointment. I hope that their wishes can be gratified."

Page and Josey had gotten the ear of the president, who said he hoped that Commissioner Sells would listen to the protests against Allen. Josey and Page had paid Sam Brown Jr. $500 to escort Chief Tiger to Washington, DC. Two interpreters, David Hodge and George Washington Grayson, also went along. Much of what transpired hinged on whom Chief Tiger listened to when Hodge and Grayson translated from English to Mvskoke and vice versa. Hodge, Brown, Sam Davis, and a former chief, Legus Perryman, were the core group of Page supporters leading the campaign to fire Allen. This group had funding from the Page-Josey camp to create a campaign of misinformation that included using intentional mistranslations from Mvskoke to English and payoffs for signatures on a petition.

An extraordinary turn of events involving Chief Tiger then took place. From what I can piece together from a series of telegrams, both Allen and Page willfully misrepresented documents they wanted Chief Tiger to sign.[11]

Tiger claimed Allen had met with him in April 1915 to discuss his reappointment, saying that he wanted to see the Tommy Atkins case through to the end. He felt he had amassed the evidence to show a web of conspiracy in a federal court. Allen reported to Commissioner Sells that Chief Tiger was "not favorable to a renewal of my contract."

After a mass meeting outside Okmulgee, the anti-Allen sentiment seemed to dominate eastern Oklahoma. Allen and his assistant, Lumpkin, gave Chief Tiger a document and told him to sign it in a Muskogee hotel. It stated Tiger's agreement to rehire Allen as national attorney for the Creek Nation. Chief Tiger later claimed, albeit through a different interpreter, that Allen had misrepresented the nature of the document. In a different telegram, however, Chief Tiger claimed that he did, indeed, have confidence in Allen, and it was the other side who was mistranslating his sentiments. [12]

Allen traveled to Washington while Chief Tiger, Brown, and Hodge were there to meet with Commissioner Sells. Allen wanted to counter the charges against him. While he was in Washington, his assistant, Lumpkin, sent a telegram from Oklahoma to report something extraordinary: Thomas Roach, an "Indian policeman" in Coweta, had spotted an associate of Page and Josey buying train tickets for Muscogee citizens who had signed the petition against Allen. Roach followed the associate, asked questions, and discovered that Long and Josey had changed the petition's language *after* citizens had signed it. Sure enough, citizens like Bunnie McCorsa began to come forward, saying that in essence they had been paid to sign a bogus document, which was now in the hands of Commissioner Sells, Secretary Lane, and possibly President Wilson. This turn of events reshaped the nature of Linnen's investigation and, indeed, the scope of the fraud allegations against Charles Page and the Gem Oil Company.

William G. Bruner, a well-respected Muscogee elder who had signed the petition, learned of the fraud and sought to set the record straight. He felt betrayed by Brown and the oilmen. When Billy Bruner spoke, people listened. He called himself "the one and only William Bruner."

Indeed, his legend loomed. In the 1880s, as a student at a mission school, Bruner had stood up to an abuser who tried to whip him for speaking Mvskoke. He dropped out of school and pursued his education with a medicine man, a *heles hayv*. Bruner had to defend his land and people against waves of invasions. Although he killed at least one white man in a gun battle, he assisted federal marshals in the investigation. He was convicted but was pardoned by President McKinley, who found Bruner to be acting in self-defense. Everyone around Tulsa saw Billy Bruner as a living legend, and although some people feared him, he was respected as an honest man.

Given Bruner's status, the telegram he sent to Commissioner Sells on July 12, 1915, is worth highlighting. "Chief Tiger is accompanied by two interpreters who are prejudiced against Mr. Allen," he wrote. Bruner recanted his signature on the petition against Allen. "The grafters are opposing Mr. Allen," Bruner wrote. "The best Indian citizens are for him."[13]

Bruner went into more detail in a letter to Sells. He was irate that the petition had been willfully misrepresented to him. He wished to strike his name from the petition and endorse what Allen was doing. "RC Allen is being made the victim of the wrath of the land grabber, of the Indian land shark and the common parasite that endeavors to prey upon Indian estates in the Creek nation. His vigorous prosecution of civil suits for the protection of the Creek nation and for the protection of the full bloods has aroused a sentiment against him by the grafters and the land grabbers who infest this country among whom are many white men some so-called prominent Indians, and in some instances, some of the courts or judges of courts."[14]

Special Investigator Linnen must have felt dizzy at the turn of events. He had stepped into a conflict that was pitting some of the state's major oil interests against the tribe—and tribal citizens against each other. Now he was finding evidence of what appeared to be a conspiracy against Chief Tiger, who had been put on a train to Washington and misinformed about Allen's work. Linnen interviewed dozens of Muscogee citizens. They either praised Allen or saw him as a usurper and corrupt figure bilking the tribe's treasury. Allen had helped secure an $800 equalization payment for Muscogee citizens, but he also had a shady past that continued to dog him. Some citizens flip-flopped in their judgment, probably because of the mistranslations denounced by Bruner.

Linnen had to consider the damning accusations against Allen on the one hand and, on the other, a resolution sent by telegram in July 1915 to Secretary Lane by the president of the House of Kings, James Smith, and countersigned by the clerk, Sam Grayson. Smith and Grayson unequivocally supported Allen:

WHEREAS said R. C. Allen has procured for the Creek people the equalization of their allotments to the extent of $800 thereby showing his fidelity and devotion to the interests of the Creek people;

IT IS HEREBY RESOLVED by the National Council of the Creek Nation that they extend to their said National Attorney their sincere thanks for the work already done by him in their behalf

BE IT FURTHER RESOLVED that we express our unlimited confidence in the ability and integrity of our said National Attorney, believing that in the future as well as in the past, he will use his utmost endeavors to secure for the Creek people all rights and interests, both equitable and legal to which they are entitled.[15]

Linnen's files fill five archival boxes at the National Archives in Washington. Evidence of Allen's corruption, drunkenness, and swindling take up several folders. Other folders attest to Allen's law-abiding crusade for justice. Thinking about the complications surrounding this man and the Tommy Atkins trials, I found my head swimming. Then I seemed to find a voice that spoke to me across the span of a century: that of J. J. Moroney, the editor of the *Okmulgee Democrat*.

Moroney wrote to Secretary Lane on May 31, 1915, with Shakespeare in mind. "Too truly does the pessimism of Hamlet's remark to Ophelia apply to Oklahoma these days," Moroney wrote. "And if you come to Oklahoma, 'I will give thee this plague for a dowry; be thou as chaste as ice, thou'lt not escape the finger of calumny.'"

Moroney channeled Hamlet's pessimism about Ophelia's chastity into a philosophy about this new, unruly state of Oklahoma. A century later, as I leafed through the 16,000 pages of documents related to fifteen years of trials, media sensations, and investigations into the Tommy Atkins affair, Moroney's dim outlook resonated with me. Thinking about R. C. Allen, Frank Long, Charles Page, Sam Brown, Ellis Childers, and sundry other grafters, I landed on another remark by Hamlet: "We are arrant knaves, all. Believe none of us."[16]

The finger of calumny had indeed grazed Allen's head, but he did not get himself to a nunnery. Instead, he went back to Muskogee, to the US District Court in the Eastern District of Oklahoma, with his scalp very much intact. Once it became clear that Page, Long, and Josey were out to remove Allen, many Oklahomans were completely outraged. Leading businessmen and clergy wrote to Washington, DC, in protest. The manipulation of the entire tribe and the misrepresentation of Allen's work to the federal government amounted to a coup attempt of Chief Tiger and his attorney. It was no wonder the *Tulsa World*, a strong supporter of Page's philanthropies, would soon turn against this man and his network of supporters.

One letter in particular stands out, written by a Muskogee accountant, J. Edgar Richardson. Richardson wrote that Long, Page, and Josey's conspiracy contravened the Ninth Commandment: "Thou shall not bear false witness." That commandment was "in this case being violated by every statement that has been made against [Allen]." Richardson then wrote something that might be one of the most incisive observations about Oklahoma ever written:

> Oklahoma is the most unruly child of your family of states, and to a large extent is being dominated by an element that in its greed for gain, places a premium on crime in high places, defies the law, and tends to make your administration the more burdensome. The man who I'm endorsing [R. C. Allen] will have none of this so far as lies within his powers; and his record shows that he is fearless in the discharge of his duties and protection of the interest of his wards.[17]

The letter reached President Woodrow Wilson's desk, and he took note of it. He told his aides that something about it spoke to him. He wanted to know more.

As the scandal around Tommy Atkins grew to encompass not only the Muscogee Nation and the oil industry but also seemingly everyday people like J. E. Richardson, Wilson had enough. He wanted the trial in Muskogee to run its course without firing Allen or removing Chief Tiger. Allen would continue to collaborate with the US Attorney's Office, even though they had their differences. President Wilson reappointed Allen as national attorney for the Muscogee Nation in 1915. Chief Tiger accepted the reappointment. The suit against Page and all the other pretenders to the Tommy Atkins fortune continued.

— CHAPTER 13 —

"THERE IS NO JUSTICE
FOR THE WEAK?"

Resistance Against Allotment

When H. L. Mott's term as national attorney for the Creek Nation ended in 1914, he left behind a damning report that he'd
written on the notorious probate system in Oklahoma. He had found
that estates inherited by Indian minors were the objects of plunder by
"professional guardians." These guardians often charged a 20 percent
commission for handling the estate, "while the cost of administering
similar estates of white children was between 1 and 3%."[1]

To make matters worse, county judges were appointing guardians
for Indian minors as political favors. They redirected funds to invest
in their own schemes. Some guardians had dozens, or even hundreds,
of wards. These guardians collected hefty fees for transactions and
often left the children destitute. Meanwhile, they subjected their wards'
legitimate needs to nickel-and-diming. Some of these cases were documented in Angie Debo's work, but others have been preserved as
private family history.

Darla Ashton, the granddaughter of a Muscogee allottee named
Millie Naharkey, told me how Millie's guardian refused to pay for
the repair to her refrigerator in the 1980s. The Muscogee woman
took an axe to the appliance and destroyed it. "Now I need a new
refrigerator," Naharkey told her guardian, listed as First National
Bank of Tulsa from documents at the National Archives. I had met
Ashton while trying to connect to people who had a living memory
of original allottees. I did not have to look far. While the history of
this conspiracy is outside the mainstream curriculum, its legacy is
ever-present in eastern Oklahoma.

"OUT OF HER PLACE": KATE BARNARD
FIGHTS BACK AGAINST THE GRAFTERS

While many white Oklahomans accepted the regime of guardianship as the natural state of things, some brave souls fought against it. H. L. Mott's report infuriated a white woman named Kate Barnard, known for her outlandish hats, steely blue eyes, and a fiery devotion to righting social injustice. Barnard came from a hard-luck Great Plains background. Her father, a widower, had moved from Nebraska to take part in the Oklahoma Territory's first big land run in 1889. Something went wrong with his land claim and he ended up not with a quarter-section of land but with a town lot. While most settlers wanted land, a lot in the booming town of Oklahoma City was still a decent reward. Kate Barnard grew up to have grand ambitions but was constrained by a patriarchal system that was only reinforced by the leading woman in the state, Alice Robertson. Barnard taught in one-room schoolhouses and also took on clerical work, running circles around the men who supervised her.

She was elected Oklahoma commissioner of charities and corrections by a wide margin in 1907. Her campaigns against child labor and for public education and criminal justice reform were wildly popular. She was a fiery public speaker and crusader against various injustices. In many ways she was the antithesis of Alice Robertson. She cared little for the "cult of true womanhood." Barnard was easily reelected in 1910 and then set her sights on a different issue. Barnard began her second term by announcing that she would direct the Commission on Charities and Corrections to call out and prosecute grafters of Indians. She announced she would push the legislature to enact laws to protect against the "definite plan to dispossess 100,000 Indians of their estates."

On November 1, 1914, Barnard published an essay in the *New York Sun* that captured her passion on the subject. It also captured her patronizing attitude toward Native Americans, which was common among progressive reformers of the era. She wrote about Native American minors:

These Indians are all government wards placed under the protection of Oklahoma by a confiding nation which believed in the honor and honesty of this state. These Indians constitute one-third of all that are left, a weak helpless remnant which once possessed the American continent. Shall we in the evening of the life of this people rob the last survivor before we pass with him down into the common silence of eternity? Shall we send the last orphan of this dying race a penniless pauper back to our common God? Shall it be said, "there is no justice for the weak in Oklahoma?"

Later in her essay Barnard appears to reference Allen's ploy to marry Cecil McKinley to Martha Verner. Although she does not name them, she references a forced marriage of a Black man to a freedperson minor girl with a $50 payout to a complicit party, which matches the details of the situation perfectly.[2] Newspapers across the Northeast reprinted Barnard's piece, but her attempt to shame Oklahoma into action generated a backlash not only against her but against her entire commission.

Powerful Oklahomans began to question her integrity. Governor William "Alfalfa Bill" Murray said Barnard was "out of her place." A retaliatory state investigation homed in on one of Barnard's investigators, accusing him of taking bribes. The investigation never really pinpointed any real corruption, but the legislature cut off appropriations for Barnard's commission nevertheless. The diminutive woman—people were often shocked when they saw that this powerful voice of righteousness came in a five-foot, ninety-pound frame—developed a heart condition. With her office stripped of funding, she decided not to run for reelection. In 1915, she founded an organization she called the People's Lobby to advocate for her core issues: protection of children, reform of prisons, and adequate funding of schools. The attacks, however, had taken a toll.

Alice Robertson, ever the defender of "a woman's place in the home," drew attention to the fact that after 1915, Kate Barnard was in and out of a sanitarium. Robertson blamed Barnard's health problems on her defiance of the natural state of womanhood. "Not many women in public life stick to their jobs," Robertson wrote. "Miss Barnard is out talking suffrage more than she is following her official duties."[3]

By 1915, both Kate Barnard and H. L. Mott had been pushed out of positions of power. The work of protecting the allottees' rapidly disappearing lands and wealth fell to the tribes and the federal government. The tribes, despite having had their sovereignty severely curtailed by the Dawes Commission, the Curtis Act, and the state of Oklahoma, fought back against the grafters in court. Although they often lost cases (the Barney Thlocco case had upheld Dawes's decisions even when they were probably based on bad information), they did see a few opportunities to reverse the plunder that Barnard had so eloquently described. The Choctaw and Chickasaw Nations were rich in coal and timber. They had some success appealing to Washington to intervene in Oklahoma affairs. Just northwest of the Muscogee Nation, the Osage Nation appeared to achieve a degree of control over their wealth by buying their reservation, along with rights to its subsoil minerals, from the government.

One opportunity for recouping land and wealth rested on the Dawes Rolls themselves. If an entity such as the Muscogee Nation could identify a deliberate fraud in the enrollment of a citizen, the allotment would be canceled and the land itself would be returned to the tribe. The key to making this strategy work, however, rested in the hands of the Muscogee Nation's national attorney, R. C. Allen.

To almost everyone's surprise, the haughty North Carolinian picked up the work where Mott had left off. He survived the conspiracy to have him fired, and then he turned his sights on demonstrating the corruption in oil leases involving Indians. On January 16, 1917, Allen appeared before the Senate Committee on Indian Affairs.[4] There he laid out the fraud involving the duplicate, nonexistent, and fake citizens of the Muscogee Nation who had been allotted land. He stated that the fight against this fraud was the "unfinished business" of determining heirship.

Allen said that when he assumed the position of national attorney for the Creek Nation, he thought his job would involve the rather tedious but predictable task of determining heirship of allottees who had died intestate. The case of Tommy Atkins appeared to be one of these difficult cases. Allen had initially accepted the theory that Tommy was deceased, his mother was Minnie Atkins, and his father was an unnamed white man, so his estate should belong to his mother. Then Allen saw that Minnie had been stricken from the tribe's own rolls.

However unscrupulous Allen's business practices had been, he took seriously his mission of recouping lost land and revenue for the Muscogee Nation. Page and Josey had failed to get him removed in 1915, so they tried another tactic in 1916. An ally in Congress, Representative James Davenport, introduced a bill in the House of Representatives that would eliminate the entire position of national attorney for the Muscogee Nation (HB 16066). Davenport was a white man from Alabama who had been adopted into the Cherokee Nation. He reasoned that the Cherokees had no national attorney, and that the entire federal government initiative of the past twenty years had been tribal termination. Davenport told Congress that US taxpayers spent $5,000 a year on Allen and his office. He wanted the whole office eradicated.

Representative Davenport seemed to be doing the bidding of the oilmen angered by Allen's actions. Allen countered with a long list of Creek citizens he had served by protecting them against swindles and outright theft. Given his important role in the Tommy Atkins trial, which was unfolding as Davenport tried to eliminate Allen's position, the bill was seen as a naked attempt at political interference. It never advanced.[5]

PROVING A LIE: ALLEN'S TOUGHEST TEST

Allen had faced down a political challenge, but an existential problem still loomed. If Allen could prove in court that the child enrolled under Creek Roll #7913 was no one's child—he was simply nonexistent—then Tommy's land would revert to the Muscogee Nation. Nancy Atkins's tenuous claim to be the mother of Tommy, verified by a notoriously corrupt court in Creek County, certainly caught his attention.

Allen most likely knew the grafter Ellis Childers, who had backed Nancy's claim. He could have gone after Childers for perjury, but he understood Childers was not so much a criminal as an opportunist. So instead of pressing charges, Allen decided to bring Childers on as a powerful asset to prove a wider conspiracy by the Sand Springs Home to manufacture their own Tommy Atkins. Childers would provide some damaging testimony about most, if not all, of the oilmen involved.

However, if Allen thought that it would be easy to prove fraud in the Tommy Atkins allotment case, he was mistaken. Page's new Minnie Atkins had a very compelling case. At the center of it was Creek Nation roll card number 2707. This card corresponded to Dawes Roll number

7913—Thomas Atkins. This card had been made up on May 13, 1901, and then submitted for citizenship certification, which was issued on June 27, 1902. The card listed the name of his mother, Minnie Atkins, of Euchee Town. Thomas was classified as a one-half-blood male who was ten years old. On the lower half of the card was a stamp from the secretary of the interior, granting the enrollment of Thomas Atkins and allowing him to select his allotment, or have it selected for him. This seemed to prove quite convincingly that one Minnie Atkins of Euchee Town was the mother of one Tommy Atkins.

Minnie tried to back up her statements about Tommy's parentage in an affidavit before Page's lawyers in Tulsa in October 1914. There she admitted to having given birth to Tommy at the home of Granny Letcher, the supposedly disreputable Black woman in Leavenworth. Minnie's statement not only provided a clear narrative about Tommy; it also gave her a rationale for her prior inconsistencies around the circumstances of Tommy's birth. She now said that she had falsely claimed Tommy was born at the Sisters Hospital "because I didn't want to tell where he was born."

During the federal trial in Muskogee, an attorney asked Minnie more questions about Granny Letcher's place. The salacious nature of the testimonies had by now reached audiences all over the Southwest. There were ladies' "sewing clubs" (gossip groups) who sent emissaries to Muskogee to listen to people like Minnie Atkins and then report back on the bits not fit for print. They devoured Minnie's testimony. There were details about affairs in the courtroom that no decent newspaper dared print. At the center of it all was Granny Letcher's place. "That was a place where men and women met for immoral purposes," Charles Page's lawyer Ben Rice said.

"Yes sir," Minnie said.

Minnie went on to say that in 1886 she had nursed another boy Tommy's age, a Black child named Walter Banks. Walter's mother had died in childbirth, so Minnie breastfed him, and some people had thought that little Walter was her son. The scene of a Native American—possibly white-passing—woman nursing a Black child constituted a scandal. But Minnie was adamant that Walter Banks was not her Tommy, as some people around Leavenworth had believed. I think, but cannot confirm, that Walter Banks was also Charles Page's backup plan, in the event that Minnie backed out of the scheme. Banks could have been the person who Page said would collect thousands of dollars for impersonating Tommy if Minnie refused to claim him. We know that Page was actively considering the alternate story of a Black Tommy in the event that Minnie got cold feet.

Minnie probably included the story about nursing Walter Banks to deflect the claims of Henry Carter. Carter was one of the many defendants in the case. His story shared some plot points with Minnie's, namely, that a child was born at Granny Letcher's to Minnie Atkins and then abandoned by Minnie. But Carter's story took on a different twist. The father, according to him, was a Black man, and he also abandoned Tommy in Leavenworth. Tommy was then adopted by a rural Black couple by the name of Carter. Thus, Henry Carter actually was Tommy Atkins.

Allen thought Carter was some kind of stalking horse for Charles Page and had no real chance of winning the lawsuit. But Henry Carter seemed to be serious. His story was backed by J. Coody Johnson, another singular figure in the Oklahoma oil patch, a Black Muscogee and Seminole lawyer and landman whom everyone knew as the Black Panther. Johnson had a vexed relationship with Charles Page, sometimes working with him, and sometimes opposing him. On the surface, Carter, backed up by Johnson, seemed to be an antagonist to Page's Minnie Atkins. Had Carter won title to the land, however, it is clear that Page would have had something to say about who actually drilled for oil.

The shifting nature of Minnie's story stirred Allen to action. He knew that Minnie wasn't simply an unreliable narrator or a person with a faulty memory; he suspected that someone was pressuring her to change her story. Allen became convinced that it was either Page or his fixer, Frank Long, and he made no secret about his suspicions. Allen was determined—obsessed—to prove that Page, Josey, and Minnie Atkins were all involved in an elaborate hoax. "I do not believe there is any question but that Thomas Atkins is a myth," he wrote to the tribe in 1915.

He underscored the importance of a favorable outcome to the Muscogees: "I have devoted a great deal of time to the Atkins case, regarding it, as I do, from many standpoints, as the most important case involving the rights of the Creek Indians ever instituted in any court."

Allen's reputation—indeed, his entire career—rested with this case. As an abstract concept, the reclassification of private allotments to public lands had mainstream political support. President Wilson had affirmed the Muscogees' right to incorporate the lands they had recuperated into the tribe's collective ownership. It was a small step forward for a nation on the brink of termination.

But proving that the individual allottees were fraudulently enrolled was easier said than done. In a private notebook, Allen set about detailing what he viewed as the facts of the Tommy Atkins case. He meticulously documented Minnie's children's lives. Everyone agreed that Minnie had had at least four children. The lives and deaths of Robert Lee Peterkin and Alice Mable Peterkin had been well documented. There had been witnesses to their births and deaths, a cause of death in each case, and their graves had been identified. Minnie's surviving children, Charley and Harvey Harrison, had also been well documented by witnesses in Colorado and on the Creek census of 1895.

Allen wrote in his notebook, "In 1903 patents were issued to said land to Thomas Atkins and they were recorded but have never been delivered to any person."[6] Allen noted that in 1905 the patents issued to the land were ordered to be held up pending further investigation. Later, a Dawes commissioner admitted that the documents had gone missing for over ten years. They were only recovered for the federal trial. It's unclear which of the three dozen or so attorneys working on this case finally found these important documents. Given their extraordinary power, not only for original allottees but for anyone trying to prove citizenship in the Five Tribes, it is almost incomprehensible that the government simply lost them.

Allen faulted the Dawes Commission for bungling the investigation into Tommy's enrollment and its poor recordkeeping. He said the government had acted "arbitrarily" in enrolling Tommy; they had lost his papers and never even bothered to physically identify the child. Allen's attack on the commission brought him into conflict with a much more powerful sovereign nation than the Muscogee—the United States of America. He was supposed to be collaborating with D. H. Linebaugh, the special assistant to the attorney general, to show that Minnie and Nancy Atkins, along with a handful of oilmen, were engaged in a fraud. But now Allen was suggesting that the federal government had been at the root of the problem in its sloppy investigation of the 1895 Creek Census. The Bureau of Indian Affairs investigator, Linnen, wrote to Washington in 1915 to complain that Allen was "not working in full accord and harmony with D. H. Linebaugh."[7]

Allen, with his hard drinking and bouts of egotism, ran the risk of undercutting the whole case in the eyes of the US attorneys. Linebaugh felt Allen's tactics were damaging the case and the reputation of the federal government in its solemn attempt to register every single citizen of the Five Tribes. Before the federal trial, Linebaugh asked the attorney general, Thomas Gregory, to remove Allen from the case. Gregory refused.

Allen continued to insist that the Dawes Commission had not done its due diligence to prove Tommy's existence. He argued that Minnie had told the truth the very first time she was asked about Tommy at Fort Lawton in Seattle in 1914. It was there that Sadie James had first told Minnie about her phantom millionaire child, to which Minnie responded that she never had a child named Tommy. Allen said that it was only Page and Long's convoluted stories that had forced her into lies in 1914 and 1915. As evidence, Allen brought up Minnie's documented actions in 1900, shortly before she left the country with Harry Folk.

In 1900 Minnie had given her brother-in-law, Thomas Holden, power of attorney over her minor children, Charley and Harvey Harrison. In that legal document there was no mention of a child named Tommy or Thomas. Minnie had been present during the 1895 annuity payment to Muscogee citizens. Allen believed that Minnie had corrected that census herself. Where someone had written "Mamie Atkins," Minnie had corrected it. Allen believed that the "error" noted beside the name Thomas had been placed there by Minnie herself or at the suggestion of Alice Robertson's sister, Augusta Robertson Moore. "If she had okehed [sic] the name Thomas it would never have been marked error," Allen said.

The Dawes Commission, Allen argued, had failed to act on that correction. Allen wrote, "The Commission acted in a hasty and loose manner when they listed [Tommy's] name for enrollment and they did so practically without investigation that the tribal roles [sic] were not dependable as evidenced by statements made by the Commission in its own report to the Secretary of Interior."

There was another problem for Gem Oil. Worldwide the price of oil was falling due to overproduction. The Cushing-Drumright Oil Field alone was producing three hundred thousand barrels a day. Flush production on the Tommy Atkins lands was about twenty thousand barrels a day, only 6.7 percent of the entire oil field but enough to be an important bellwether for the industry. As US entry to World War I approached, this small field—less than fifteen miles long—was producing 17 percent of all the petroleum in the United States and 3 percent of the world's consumption of oil.[8]

The quality of the oil was more important than the quantity. The petroleum coming out of the Cushing-Drumright Oil Field was considered the best in the world. It commanded higher prices than oil from Russia, Mexico, or other important oil producers. The oil was easy to refine, unlike the "sour" oil coming from elsewhere. Sour oil was corrosive and needed extensive treatment; Cushing-Drumright oil was perfect for airplanes, trucks, tanks, and ships. The price per barrel had declined by about 33 percent since 1914.

Page had appealed the receivership by offering to post a large bond on the land's oil production. That would function, essentially, as collateral. The receiver for Gem Oil's operations was J. W. McLoud, the solicitor general for the Midland Valley Railroad. He appears to have been a business associate of Charles Page, but he noted something disturbing in a report to Judge Campbell: Allen and Linebaugh's evidence that Gem had started a secret operation to extract oil from Tommy's allotment but store it outside his land in steel tanks. McLoud backed up the accusation, noting that Page and Josey bought forty acres of land just beyond Tommy's allotment, "for the purpose of a tank farm in connection with the Atkins farm. They had completed three steel tanks and had a fourth tank nearly completed, and the grade made for a fifth tank, on said forty acres; that Page and Josey have since sold said fourth tank to the McMan Oil Company, leaving three completed steel tanks which are connected with the Atkins property by the necessary pipelines." These tanks held something like 55,000 barrels of oil, ready to be sold to Standard Oil and transported via pipelines to market.[9]

Allen and Linebaugh wrote that agents from the Gem Oil Company "have unlawfully entered upon said lands and have prospected and drilled thereon for oil and gas."[10] Allen and Linebaugh alleged that Gem workers were siphoning or transporting oil from the Tommy Atkins lands and putting it elsewhere, so that government and tribal officials could not realistically estimate the true value of the minerals.

"A MOST UNSAVORY MESS"

Before 1917, Page had contended that Tommy's existence, or lack thereof, was irrelevant to the legal basis of his lease. That should have been all Judge Campbell needed to know. But Judge Campbell seemed to be changing his mind. Now he wanted to hear evidence about whether Tommy existed. Campbell had found nothing precluding the government from reexamining tribal rolls. If someone's claim to a piece of land was based on a fraud, it seemed reasonable that the fraud in question should be examined.

The *Tulsa World*, which had mostly sympathized with Page during the receivership trial of 1915, had begun to evince skepticism by 1917. That was when the lawsuit to entirely cancel the patent finally came to trial in Muskogee. As the trial dragged on, the paper started to view philanthropist Page as more like mob boss Page. The *Tulsa World* published a host of stories about Page being the cause of a multitude of public nuisances and scandals. On March 3, 1917, to cite one example, the paper published an article titled "Dr. Jekyll and Mr. Hyde," in which a Sand Springs resident recounted "how Page robs his own town." The paper often illustrated stories about Page with cartoons of him as a fat tycoon loaded down with bags of money and chomping on an old stogie. Another cartoon presented Page as an octopus. It was a familiar metaphor for the Standard Oil Company that captured the public's fear of resource giants and captains of industry controlling government policy, fixing the price of a valuable commodity, and squeezing out competition.[11]

When it came to the Tommy Atkins federal court case, the *Tulsa World*'s story dispensed with any charade of objectivity, noting that "slowly but surely, and with evenly directed blows, the government has torn down his house of cards." Then the writer went in for the coup de grace: "Few remain . . . who believe that he even has a 'fighting chance' in the Tommy Atkins case. Great surprise is expressed by many that Page should have become so seriously involved in what appears to be a most unsavory mess."[12]

A pro-Page newspaper, the *Tulsa Morning Times,* countered the *Tulsa World*'s attacks on Page with some cutting prose of its own. On June 11, 1917, in a boxed inset on the front page, the *Morning Times* said the *World* was printing "libel" to which "Charles Page would be justified in responding with a shotgun."[13]

— CHAPTER 14 —

"WHAT A FOOL WE HAVE BEEN"

The Atkins Sisters Face Off in Federal Court

On May 11, 1917, Minnie Atkins sat in the federal courthouse in Muskogee, awaiting the arrival of Judge Ralph E. Campbell, who would preside over *United States v. Atkins et al.* The federal government and the Muscogee Nation were the plaintiffs. Among the defendants were some of the most recognizable oilmen in the industry, Minnie and Nancy Atkins, Henry Carter, and a man named Quentin Garrett who had filed on Tommy's allotment in case everyone else's claim fell through. Two lawsuits in Creek County had only added to the intrigue and mystery; now the federal government and the tribe sought to cancel the entire allotment and return the land to the Muscogee Nation.

The courthouse, built only two years prior, embodied the transformation of eastern Oklahoma from a cattle-grazing backwater into a center of American energy power. Taking up an entire block of Broadway, the building was noted as the greatest "architectural achievement in the state" when it was finished in 1915.[1] The imposing symmetrical neoclassical gray Indiana limestone building looked like it belonged on Pennsylvania Avenue in Washington, DC, not in a provincial railroad town like Muskogee, Oklahoma.

There were five possible outcomes to the trial: (1) the allotment was canceled entirely and the land reverted back to the Muscogee Nation; (2) Charles Page's team convinced Judge Campbell that Tommy existed and that Minnie was his mother, which allowed Page to continue his drilling operations on the land; (3) Henry Carter was recognized as the real Tommy Atkins and was given the land; (4) an alternate Muscogee claimant named Quinton Garrett got the land; (5) Nancy Atkins was recognized as the heir to Tommy Atkins, meaning the allotment

150

was hers. At stake was an oil fortune estimated at $10 million ($236 million in 2024 dollars).

A *Tulsa World* reporter noted that Minnie sat near a railing with her husband, Harry Folk, and stared blankly out a window. Minnie tried to ignore the hundreds of reporters, lease hounds, and gawkers, but one woman, with poor eyesight, caught her attention. The woman felt her way down an aisle, groping the benches to find a seat facing the judge. It was her sister, Nancy Atkins. The sisters turned to face each other. "Minnie was so overcome that she broke into tears and had to be led from the room by her husband. Nancy bowed her head and held it in that position most of the morning," the *World* reporter wrote.[2]

Judge Campbell entered the courtroom. He was no stranger to Oklahoma politics or Native American land controversies. Judge Campbell had been chairman of the Republican Convention in 1908 and had been nominated by President Theodore Roosevelt to be the first federal district judge in the new state. He was a rising star in Republican politics, but the Atkins trial was draining him, mentally and physically. Hundreds of witnesses, dozens of defendants, and a press corps calling the trial the most litigated case in the history of the state—it was wrecking Judge Campbell's health. Page's response to the receivership Campbell had ordered in 1915 had been to fight, to ruin reputations and careers (including R. C. Allen's), and the judge was worn out. The receivership ordeal on its own led to the corruption scandal involving the possible kidnapping of Chief Tiger and the intervention of Representative Davenport, who had tried to eliminate the very position of national attorney for the Muscogees. And things were just getting started.

Page's business partner, R. A. Josey, was no longer involved. Josey had Texas swagger but not enough endurance to keep up with multiple layers of intrigue and dirty tricks. At some point before the 1917 trial, Josey sold his interest in the Gem Oil Company to Page.

All eyes must have been on Judge Campbell as he acknowledged the mosaic of alliances that made up both the defense and the prosecution. On the prosecution side sat a team from the Department of Justice, headed by Linebaugh; Allen, national attorney for the Creek Nation, was helping to coordinate the case. The prosecution also included Frank Montgomery, the probate attorney in Indian affairs. The plaintiffs' star witnesses were Bettie Mann and Sadie James.

The prosecution was not a happy family. For Allen this trial was personal—since Page and Josey had tried to "get his scalp" in 1915, he had wanted nothing more than to take them down and expose them as gigantic frauds. The US attorneys, on the other hand, saw their task as rather narrow: to prove that the enrollment of Tommy Atkins was invalid so that his land could be returned to the tribe.

On the defendants' side were forty individuals and corporations that formed a microcosm of unruly early Oklahoma society. Among the defendants were Nancy Atkins; her guardian, Micco T. Harjo; a freedman Creek attorney; Henry Carter; and, of course, Minnie Atkins and Charles Page.

If Page was nervous that the majority of his wealth was now tied up in this convoluted case, he did not show it. Page played the role of the unaffected, bighearted philanthropist, maintaining a guileless attitude when he took the witness stand. Bettie Mann and Sadie James would testify that Page had hired them to deliver him sworn testimonies from Leavenworth residents that would support his version of the Tommy Atkins story. But who was Judge Campbell going to believe: the notorious Sadie James or Daddy Page?

Assistant US attorney William German had gotten under the skin of Page and Long. The oilmen squirmed in their seats when German pushed them to explain their changing stories. German asked if Page had pressured Minnie to change essential facts about Tommy after Nancy's initial victory.

"What do you mean?" Page said. "If there's anything wrong with our lease or the allotment, we told [Nancy's team] we would give them a quitclaim deed immediately and claim no more interest in the matter."[3]

Oilmen and reporters from across the state packed the public viewing area, wanting to see how a federal court would deal with a case that went to the heart of the issues of the day: oil and gas leases, Indian citizenship, identity, and land tenure. Powerful newspapers and their publishers aligned themselves with various sides. The *Tulsa Democrat* reported the trial from the perspective of Minnie Atkins and Charles Page, as did the *Tulsa Morning Times*. The *Sapulpa Daily Herald* clearly favored the claims of its hometown businessman, Hugh Bartlett. The *Leavenworth Times* in Kansas seemed to delight in the twists and turns that two of its famous former residents, Minnie Atkins and Sadie James, provided. The *Muskogee Times-Democrat* did not seem to have a favorite, but it could barely conceal its animosity toward the Muscogee Nation and the federal government.

Eugene Lorton's *Tulsa World* was the wild card. Up until this point, Lorton's newspaper had regarded government interference as an obstacle to capitalism's relentless march of progress. In the summer of 1915, the *Tulsa World*'s flattery of Page had been continuous. "Charles Page has transformed wilderness into fertile valley" ran one subhead. Page could boast of around one million riders annually on the Sand Springs Interurban Railway that he had built—not just commuters but also pleasure seekers visiting Sand Springs Park, where Page's restless ingenuity and drive had built "great recreation and picnicking grounds, with zoo and lake and flower gardens and open air band concerts three nights each week."[4]

But on May 4, 1917, the *Tulsa World* began to shift its narrative about Page, claiming that Page may have known that Tommy was a fiction all along. "Mother Admits 'Tommy Atkins' Just a Myth," ran a *World* headline on May 9, 1917. A few days later, the *World* quoted Bettie Mann's testimony in which she stated that she had met Page in 1914 and informed him that Minnie had never had a son named Tommy. Mann had admitted to Page that Minnie's original lease was a forgery, and that it was better to drop the whole thing. Page had disagreed. "Well," Page had said to Mann, "it doesn't make any difference. We will have Tommy fixed up all right."[5]

As the *Tulsa World* pivoted in its portrait of Page, the oilman fired back. Page's newspapers attacked Lorton personally, calling him a "wife deserter," and threatened the *World* with a libel lawsuit. The *Tulsa Tribune* accused Lorton of being a tax dodger; the *Tulsa World* made similar accusations against Page. The *Tribune* gave a column to an anonymous employee of the newspaper who wrote: "Eugene Lorton is an unprincipled grafter; he is a sneak and real men feel a sickening disgust when they look upon his putrid face and read his lying accusations."[6]

Still, Page's team found itself in an awkward position, having to explain why Minnie had changed her stories about Tommy in sworn statements three times, including one in which she had said that there was no Tommy in the first place. The *Tulsa World*'s reporters noted the curious strategy Page's legal team developed in attacking the credibility of their codefendant, Minnie: "Page's attorneys in open court evince a strong inclination to throw poor old Minnie, Tommy's alleged mother, into the discard and rest the Page claims upon his lack of knowledge of the nonexistence of Tommy."[7]

In the eyes of some, Nancy Atkins, represented by Napoleon B. Maxey, seemed to have a weaker case than her sister. Her witnesses were Wagoner grafters and Atkins's cousin Ellis Childers, the scandal-ridden ex-treasurer of the Muscogee Nation. Her financial backers—J. A. Ferguson, a lumber tycoon from Fort Smith, Arkansas, and J. B. White, a shady Tulsa oilman—were hardly prominent figures like Charles Page. The Wagoner *Times-Democrat* may have loathed Page, but it did little to endorse Nancy's claims. They paper used racist tropes to call her credibility into question, often labeling her a "mulatto" even though she was not of African descent. The *Morning Times* noted that most of Nancy's witnesses were "negro," while Minnie's were white people of good character.

However, as the trial to decide *United States v. Atkins et al.* began, there were certainly a few betting men among the throngs of people gathered to watch, and to those making the odds, Nancy must have been the favorite. Important publications like the *Tulsa World* were turning their backs on Page. Judge Campbell had tried to put Gem Oil Co.'s operations in a receivership. Moreover, Nancy's lawyers had proved in Creek County Court that Bartlett's Minnie was a forgery. And unlike Henry Carter and Minnie Atkins, Nancy did not have to convince the judge that their claims rested on a series of mistaken identities. People around Wagoner knew Nancy Atkins, and plenty of them were ready to swear that her one child was a boy named Tommy.

"THIS CHILD WAS A GIRL": THE PRESSURE ON NANCY

Nancy Atkins testified that she had become pregnant in 1890. The pregnancy had most likely been the result of a sexual assault by a man whom she would not name. When attorneys pressed her to name the father of her child, she only replied, "That is one thing you will never find out."

As her pregnancy progressed, Nancy moved to Wagoner, where she found work as a laundress, first at the Bernard Hotel, then at the

Brown Hotel, where she went into labor on a September day. Her baby was born at the home of a Wagoner midwife named Elnora Williams. Nancy could not afford to leave her job at the Brown Hotel, so when she went to work, she would leave the baby with a woman named Betsy Birney and then return to see the child in the evenings.[8] Dozens of witnesses corroborated these details: they remembered seeing Nancy with a child named Tommy in Wagoner; some of them recalled Nancy calling the child "my boy."

Nancy stayed in Wagoner throughout the 1890s. When she was not working, she was occupied with children, including her sister's boys, Charley and Harvey, whom Minnie had brought to her in 1895. Sometime in 1899, word went around Wagoner that Nancy's child, Tommy Atkins, had died at the age of eight or nine. A Wagoner resident named John Ford said he'd pitched in twenty-five cents to help bury the boy. For a time that was all the world knew of Nancy Atkins and her baby.

Shortly after Tommy was born, Nancy got into "a little scrape" with Betsy Birney. She had taken mail that did not belong to her, and Birney turned her in. Nancy was shipped away to a federal prison in Detroit, where she served six months of an eight-month sentence for mail fraud. She came back to Wagoner on July 2, 1900. She had nowhere to stay except a tent behind the general store. Her cousin, Ellis Childers, took up a collection to find Nancy a home and the extended care she needed to get back on her feet.

This was Nancy's story, and it seemed solid. When the prosecution cross-examined her witnesses, however, they wavered on the years of Tommy's birth and death, casting doubt on Nancy's credibility. Wagoner resident John T. Beard remembered seeing Nancy pregnant in either 1888 or 1889, not 1890. Beard remembered contributing money for the child's funeral expenses but upon further recollection placed the death in 1901 or 1902.

Wagoner resident Andrew Jackson had also helped out with Nancy's child's funeral, but he remembered its being in either 1902 or 1903.

Another of Nancy's witnesses, Jim Dyer, had his credibility attacked by a prosecution lawyer, C. B. Stuart. "This witness admits being the identical Jim Dyer who was convicted for being constructively present at the Blackstone robbery," Stuart wrote in a brief regarding Nancy's claims. "He admits that he was pretty wild along about the early nineties and that he went to Wagoner to frequent the gambling shops and it was on these occasions that he would see Nancy Atkins."

Another witness, Kirk Turnbe, testified that he had gone into town one day in 1892 to have some horses shod. He heard Nancy Atkins outside on the street "hollowing [sic] for her boy Tommie [sic]." Turnbe said that he had seen Tommy, and he had been a sickly boy of about ten or eleven years old. This would have put his birth year several years earlier than 1890, contrary to Nancy's claim.

Stuart asked Turnbe if he was sure Tommy was Nancy's own child. It was a line of questioning that Stuart took with many of Nancy's witnesses. Stuart reminded the court of how Nancy had found a home among Wagoner's Black community, and he shared testimony that had been given by one Chaney Trent at the time of allotment. Trent, a Black woman who had been declared an "intruder" from the States by the Muscogee National Council, had been determined to prove that her paternal grandfather was the famous Lighthorse captain Thomas Atkins and that she therefore was a Creek by blood and entitled to allotment. Ellis Childers had supported Trent's claims, and eventually found a home for her and her siblings in his tribal town, Cheyaha.

Stuart saw a new strategy unfold. If old Thomas Atkins had been the father of Dick Atkins by an enslaved Black woman, and if Dick had a son named Tommy as well, then maybe Nancy's child was not her Tommy but rather Dick's child. Stuart's strategy became clearer as more and more people testified to Nancy's care of the mixed-race Tommy. Stuart allowed that Nancy had had a baby named Tommy. But that child had died hours or days after birth. The boy that had been seen in Nancy's care had, in fact, been her nephew, a son of Dick and Sally Atkins. Although Stuart did not explicitly state it, he implied that Nancy had compensated for the loss of her own child by effectively adopting her nephews as her own children. It was an interesting theory. At the time, Stuart and Page had no idea that Sally Atkins would later take that theory and run with it, leading to yet another existential challenge to the Page oil fortune.

After Nancy's witnesses had been questioned, it came time for Nancy herself to take the stand. Assistant US Attorney German questioned her first. Rather than asking her directly about the child,

German asked her about a sworn statement she had made in 1914. (At that point the Creek County lawsuit had been decided in her favor, but H. U. Bartlett was preparing to appeal.) In the statement, drawn up in the law offices of Lytle and McDougal in Sapulpa, Nancy had said that her child was a girl, not a boy.

Nancy now said that she had lied in the statement—she had been desperate for money at the time. She needed clean clothes and permanent housing. One day Bettie Mann approached her with a proposition on behalf of Bartlett. If Nancy would go to Bartlett's office and sign a paper saying her child had been a girl, Bartlett would give Nancy $2,000. Bettie took Nancy to a hotel in Sapulpa and gave her a clean set of clothes and five dollars in spending money. A man named Lytle, Bartlett's representative, told Nancy that she could get the $2,000 for signing the statement, or else they would have her sent back to the penitentiary for drinking alcohol. Nancy had already done two stints in prison. She was caught in a bind. Nancy admitted that she pondered Bartlett's proposition.

Nancy's lawyer, Maxey, realized his client's entire case might fall apart before she even had a chance to swear to Judge Campbell that Tommy really had been her boy. The government attorneys were making Nancy a pawn in a game she did not understand. Nancy had been caught up in the greedy machinations of oilmen, just like her sister, Minnie, had.

Finally, Maxey had a chance to question Nancy himself. He asked her when Tommy had died. "Well," Nancy said. "I don't know how old he was when he died. He was about—I don't know the year, but as near as my recollection can get at, he died in '90."

"Ninety or nineteen hundred?" Maxey asked.

"Nineteen hundred," Nancy said. She paused. "I guess."[9]

Nancy's noncommittal answer caught the attention of the government attorneys, who objected to Maxey's attempt to lead the witness into swearing to a life story that she did not seem to believe herself. It is impossible to know why Nancy, who might have held the strongest hand of all the defendants, was now filled with doubt.

She had already convinced the Creek County judge back in 1914 that the boy had been her own and had a long list of witnesses to back her up. Perhaps it was the emotional brush with Minnie during the trial, or the onslaught of questions about her traumatic past by attorneys on all sides. The threat of jail time for perjury loomed, as did retribution from agents of oilmen known to wield a stick when a carrot would not suffice.

As the trial wore on, it was clear that Nancy still had a case, but she, like Minnie, would have to admit to previously lying about her own child in order to win. She gave the court more details about her encounter with Bartlett during the Creek County case.

"What they wanted me to do was to say the child was a girl," Nancy told Judge Campbell. "The best thing I could do was claim this child was a girl."

"I WASN'T THAT BIG OF A FOOL": NANCY'S STORY CHANGES AGAIN

Bartlett's associates had kept Nancy in the Sapulpa hotel for days. She was unable to decide whether she should lie and take the money, or risk being sent back to jail if she refused. She left Sapulpa and went to the house of a Mrs. Yarboro, who was fixing a dress for Nancy in Nowata. Nancy went into Mrs. Yarboro's dining room, and sitting there was another woman she did not recognize—a Black woman in her late forties with a slight build.

"You don't know me, do you?" the woman said.

"No," Nancy replied. "You got me bested."

The woman asked Nancy about Minnie. Nancy was shocked this stranger had shown up at her friend's house to ask about her long-lost sister. Nancy told the stranger that her older sister was dead.

"No, she ain't," the woman replied. "Minnie is living just as you is today."

Nancy recounted to Judge Campbell how this woman at Mrs. Yarboro's offered to take her to meet Minnie. "I don't want to go anywheres with you," Nancy said, sensing the visitor meant trouble.

The unknown woman tried a different strategy. "You ought to be ashamed of yourself," the woman said. Nancy had lost contact with her sister, and both sisters were being stubborn. This stranger somehow knew that Minnie and Nancy had once had a deep bond but had become estranged. The shaming exposed a wound between the sisters. "My sister don't think enough of me to come to me," Nancy said. "And I think less of her."

Nancy walked toward Mrs. Yarboro's back door. As she started to leave, Mrs. Yarboro called her back inside. "You are not going to leave here," Mrs. Yarboro said. "They will certainly make away with you."

Someone, in other words, had a plan to kidnap Nancy. The strange woman was Sadie James, and she was working for Bartlett. She had instructions to send Nancy to Tulsa, to the Brady Hotel, one of the finest hotels in town. Nancy would be given an allowance, new clothes, and protection from other grafters. Nancy accepted James's proposal.

As Nancy rested up at the Brady Hotel, she was visited by Bettie Mann. It wasn't clear to Nancy whether Mann and James were on the same team or working for different oilmen. Mann had found the original fake Minnie Atkins in Kansas in 1912 and been convicted of forgery. Now she was out of prison and working for Bartlett again. Mann urged her to take Bartlett's $2,000 and be done with the entire drama.

"What a fool we have been," Nancy said. "Why didn't we let me claim that child and make some money? I could have been Tommy's mother just as well and we could have had a lot of money now."[10]

Nancy decided to go along with the plan. She wrote an affidavit in the law offices of Lytle and McDougal in Sapulpa saying her child had been a girl, and she had died shortly after birth. This was a direct contradiction of what she had said at the Creek County trial. Now, as she sat on the witness stand at the federal trial three years later, she claimed that she regretted the decision. But her attempt to reassert her parentage over the one true Tommy Atkins came off as utterly unconvincing.

Attorneys on both sides cross-examined Nancy over several days. At some point Nancy broke down. Asked repeatedly about the dead baby girl or boy, she stopped answering the lawyers' questions.

Judge Campbell urged her to speak up, but by May 16, 1917, she could no longer withstand the inquisition. That was the day that Maxey's scheme to prove that Nancy was the mother of Tommy Atkins broke down in front of the court. Maxey asked his client:

Q: Did you know Thomas Atkins?
A: I don't know anything about him.

Maxey had been practicing law in Indian Territory for decades. He had seen and heard it all, but Nancy's steadfast denial shocked him. Attempting to recover, Maxey asked Nancy to reaffirm the testimony of the gravedigger.

> Q: Isn't it a fact that he was one of the men who dug the grave for your son, Thomas Atkins?
>
> A: No, Sir, indeed he didn't. I didn't have any son Thomas Atkins.[11]

Maxey was stunned. Nancy had been coached to look Judge Campbell in the eyes and say: *Tommy Atkins was my child and Charles Page has concocted a story with no basis in reality.*

Maxey began to badger his own client.

> Q: You just signed anything that they brought to you, if they paid you some money?
>
> A: No, I wasn't that big of a fool.
>
> Q: Well, they did pay you some money, didn't they?
>
> A: Yes, Ellis [Childers] gave me fifty dollars.

Maxey belittled Nancy for taking such a paltry sum for so rich a land.

> Q: That fifty dollars looks good to you?
>
> A: No sir, I had more money than that at times.
>
> Q: But you took it, didn't you?
>
> A: Why sure.[12]

If Maxey was too angry to realize what was really going on with Nancy, another of the defense attorneys, a man named McGraw, had deduced what had really happened. Powerful people had threatened Nancy if she continued to insist that she had a boy named Tommy. He asked Nancy if she had been threatened with prison time if she did not cooperate with the plan to make Tommy the child of Minnie. "You were afraid if you didn't change your testimony, you might get in trouble?" McGraw asked.

Nancy was evasive. She admitted that several people had pressed her to change her story, but she would not name them in the courtroom. Backed into a corner, Nancy blamed the whole scheme of bribery, false testimony, and witness tampering on a group of "colored folks up [in] Nowata."

At this point, the federal government's entire case against Atkins et al. was verging on becoming a theater of the absurd. Judge Campbell realized that, after hours of interrogation from all manner of attorneys, some from the government and some from oil companies, Nancy would remain an enigma. Campbell tried to intervene. He questioned Nancy:

> Q: Do you want to tell the truth? The court wants you
>   to tell the truth.
> A: I would rather not have anything to do with it.
> Q: Was Thomas Atkins your son?
> A: He is supposed to be.
> Q: Was he or was he not; answer the question.
> A: Yes, sir.

— CHAPTER 15 —

"NANCY SHATTERS OWN CHANCE"

The next day, May 17, 1917, the *Tulsa Morning Times*, one of the three newspapers Charles Page owned in the Tulsa area, noted that Nancy had essentially destroyed her own case. "Nancy Shatters Own Chance for Leases," the headline proclaimed. That same day, the *Morning Times* published a column defending Page against that "slime-reeking viper" of a newspaper, the *Tulsa World*. One of the *World*'s biggest sins, in the eyes of the *Morning Times*, was that it gave over large sections of print to Sadie James's testimony.

The trial generated enough rumors and innuendo to fill months of column space in newspapers. The salacious details had a soap-opera-esque quality that must have delighted many readers. Beyond the gossip around these singular characters was an issue that few reporters bothered to note. *United States v. Minnie Atkins et al.* cut to the heart of what it meant to own land in the United States. In 1803 with the Louisiana Purchase the federal government had bought from France lands that stretched from Louisiana to the Dakotas. The area that became Oklahoma was set aside as Indian Territory in the 1820s and was later specifically demarcated as the property of various tribes through the 1830s. In 1907, it became no longer owned by the tribes but by specific citizens of those tribes in the form of allotments. The land had been deeded by Washington to these individuals as a land patent. Therefore, in order to revoke that patent, a federal judge needed to see compelling evidence that there had been fraud in the creation of the patent in the first place. The problem for Judge Ralph Campbell was that the case had opened a Pandora's box of fraud, identity theft, and conflicting notions of sovereignty.

The original Creek censuses of tribal towns, compiled in 1890 and 1895, were at the heart of this controversy. These census documents showed a grouping of people belonging to Euchee Town living together in 1895. The last roll from that year grouped a Thomas Atkins with Minnie, Nancy, and a man named Ed Schrimsher. The Dawes Commission had started with that census when compiling its definitive list of who was a Creek citizen entitled to a land allotment. Tommy's allotment, therefore, and the subsequent leases, deeds, and inheritance derived from it, all ultimately stemmed from that census. But the federal government had the right to expunge or add citizens as it saw fit.

Questions were raised about this odd grouping of the Atkinses and Ed Schrimsher. People remembered the accusation that Minnie had placed a Thomas on the roll to collect an extra $14.40 payment from the federal government in 1895. Back then, the thinking of the National Council of the Muscogee Nation was that Minnie had left the nation with an extra payment to Thomas. Most people believed Minnie was dead. However, the Dawes Commission did try to locate her, sending letters to various military forts that were returned to sender.

One of these letters had reached Minnie around 1903, after she had moved in with Harry. They were living in Missoula, Montana, when Harry opened a strange letter from the Dawes Commission one day. The letter stated that Minnie Atkins was the mother of the deceased child Thomas Atkins, and that his citizenship had been certified and his allotment was ready for selection. Harry asked Minnie about it. She said that it must have been some sort of mistake. They burned the letter and Minnie pleaded with Harry to leave Missoula.[1]

When Commissioner Bixby finally struck Minnie from enrollment in 1907, he admitted he could not fully explain what had happened to her. A closer inspection of the records reveals that Minnie may not have stolen anything, and that her supposed crime was part of a false narrative that shifted blame onto Minnie when the fraud—if any had occurred—belonged to someone much more well connected and powerful in the tribe: Sam Brown, the hereditary Euchee chief, who had overseen the original census.

So much of the confusion in all the various cases hinged on a strange annotation on the Muscogee receipts for the 1895 payment. Someone had scribbled in a bracket next to the names of Thomas and Mary Atkins the phrase "error of one." To complicate matters, over "Mary" was written another name, that of Alice Mable Peterkin—Minnie's daughter, who had died at the age of one in 1889 and was buried at Fort Logan National Cemetery. Was the name Thomas the error? Or the name Mary?

Ed Schrimsher, a cousin of the Atkins sisters, aimed to clear up that 1895 census during the federal trial. Schrimsher had been there when Sam Brown put down names of a family grouping. Schrimsher himself was listed at the top of the grouping. He was a cousin to the Atkins women. He said that neither Thomas nor Mary had been a mistake. Schrimsher had for a time lived with Nancy.

One day in 1895, Schrimsher went to a butcher shop in downtown Muskogee. Dick Atkins came in and asked him what he was doing in Muskogee. "I am making up a list to get some of that Creek money," Schrimsher said, referring to the allotments.

"Put my boy down," Dick said.

"Which one?" Schrimsher asked.

"Tommy," Dick said. Schrimsher knew Dick's Tommy Atkins. Like so many Black and Native American people in this story, Schrimsher had been in and out of prison. He knew all about the contentious relationship between the two Richard Atkinses. Now Dick was asking his Thomas to be included in a family grouping with the non-Black Atkinses. This gave Schrimsher pause. He recalled that there had been a debate within the National Council of the Muscogee Nation about whether to enroll Dick and his children. Dick had been classified as an "intruder" by some, but the Childers brothers and other Muscogees prevailed on their National Council to accept them, not as freedmen but as "Creeks by blood" owing to Thomas Atkins's paternity of Dick.

Ed Schrimsher found Sam Brown in downtown Muskogee. Brown was the most powerful Euchee in the Territory and carefully guarded who would be listed as part of his tribal town. Brown pulled out a notebook and wrote down the following grouping:

Ed Schrimsher

Mamie Atkins

Charlie Atkins

Susan Atkins

Thomas Atkins

Nancy Atkins

Later, in Brown's list, "Mamie" was crossed out and rewritten as "Mary." After Brown submitted this list to the National Council, "Mamie" was again corrected to "Minnie" and Susan was corrected to "Alice." In brackets next to "Alice" and "Thomas" was the phrase "error of one." What this meant, and who the error referred to, would be an ongoing mystery.

Schrimsher himself never received his $14.40 in 1895. When he approached Sam Brown about it, Brown said that Minnie had taken Schrimsher's payment. Minnie denied this to Schrimsher. So, while everyone seemed to believe Minnie had committed a fraud, and she herself admitted she had down something illegal in conversation with Sadie James, it is far from certain if Minnie did, in fact, draw this extra payment. If she never took a payment for Thomas Atkins, then the entire case might have collapsed. Even though Minnie changed her story several times, she did continue to insist that she took the payment.

Sam Brown, a star witness for Charles Page, had a slightly different version of how the census had been compiled. He said that when it came to this family grouping, he had relied on the testimony of John Davis, another cousin of the Atkins sisters. This was significant. If any errors cropped up with payments, Brown could blame it on Davis. While Brown's testimony helped establish the Minnie-as-mother theory, an important fact came to light after Judge Campbell's decision. John Davis had been in a federal penitentiary in 1895, so there was no way Brown could have received information from Davis. During the federal trial Brown was either lying for Page or having a serious lapse of memory. Still, his belief that the 1895 Tommy was Minnie's son was consistently cited as a keystone in Page's case.

Page's lead attorney, C. B. Stuart, walked through the events of 1895 carefully. Euchee Town King Sam Brown had been present when the Euchees had gone to the Muscogee treasury to withdraw their $14.40 payments. Stuart called on Brown, who had been present when the Euchees had collected their payments, to clarify whom, exactly, the names Thomas and Mary in that 1895 census had referred to.

Brown stated that the Thomas and Mary Atkins on the rolls referred to Minnie Atkins and her child, Tommy. He rejected the theory that the names referred to Dick and Sally's children because, he said, the Euchees would not admit anyone of "mixed" blood. Stuart pressed Brown to clarify what he meant by "mixed," asking: "Mr. Brown, do you know whether or not the Euchees ever admit into their membership of their tribe any persons of Negro blood?"

Brown hesitated before he answered. "Is that the question?"

"Yes, sir."

"That is one thing that was forbidden fruit among the Euchee Indians, to allow any other tribe or belonging to any of their tribe to—"

"Of Negro blood," Stuart interrupted.

"Or tribe," Brown continued. "That is, ever since I have known them."

It was an odd manner of speaking for Brown to refer to the Euchees in the third person—"them." Brown's testimony grew disjointed. He sounded like someone trying to back out of a corner—he did not want to definitively state that Euchees had never mixed with people of African ancestry. He allowed that there had been at least one person among the Euchees who did have African ancestry. "I will state there, they might think we had—John Buck was mixed so they will know."

"THERE WAS SO MANY TOMMYS": ELLIS CHILDERS ATTEMPTS TO CLARIFY MATTERS

Nancy's team seized on the uncertainty to advance the theory that the Thomas in this grouping in fact referred to Nancy's child. They had a witness, Ellis Childers, who remained firm in his belief that Tommy had indeed been Nancy's son. On the surface, it seemed like Childers would be a star witness for Nancy. He was a Carlisle alum and three-time speaker of the House of Warriors in the National Council. He had been praised at Carlisle as a model student and was a gifted public speaker in English. But there was a cloud over Childers's reputation.

Assistant US Attorney German questioned Childers's credibility. In 1898, during his tenure as treasurer of the Muscogee Nation, $93,000 worth of improper financial warrants had been discovered in the nation's accounting records. The warrants were, in essence, checks good for payment directly from a fund in the Muscogee Treasury, which in turn was funded by the US Treasury. The warrants were in a book that was stolen during a trip to Tulsa made by the former chief, Legus Perryman. Whoever stole them the warrants had sold them to people who could use them to write their own checks for whatever they wanted.

Childers had been tasked with making sure that the fraudulent warrants never resulted in actual payments. Along with a committee of leading citizens, he was supposed to track down and cancel these missing warrants. Instead, Childers used some of the warrants to benefit himself. An assistant secretary of the interior noticed something suspicious about some of the warrants and ordered an investigation. This led a federal judge to impanel a grand jury. One of the men accused turned state's evidence and named Childers as the ringleader of the conspiracy to defraud the US Treasury.

The whole episode was a tremendous embarrassment to the Muscogee Nation at a time when many white reformers were arguing that the Muscogee could not be trusted to responsibly manage their own affairs.[2] Childers was convicted by the federal government of conspiracy and served time, starting in 1899.

Childers had somewhat rehabilitated his reputation by the time of the Atkins trial. However, the mere mention of the warrants scandal by Assistant US Attorney German cast a pall over his testimony. German also pushed Childers to recount how he had lobbied the Muscogee National Council in 1890 to accept the freedman branch of the Atkins family—Dick and Sally Atkins, along with their twelve children—into the nation as Creeks by blood. Childers admitted to seeking revenge on other people in the National Council who tried to strike some of his town's citizens from their place in the Nation. Childers explained to politicians in Washington, DC, that he wanted to stand up for the people of his tribal town first and foremost. Childers now evaded German's questions on this incident, wanting to distance himself from the whole affair.

German's questions grew more and more pointed as he recalled how Childers had, years prior, misled the government about what he had known about Nancy Atkins. Childers had presented himself as a disinterested party, when in fact he had had Nancy virtually kidnapped and detained at his house. "You kept [Nancy] there for several months to keep anybody from making a statement to her," German said.

Childers did not dispute that version of events.

Nancy's odds of triumphing in the case seemed to be dwindling. Her main ally, Ellis Childers, appeared to be a second-tier grafter, while her attorney, Maxey, struggled to keep their side's story straight.

Childers was confident that Nancy had birthed a boy shortly before 1890. One day around that time, a relative of Childers's told him their cousin Nancy was sick from childbirth complications. The relative suggested taking up a collection to help Nancy, who was still living in her tent. Childers put in $5. With the money, Nancy took up residence at Betsy Birney's house, where she convalesced. Childers went by Birney's house ten days after the collection and saw Nancy with a living baby. He could not state whether it was a boy or a girl.

About a year later, Childers saw Nancy and the child walking around Wagoner. Someone told him that the child's name was Tommy Atkins. Time went by and Childers again saw Nancy with a boy running around the streets near the Davis and Jones store. The child was between two and three years old at that point. In 1895, when Childers was among the group of Muscogee officials tasked with distributing the $14.40 per capita payment from the federal government, he was contacted by Sam Brown, town king of the Euchees. "He needed me to help him verify three families of Euchees that lived in our section of the country," Childers said.[3]

Brown wanted Childers to look over the names, taking special note of a Thomas Atkins who had been grouped with several names that seemed out of place, including one Mary Atkins. Childers knew a Mary Atkins, but she was the daughter of Dick and Sally Atkins, the Black branch of the family.

None of this clarified who the mother of Thomas was. After Childers had finished giving his testimony, Judge Campbell tried one last time to set the record straight with Nancy.

"Just tell the court what the truth is about that child," Campbell said.

"My child was a boy sure enough," Nancy said.

"Look at me and talk loud," Campbell said.

Nancy explained that her eyesight kept her from maintaining eye contact. She had been born cross-eyed and had developed a cataract.

"All right," Campbell said, "look at me anyhow."

Nancy said that the boy had lived to be at least eight years old. She understood that his name had caused confusion. If she had it to do over again, she would have picked a different name. "I named it Tommy," Nancy said, "but at the time I didn't know there was so many Tommys, so many boys in the Atkins family named Tommy, I wouldn't never named him. I would much rather have named him after my brother, but after Minnie had one named Lee, I just called mine Tommy."[4]

Judge Campbell seemed skeptical. Nancy, like Minnie, had changed her story many times, and there were those disturbing issues concerning Ellis Childers's credibility.

To close his case on Nancy's claim, Stuart discussed the testimony of Henry Anderson, the Wagoner resident who had seen his employee bury Nancy's dead child. But Anderson could not remember the year—whether he had seen the dead child being buried in 1900, 1901, 1902, or 1903.

"Now the testimony of Anderson is to a concrete fact about which he could not be mistaken unless he was a clean-cut perjurer," Stuart wrote, noting that the government had called Anderson as a reputable witness with no interest in the case, nor any animosity toward Nancy Atkins.

"Witnesses swear that this child was practically born dead," Stuart said, addressing Judge Campbell. "Supplemented with the testimony of Henry Anderson, who stated he saw Nancy's dead child in a box as it was being buried behind Elnora Williams's house, was a statement by Bettie Mann, who came across Nancy early in quest for Minnie. Nancy told Bettie in 1912 that her only child had been born dead. If Nancy cared for a Tommy Atkins around Wagoner, it was not her Tommy. This child belonged to someone else entirely."[5]

A *Tulsa World* reporter noted that Nancy Atkins sat with her head bowed as C. B. Stuart rehashed the tragedy of her short-lived Tommy. It was clear that her claim to the land, and its massive fortune, had been gutted.

This point in the trial marked the end of an uneasy alliance that had been forged between Page's team and the federal government when it came to Nancy Atkins. They had both wanted to destroy her claim. Now that this had been done, the government had to go back on the offensive against Page and prove that his claim on behalf of Minnie was just as fraudulent.

Once it became clear that not even Nancy herself believed in her case, Childers started working for the government and the tribe as an interpreter. Nancy's chief attorney, Maxey, chose to refocus his efforts on how Page and Long had conspired to manufacture a Tommy of their choosing. Nancy would not win title to the land, but she could expose others involved in the fraud.

Maxey brought to the stand Henry DeWitt, a Muscogee citizen who had known the Atkins sisters since their girlhood and asked him about the affidavit Nancy had signed stating that her child had been a girl. DeWitt recounted that in 1914 he had volunteered to help find Nancy Atkins and bring her to Page's office in Tulsa. DeWitt went with Sam Brown Jr. to Nowata to find Nancy. By this time, his father was virtually retired from public life. He put more and more of his work in the hands of his son, whose reputation quickly came under fire. Young Sam stiffed people on invoices, ran around with shady oilmen, and did not seem interested in his father's main mission in life—preserving the distinctness of the Euchee people within the Muscogee Nation.

Nancy was afraid of Brown Jr., possibly due to his reputation as a grafter. She felt comfortable with DeWitt, so he accompanied her to Tulsa. However, Nancy balked when they got to Page's downtown office and Long presented her with the affidavit to sign. With Nancy refusing to hear them out, Long leaned on DeWitt, badgering him to sign Nancy's name to the affidavit. DeWitt bristled. "I told Long that the child was not a girl but a boy," he said. "If I made any affidavit, it would not be like Long wanted."

"What difference does it make to you whether it was a boy or a girl?" Long said to DeWitt.

DeWitt countered, "Hundreds of people up in this country would know that was false."

The meeting turned tense. Long stood up and left.

As they went back to the car, DeWitt asked Sam Brown about his affidavit. Brown admitted that he was working for Page and Long to secure Minnie's claim to the Tommy Atkins allotment. Brown knew that his work for Long and Page could put his reputation and, indeed, his livelihood, in jeopardy. But the potential rewards may have included some subsection of oil land for himself, or monetary rewards for the rest of his life.

With DeWitt's testimony now added to the record, there was new pressure on Page and Long to prove that they were not the grafters depicted in DeWitt's narrative.

Sam Brown Sr. remained the indispensable lynchpin between the old Muscogee Nation, its allottees, and Page's ambitions to grow the Sand Springs Home into "the Industrial Center of the Southwest." Brown Sr. was not only the supervisor of the 1895 Euchee census but also a political mover inside the Muscogee Nation. In 1916, Brown formally transferred his roles and responsibilities to his son.

For most of their careers, the Browns had done the bidding of Charles Page and the Sand Springs Home, but unlike so many other figures in this story, Sam Brown Sr. did not exit the stage at an early age. When he finally died, in 1935 at the age of 102 in Sapulpa, he was remembered as "the last of the Indians whose sweep of memory included the ante-bellum days in Indian Territory."

By that time, Brown was no longer sure that the interests of the Sand Springs Home were the interests of the Euchee people. But also, by that time, many Euchee people were not sure if Sam Brown should have ever represented them in the first place.

THE SAM BROWN INTERLUDE

*I*n 2021, Apollonia and I drove down from Tulsa to the Oklahoma History Center in Oklahoma City to check out the Brown family archives. Sam Brown's name had popped up everywhere we looked for Tommy Atkins—in Creek County, Sand Springs, Tulsa, and the Western History Collections at the University of Oklahoma. He seemed to be one of those people in the background of everything. Google searches led to some wild theories about his life—that he had not been Euchee by blood at all but rather a Jewish boy adopted into the tribe by a Muscogee woman in Arkansas. There is much speculation from genealogists about Brown. He reportedly insisted that he not only held a hereditary title as king but that another ancestor was Texas governor Sam Houston.[1]

The collections contained materials that had belonged to Samuel W. Brown and his son, Samuel W. Brown Jr., both of whom had held the title of hereditary chief of the Euchees (also spelled Yuchi). There were logbooks, letters, postcards, and certificates of recognition. As I looked at the materials, my first impression of Brown was of a distinguished elder statesman, businessman, and advocate for Native American rights. There was a letter to him from Will Rogers Jr. recognizing Brown for his hard work on behalf of Native Americans. There was a photograph of Brown Jr. visiting the ancestral lands of the Euchee in Georgia in which he wore a full feathered headdress while being received by dignitaries there. Muscogees almost never wear Plains-tribes-style headdresses, and Apollonia laughed when I showed her the photo. White folks could not resist the allure of an Indian in a headdress, she said.

As I leafed through the yellowing documents, I started to cobble together a portrait of a more enigmatic man. The many obituaries that *ran for him repeated the story that Brown had been the biological son of Sam Houston. There was some evidence for this. Brown's appearance was ethnically ambiguous: he had bluish eyes, a wispy goatee, and a gaunt face that some described as looking Mongolian. Houston had had a brief affair with a Euchee woman named Suttah, who had given birth to a son in Van Buren, Arkansas, in 1843.[2]*

A more likely story was that Brown's father had been a soldier in the US Army, and that he was part Scottish by blood. As a child, he had been sent to a school run by a Native American named S. C. Brown, who had lent his last name to young Sam. In the 1850s, he attended the same school as Minnie Atkins at the Tullahassee Mission, and then left Muscogee Nation for New Mexico. He returned during the Civil War. Brown fought in the war on both sides, first for the Confederacy, which he claimed to have done out of self-preservation. In 1863, he joined the Union Home Guard and reached the rank of captain. Brown spoke five or six languages and proved adept at understanding the concepts of landownership in white society. His obituary claimed that he was one of only five people in the world who spoke Yuchi, Mvskoke, and English with the fluency of a native speaker. He accumulated around seven hundred head of cattle and sixty stock horses and mules. He established a store south of Tulsa and fought off notable outlaws, including Belle Starr. He sold off the store but still maintained about two hundred acres of fenced farmland.

The discovery of oil in Indian Territory in the early 1900s was a crucible for Brown. The unique system of allotment in early Oklahoma gave him an incredible amount of power as a guardian, a translator, and a broker. He ran his farm as a private enterprise. Charley Guthrie (the father of Woody Guthrie) wrote to Brown to offer him "a cut" for any Indians he would bring in to register with the Dawes Commission. It is unclear what Guthrie's scheme was, but in all likelihood it was obtaining guardianships.

Brown walked around with little notebooks and he claimed to have personal documentation of every Euchee child born in the Muscogee Nation. As the Atkins trials showed, Brown did not always know who was related to whom, and who had what degree of "blood." He could be forgiven for not having an encyclopedic knowledge of how his people's lives translated to the arbitrary ways of white society— except for the fact that he imposed his own interpretations on what were debatable concepts, in particular the notion of the hereditary kingship that he claimed to hold. A friend of Brown's remembered that he would slap himself on the chest and proclaim, "I am a king!"[3]

Apollonia introduced me to a Euchee elder who urged caution when talking about hereditary powers. It evoked the idea of European dynasties, and that was not the reality of Euchee government, he said.

When Brown Jr. inherited the title of town king, he found himself confronted by other Euchees who believed the very concept of inherited power to be an invention. The cultural anthropologist Pamela Wallace has noted that many Euchees believed that Brown Jr. was trying to con them. "There is considerable confusion of 'Chief' Brown and his role," Wallace wrote. "Leaders of E.T.I. and E.U.C.H.E.E. [contemporary Euchee organizations] feel that the title of Principal or Hereditary Chief that Brown assumed was a 'self-appointed' title with no meaning."[4]

When I talked this over with Apollonia, I remarked that the Brown men—junior in particular—seemed to be at the heart of the confusion around Tommy Atkins. They used the term "town king," or micco, to justify their power grabs. This did not sit well with Apollonia. The idea that a micco could be corruptible or greedy was anathema to her cultural knowledge. A micco was a universally trusted figure in Mvskoke culture. If Brown Jr. had been engaged in dubious business practices with Charley Guthrie, Charles Page, or anyone else, he could not, by definition, be a micco. She was so bothered by the idea that a micco would participate in a fraud that she proposed we drive to see an acquaintance of hers in Sapulpa. The friend was a scholar who had devoted his life to the maintenance of the Yuchi language. If it had to do with Euchee customs, then this man would have an explanation.

We drove up the turnpike to Sapulpa and down South Main Street. It looked like typical small-town Oklahoma—pickup trucks, cannabis dispensaries, gracious old houses fallen into disrepair, sparkling new and incredibly large gas stations. In a rambling stucco building was the office of the Yuchi Language Project, where English is rarely heard. At the time we visited, there were only three Native speakers of Yuchi left in the world. The executive director was trying to change that, one child at a time. We asked him about Town King Sam Brown. What he said has stuck with me: "Brown was not who he said he was."

It was unclear if he meant Sam Brown Jr. or Sr. In any case, Brown Jr. was not nearly as popular as his father. Wallace's dissertation is filled with accusations against the man. There are stories of loans extended to Brown Jr. for various causes that the "town king" ended up spending on a new pair of Justin cowboy boots.

Harry Folk knew that Minnie Atkins's claim rested on Brown Sr.'s story. After Minnie's death, Folk periodically wrote to Brown, including a series of payments to him as a gift. Folk was careful about the implications of this payment to Brown. "I realize that I am not obligated to you in any way Mr. Brown," Folk wrote in 1925, "but I merely send you this present as a gift in the hopes that it will bring more happiness to you and your family."⁵

Brown Sr.'s relationship with the Sand Springs Home became even more complicated after the death of Charles Page in 1926. The home gained title to Brown's lands, and the Euchee leader soured on its new relationship. Brown felt the Sand Springs Home owed him money after all he had been through during the Atkins trials. But somehow the home ended up owning Brown's land, and he was often in debt. In 1931, a Tulsa attorney, B. F. Ingraham, wrote to Brown urging him to pursue legal action against the home. "If anyone was indebted to you," Ingraham wrote, "it was the Sand Springs Home, who now holds the title to your land through fraud."

Ingraham continued: "I am indeed sorry that you lost your property to the Sand Springs Home, and I think you are sleeping on your rights by delaying bringing an action to set aside the sale of your 40 acres and for damages."⁶

Piecing together the letters from Harry Folk, Ingraham, and the home's attorney, Paul Pinkerton, the picture becomes clear. Page's interests in the Tommy Atkins case hinged on the continued avowal by Brown that Minnie was Tommy's mother. But Brown had never seen Minnie at Fort Leavenworth or Fort Logan. He had based his testimony on secondhand information that was at best an educated guess and at worst, a lie funded by the Page interests. Brown, however, had misgivings. He knew it had been a mistake to give Frank Long valuable documents relating to the Euchees. An even bigger mistake had been trusting the Sand Springs Home to take care of the Euchee cemetery near Jenks.

Sam Brown Jr., for all of his character flaws, in the late 1950s decided to take on his father's former benefactor and right a historic wrong. During the Atkins trials, Frank Long had "borrowed" the original tribal rolls of 1895 on behalf of the Sand Springs Home. They were never returned. Although copies existed and had been preserved, Brown Jr. fought to get the original rolls back. By the late 1950s, Brown Jr. was threatening legal action against the home to force their return.

Brown Jr.'s lawyer, J. S. Severson, warned him against the move. No one dared take on the Sand Springs Home, even three decades after the death of Charles Page. Brown Jr. was unfazed. On April 15, 1957, Brown demanded that the home return what was rightfully the property of the Euchee people: "1. One red book-marked journal, containing his personal accounts of the Euchee town roll of citizens. 2. One book containing personal accounts of S. W. Brown and enrollment of citizens of the Yuchi tribal town, of 1895, of which he was king."

"These rolls have an important public interest not only for their value from a historical standpoint, but because of the facts of heirship as set out on those rolls," Brown wrote.[7]

The only response from the Sand Springs Home came in the form of a letter reminding Brown that he was still in debt to them. By this point, Harry Folk was dead and the venerable old Chief Brown had also passed from the earth at the age of 102. Brown Jr. told a Muskogee journalist that his father had simply guessed at the name of Minnie's children.

Brown wasn't done. In the summer of 1957, he discovered that the Euchee burial ground in southwestern Tulsa County, which dated back to the 1890s, had been effectively wiped out by the Sand Springs Home and that the grounds had just been sold to a well-known Tulsa developer, Evan Durell.[8] More than one hundred Euchee people had been buried there, including several Civil War veterans. The Euchees had landscaped around the cemetery to mark the area, and some of the gravestones had been elaborate affairs. Brown said the home had plowed over everything, including the gravestones of some of his relatives, prior to putting the property on the market. By the time Durell bought it, it was a grassy field, ready for suburban development.

It was an abhorrent crime, but there was no legal remedy. That land had been allotted, then sold to the Sand Springs Home, which in turn had sold it to Durrell. They had destroyed the cemetery beyond recognition, but, as Brown's lawyer noted, the statute of limitations had passed.

A year after his futile attempts to seek justice with the Sand Springs Home and Durrell, Sam W. Brown Jr. was dead. Although he had lived most of his adult life in Texas, Brown's funeral was held at the same place as his father's: Little Cussetah Indian Church in Sapulpa. He could not be buried in the Euchee burial ground that he had fought in vain to have restored.

Today, those six acres, with the Euchee remains in the soil, are now covered by a Candlewood Suites Hotel, a FedEx drop-off box, and the offices of Gateway Mortgage, a company founded by Oklahoma governor (and Cherokee citizen) Kevin Stitt.

If Stitt has been known for one thing, it is his vehement opposition to tribal sovereignty.[9]

Amid all the stories and counter-stories, a theme was emerging: everyone in the Tommy Atkins story had manipulated, fabricated, or simply made up part of their life story to get ahead in a new society. Sometimes, as in the case of the Mvskoke people, it was a survival strategy. Other times, as in the case of Charles Page, it was a branding and public relations move. I was becoming cynical. All the potential good guys in this story had been revealed to have some terrible flaw. Frank Montgomery was supposed to be the US probate attorney who saw the fraud for what it was. Lurking inside Montgomery, however, was something dark indeed. In 1931, the attorney returned home for lunch to find his twenty-four-year-old daughter at home with her baby. His daughter had divorced her husband. Montgomery went into the child's room and shot the baby in the crib. He then turned his weapon on himself. When his wife and daughter came in, they found Montgomery and his grandchild dead.[10]

Even Saint Angie, Dr. Angie Debo, had failed to see the fraudulent practices of Charles Page and the Sand Springs Home. Meanwhile, the bad guys were turning out to be way smarter than I had given them credit for. I had by this point read hundreds of letters and briefs by Frank Long, the man who did Page's dirty work. He might have *had the brightest mind in this entire cast of characters. He had an encyclopedic knowledge of who was connected to whom, what the law said, and what Muscogee custom dictated. All of that intelligence was marshaled for one purpose—to control land, people, and money. Money and power corrupted everyone. However, I also believed that, at the end of it all, there was such a thing as the truth. And we'd get to that truth eventually.*

— CHAPTER 16 —

"YOU KNOW HOW A WHITE MAN IS ABOUT MONEY"

Sadie James Reveals All

O n an unseasonably warm day in November 1917, Charles Page admired downtown Tulsa's first true skyscraper—the new Exchange National Bank on the corner of Boston Avenue and Third Street. This was where he had put up a bond to keep the oil flowing from the Atkins lands. It was unclear whether Exchange National had counted the bond against his balance sheet, so Page went there himself to find out. The building was every bit as modern and ornate as anything in Chicago or New York City, and the whole city turned out to celebrate its opening.

The two-story terra cotta base featured a stunning Beaux Arts design, with intricate metal work on the outside and a steel frame structure supporting all ten stories. The inauguration of the building seemed to presage Tulsa's coronation as the Oil Capital of the World. The Cushing-Drumright oil patch itself was a notoriously crime-ridden place, but money would be safe here in the bank. The building had fourteen-inch walls of concrete and steel, along with a steel safe whose door weighed seventeen tons.[1] Bandits and highwaymen might pick off small-time oilmen on the road to Drumright, but if the oilmen got their money to the Exchange National Bank in Tulsa, it might as well be in Fort Knox. Tulsa boosters had taken out a full-page ad in the *Washington Post*, boasting that deposits in the city's banks totaled more than those of some entire states in the Union. The president of Exchange National Bank, Harry Sinclair, was also the president of Sinclair Oil and Refining Corporation, one of the ten largest oil companies in the nation. Page was one of many oilmen who would establish an office here at the bank, one from which he would formulate dreams every bit as ambitious as Sinclair's. The bank was delighted that Page would lease an office in their building; it counted on the deposits of millionaires as a vote of confidence in its solvency.

An orchestra played patriotic songs and employees handed out cigars to visiting bankers. At one point during the opening ceremony, Page cornered Earl W. Sinclair, the vice president of the bank and Harry's brother. According to one report, Page suddenly remarked, "Earl, if it's not too much trouble, I'd like to know what's my balance here."

"No trouble at all," Sinclair replied.

Sinclair gave instructions to a teller to find Page's balance sheet, then reported, "You have on deposit today, Mr. Page, $1,786,214.17."

"Thank you," replied Page.

It was the response he wanted. That figure meant that Earl Sinclair had not subtracted from his account the $950,000 bond Page had put up in 1915 to continue operating the Tommy Atkins oil field. Subtract that figure from what the teller had calculated, and Charles Page was no longer a millionaire. Then subtract the hefty legal fees, various payments to friends, witnesses, and secret agents, plus another $40,000 in interest payments from the bond also coming due, and Page might have been in financial trouble if the bank realistically counted all of Page's liabilities. But Exchange National Bank believed in Page. The bank needed to believe in Page. If the Muscogee Nation could recover land and riches for fraudulent transactions, there was no telling how much money and land might suddenly be up for grabs. Not only the Tommy Atkins riches would be in question; there were the claims in Glenn Pool, in Sand Springs, the Emarthlas, the Naharkeys, the Adamses.

If the Tommy Atkins case was an unsavory mess at that point, it was about to get a whole lot messier, thanks to a remarkable antihero who, by a strange twist of fate, happened to be a close acquaintance of Charles Page, H. U. Bartlett, and Minnie Atkins.

This is the story and testimony of Sadie James.

THE NOTORIOUS SADIE JAMES: ENTREPRENEUR

It is hard to imagine a more unlikely pair of allies than Sadie James and R. C. Allen. Here was Allen, an aristocratic white Southerner who had used racist slogans on his way to a judgeship, relying on the testimony of a Black woman whose mother had been born into slavery and who went on to run what a US census taker described as a "house of ill fame" in Kansas. Allen had made himself modestly wealthy by using dubious methods to secure land titles from Black freedpeople around Coweta and Wagoner. James had used her savvy to start a hotel for Black people, the Brooklyn Hotel, in Sapulpa, Oklahoma, and then offered illicit services to well-connected white and Black clients in Tulsa. Allen had run a law practice noted for stiffing its clients and misrepresenting the facts. James ran an establishment noted for fights, bootlegged whiskey, and women of the night.

Two themes unite this unlikely duo: a tendency to play fast and loose with the law in pursuit of an advantage over rivals, and a desire to finally let the truth be known about the myth of Tommy Atkins. Allen had awakened to the massive scale of fraud being perpetrated on Muscogee allottees after he became national attorney for the Creek Nation in 1914. He seems to have bucked the oil interests that had installed him in the position, instead exposing the grafters who were pillaging the estates of his clients, the Muscogee people. Of course, Allen's motives were not entirely pure: if he recovered the land for the Muscogee Nation, the tribe would be able to lease out the land and would then, presumably, pay Allen a handsome fee. And an unconfirmed rumor circulating around the Hotel Tulsa had it that Allen already had another Muscogee citizen in mind to claim the allotment— along with an oil and gas lease ready to be auctioned to the highest bidder. If true, it was plausible that even if Allen won the case, yet another grafter would end up owning the land.

Such machinations were exactly the stock and trade of Sadie James. She had parlayed her connections as a proprietress of a roadhouse into liaisons with people like Charles Page. Her existence and continuing prosperity were, however, much more tenuous than Allen's. Like other enterprising Black businesspeople in Oklahoma at the time, she was constantly subjected to swindling, double standards, and the threat of violence. If getting ahead in life meant playing both sides of the rivalry between Page and the Sapulpa oilman H. U. Bartlett, James would do so.

James's access to Page and Minnie Atkins put her in a unique position. She had befriended Minnie as a young woman in Leavenworth. Her acquaintance with Page was probably initiated through her roadhouse, where Bill Creekmore, "the King of Oklahoma Bootleggers," supplied her establishment with whiskey. When someone accused her of bootlegging, she said it was totally unnecessary, that Creekmore supplied whiskey for so many people he was untouchable. Creekmore had become quite wealthy from his liquor trade and laundered some of his dirty money in real estate. James said that Creekmore and Page were friends, and often discussed deeds that might be obtained by unorthodox methods in Page's office.

At one point, Page suggested that Creekmore be the name on the deed to Tommy's land. Page did not want to be listed as the owner, since it might attract bad publicity. "I have a lease and I don't want the deed, but, Bill, you take it," James heard Page say to Creekmore.[2]

It's unclear why Creekmore opted out, but it might have presented legal complications for him as well; Creekmore was in and out of prison from convictions for gambling, bootlegging, and other crimes. Despite the legal troubles, he was a well-known operative in the Democratic Party. The connections between respectable Tulsa and the city's underworld were intimate, even though the city's newspapers sought to portray the place as a safe, prosperous site of all-American values. Sadie James said out loud what was usually only whispered in the gambling dens and suites at the Hotel Tulsa. Her testimony at the 1917 trial enthralled everyone, although it was quickly repressed and eventually forgotten.[3]

THE ROYAL CHEROKEES AND LOYAL ETHIOPIANS

James's mother, Carrie Belle Ross, had been born in the Cherokee Nation in 1852 as a slave of a Cherokee citizen, Lewis Ross. In 1866, the Cherokee Nation entered into a treaty with the United States that, among other things, granted Cherokee citizenship to freedpeople born among the tribe. By 1875 Carrie Belle Ross had returned to Lightning Creek, the place of her birth in the Cherokee Nation, to claim her place on the nation's rolls. Her name appears on an 1883 payroll of the federal government to Cherokee citizens, but it is possible this reference is to another person. (Ross is a very common Cherokee surname.)

When the Dawes Commission began their censuses in the 1890s, they were skeptical of Ross's claim. The Cherokee Nation advocated excluding her, arguing that she was either a Muscogee freedperson or an intruder, reflecting a larger unwillingness on the part of the tribe to accept Black members. Her case remains a mystery. Lewis Ross did hold many people in bondage, perhaps as many as 150 at one time. But given that documents counting enslaved people, called "slave schedules," did not include vital statistics about them as individuals, it was exceedingly difficult to prove that any one person, post-Emancipation, was the former slave of someone like Lewis Ross or Benjamin Marshall.

Carrie Ross persisted in her efforts, but the commission continued to rebuff her. In 1896, Cherokee citizens received a per capita payment from the federal government as part of a deal in which the tribe forfeited title to a swath of territory known as the Cherokee Strip. Carrie and Sadie Ross received no such payment. In 1901, Carrie and Sadie Ross were rejected for allotment by the Dawes Commission on the grounds that they had not been counted on any census nor were they entitled to payment in 1896. Meanwhile, well-connected white impersonators were finding their way onto the Cherokee rolls. This clearly embittered Carrie Ross, who went about the Southwest claiming to be part of a group called the Royal Cherokee and Loyal Ethiopians, championing the cause of rejecting Oklahoma statehood, and trying to enlist anyone who would listen.

Sadie Ross married her first husband, Edward Carris, when she was seventeen. Together they had one daughter, Eva, who accompanied and lived with her mother her entire life, never having children of her own. Sadie's marriage with Carris quickly dissolved. She would go on to marry seven or eight times, relying on these husbands mainly for protection rather than romantic love. Sadie took on a multitude of last names: Ross, Johnson, Harris, Curtis, Carney, James.

Carrie, Sadie, and Eva Ross traveled around the region trying to find a suitable home for the Royal Cherokee and Loyal Ethiopian movement. The Southern states did not suit Carrie Ross at all. She later told the *Tulsa Post*, "Texas was hell and Arkansas her wayside station."[4]

The family finally settled in Tulsa, probably in or around 1909. Tulsa was a wild and lawless town run by transplanted Southern bigots, to be sure, but it afforded the family some measure of freedom. The Black neighborhood of Greenwood in particular offered opportunities not available to Black people elsewhere in the South or Southwest. Tulsa newspapers saw Carrie's pronouncements about her royal lineage from Ethiopia and the Cherokee Nation as a source of good copy, but her criticisms of statehood as a project of white supremacy must have caught the ear of some people in Greenwood.

Carrie considered herself a prophet, and her message had by now expanded into a Christian-inspired Black nationalism, a gospel well ahead of its time. The Christian part of her message might have had mainstream acceptability, but Carrie insisted that Christ would have been eager to strike down Jim Crow statutes and the grandfather clause, both of which were the law of the land in Oklahoma.

Sadie and Eva accompanied Carrie on her mission of spreading the gospel of Black Christian nationalism for many years, but once Sadie became interested in business opportunities in Tulsa, she and her mother parted ways. This was understandable. Carrie refused to recognize the state of Oklahoma as an entity with any political legitimacy. She was not opposed to white settlers per se but believed they should live and worship with the "Royal Cherokee and Loyal Ethiopians of Indian Territory," who were the true "natives by birth" of the place. "We don't care if the poor whites take all the work," Carrie wrote in a newsletter in 1911, because the Royal Cherokee and Loyal Ethiopians were "a God chosen race."[5]

Unlike her mother, Sadie made no grandiloquent statements about race, politics, or religion. She did, however, understand that everyone, regardless of race or religion, was susceptible to the mortal sins of greed, lust, and pride. Sadie saw that the new class of white men flooding into Tulsa were arrant knaves, all. If they wanted bootlegged whiskey, poker games, and interracial encounters, she would provide that.

Sometime around 1910 or 1911, Sadie James started operating a roadhouse in Greenwood called Sadie's Bucket of Blood, most likely leased from the well-known Black pioneer O. W. Gurley.[6] Ottowa Gurley was a successful businessman originally from Arkansas and one of the first investors in Greenwood. While other African American newcomers like *Tulsa Star* editor A. J. Smitherman argued for militant Black self-defense, Gurley sought cooperation with Tulsa law enforcement. Gurley worked with Tulsa County's lone Black deputy sheriff, Barney Cleaver, to try to balance Greenwood's growth with white Tulsa's fear of Black power. While white newspapers demonized Greenwood as a place of sin and lawlessness, much of the illegal activity there was, in fact, financed by white bootleggers like Bill Creekmore.

In the early 1910s, Gurley and Cleaver decided they needed Sadie James to leave Greenwood. Her place of business had garnered a notorious reputation; depending on whom you asked, it was a hotel, a brothel, a saloon, a juke joint, a dance hall, or possibly some combination of all of these. As tales of miscegenation swirled about her business, James continued to live in the heart of Greenwood. This was dangerous business, as interracial marriage was illegal in Oklahoma.

And no matter how many editorial columns derided her business as dangerous and immoral, she never lacked for clients, Black or white. One article told of a visiting laborer who went all over Tulsa looking for a beer in this nominally "dry" town. He found he could slake his thirst at James's roadhouse while playing roulette and craps. In a town where bootleggers operated freely in downtown hotels Sadie was a pioneer of "stockinglegging." She regularly supplied Tulsa women with their own access to whiskey pulled from her silk stockings.[7] Much of this underworld was an open secret.

Later, in 1942, my great-grandfather, Police and Fire Commissioner Russell Cobb, complained about the power of Tulsa bootleggers over his police force. Cobb told the *Tulsa Tribune* that he had been offered a $1,000 bribe to look the other way when it came to roadhouses in Greenwood. In 1966, his son, Russell Cobb Jr., was a member of a grand jury investigating the bootlegging ring of Cleo Epps, "Oklahoma's Bootleg Queen." Cobb admitted to accepting a payment from Epps and then recommending a lenient sentence for her. Epps wound up murdered in 1970.

Sadie James, on the other hand, had nothing to hide. James's mother did not approve of her daughter's entrepreneurship. Carrie Ross took to the streets of Greenwood, and the pages of the *Tulsa Post*, to denounce her daughter. "I did all that I could to teach my daughter Sadie Johnson and my granddaughter Eva Holmes the way of right," she wrote. "But I have failed. Therefore, I have put them in His hands that they may get straightened out."[8]

"TELL THE LORD ANY DARN THING YOU WISH": SADIE'S FIRST TRIAL

In 1911, Sadie James was living with a man named Walter Agnew. James relied on Agnew for protection, but the man professed his love to her. One day, James caught Agnew stealing cash from a dresser drawer in her home. She told him to leave and never come back. Agnew believed that James's real motivation for kicking him out was because she was interested in another man, and he became jealous. Fearful that Agnew might turn violent, James armed herself with a shotgun, which she kept by her side at all hours. One Monday night, she was at her roadhouse when she heard someone trying to force his way through a locked back door. She yelled at the intruder to stop—if he came through the door, she would shoot.

The intruder broke down the door. James fired three times. Agnew later died in the hospital, and James was indicted for murder. Police raided the roadhouse, where they found liquor and gambling paraphernalia. The press ran sensational articles, describing her as a "murderess." At the trial in 1913, James finally had an opportunity to tell her side of the story.

She told how Agnew had become drunk the morning of the killing. Not only had he already stolen from her, but now he was demanding more money. When James would not give in, Agnew grabbed a long knife and assaulted her.[9] He accused her of dumping him for another man. James felt her life was in danger. Agnew's assault, his threats, and the break-in made her actions justifiable homicide, according to James's attorney, a white man named C. S. Walker. He had once been the city attorney for Tulsa and had an unsavory reputation. Walker received hate from the white press for defending Sadie James, but he made no apologies.

James's story of self-defense won the day—she was acquitted in July 1913. The *Tulsa Democrat* called the verdict an "outrage." A county attorney agreed, filing a motion to summarily discharge the entire panel of jurors and retry the case (though the motion went nowhere).[10] The *Tulsa Star*, a Black-owned newspaper, noted that James's daughter, Eva, had accosted Deputy Sheriff Cleaver for his botched attempt to gather damning evidence against her mother. The *Star* reporter quoted Eva as saying that she "was going to the Lord in prayer and ask him to rain down shower after shower of eternal wrath and damnation upon [Cleaver's] head."

Cleaver smiled back at her. "That'll be all right my dear Madam," Cleaver was heard to say. "Tell the Lord any darn thing you wish."[11]

Cleaver would go on to become an associate of Charles Page.

"BETTIE IS GOING TO DOUBLE-CROSS YOU":
SADIE JAMES AND H. U. BARTLETT

Considering the reputation of Sadie James, H. U. Bartlett must have been willing to take a few risks when, in 1914, he chose to employ the hotelier to help him find the real Minnie Atkins. He had already employed James once before, in 1912, when she and Bettie Mann had found him a fake Minnie Atkins in Lawrence, Kansas. Now, if Bartlett could find the real Minnie, he could wipe away the stain of embarrassment from the forged contract with the fake Minnie in Kansas. Once he heard that James had known Minnie from her Fort Leavenworth days, he saw an opportunity.

Bartlett offered James a finder's fee of $1,000, plus expenses, if she could locate the real Minnie. James demanded $2,000 ($60,000 in 2024 dollars). Bartlett agreed, but on one condition. "Sadie," Bartlett said, "you will have to let Bettie [Mann] come in on this, she has been working for me so long I will have to let her have a part of it."

Sadie did not want Bettie to be a part of her scheme. She tried to talk Bartlett out of it. "Mr. Bartlett," she said, "I have never said anything to you before about it, but Bettie is going to double-cross you." In fact, the opposite had been the case during their last heist—Bettie Mann had taken the fall for Bartlett when the fake Minnie had come to light. Mann alone of the three conspirators had been charged with forgery, with Bartlett claiming not to have known about the fraud, and Sadie somehow escaping prosecution.

James ultimately agreed to work with Mann and to split the finder's fee with her. The two planned to set out for Kansas, Minnie's last known location. The pair went to Mann's house in Sapulpa to discuss their strategy and compare notes. If they were going to bring Minnie back to Oklahoma, Mann figured that they should probably notify her sons. They called Harvey and he came to Sapulpa, but they ultimately decided to not involve Charley. Mann said that whereas Harvey was dark, Charley "thinks he is a white man."[12]

Mann and James told Harvey that they would be looking for his mother and showed him a picture of Minnie. James said it was a photo that Minnie had given her from "the college," most likely a reference to the Carlisle Indian Industrial School; it was probably an official school portrait. James asked if Harvey wanted to see his mother. James later recalled Harvey's reply: "Any woman that would go away and leave [him] as she had done, he didn't want to see her."[13]

James stayed in Sapulpa with Mann but kept her at arm's distance, suspecting her of plotting some sort of treachery. One day, James spotted Mann talking to a man named Charles Haskell, at the train depot, and assumed it was about the Tommy Atkins affair. James mentioned the name Haskell at trial, and the attorney C. B. Stuart interrupted.

"Who is he?" Stuart said.

"C. S. Haskell, from Oklahoma," James said.

"Governor Haskell?" Stuart replied.

"Yes, Governor Haskell," James said. "I am talking about Governor Haskell."

"You mean C. N. Haskell, don't you?"

Stuart was trying to embarrass James. The court laughed at James's mistake, and R. C. Allen called for quiet. Stuart had been the US court judge for Indian Territory and the first president of the Oklahoma Bar Association. Charles N. Haskell was Oklahoma's first governor. The normally bombastic R. C. Allen objected to Stuart's attempt to ridicule Sadie James. People were "indulging in talking and laughing to such an extent that neither the witness or counsel could understand the questions and answers."

Some of the courtroom chatter might have concerned the scandalous news about Haskell, who was apparently looking for an angle on the Tommy Atkins lands himself. Haskell had recently been the subject of a grand jury investigation regarding the town lot frauds mentioned previously. He was indicted twice by the federal government. It was widely understood that Haskell had a role in manipulating the market for lots in Tulsa and Muskogee, even though he was not convicted of any outright conspiracy.

One of Page's lawyers asked James why she did not attempt to talk to the governor. James knew that Governor Haskell wanted nothing to do with her, or with any Black people for that matter. According to Mann, Haskell said that "he had been burnt by enough educated negroes in Oklahoma . . . he didn't want anything to do with the deal."[14]

That was the last Mann or James saw of Governor Haskell.

Mann and James each received an initial payment of $100 from Bart-lett to cover their travel expenses. It was important to keep them happy—Mann had also been approached by Frank Long for her ser-vices in finding Minnie. James had heard the name Frank Long, but—not knowing that he worked for Page—assumed he was a small-time player. "Long ain't got no money," she said.[15]

Mann took the 6:20 train to Kansas City on a Friday in May 1914, but James stayed behind. James was exasperated that she had to work with Mann, a con artist who also seemed slow, dull-witted, and untrustworthy—a snake in the grass. Later in May the pair met up in Portland, Oregon, to find Micco T. Harjo, Nancy Atkins's Black Muscogee guardian, who had relocated there. Harjo claimed to have intelligence about the real Minnie Atkins, but once they'd had a chance to question him in person, James realized that he knew nothing. Their Portland trip had been a waste of time.

Mann and James decided to split up again. James went to check on a certain Mary Hamilton in Denver, who remembered something about Minnie being with a Sergeant Folk after the war in the Philippines. Hamilton also claimed to possess the only photograph of Tommy Atkins, and James was determined to see it.

Mann and James met up again in Seattle but decided to cover different ground. Mann asked around in the hotels that served white clients and James in the hotels catering to a Black clientele.[16] James heard something about a couple in Vancouver who seemed to match Minnie and Harry Folk's description—a Native American woman traveling with an army bandleader—and started making plans to catch a train to Canada. Someone asked her if the Vancouver she was looking for was not in Canada but rather was a small town across the river from Portland, in Washington State. There she found a veteran in a coal yard outside the army barracks. James showed him a photo of Minnie. The ex-soldier recognized the woman in the picture and said he knew her husband. For the first time, someone from Minnie's past had connected her to her new life with Harry Folk.

James went into a soldiers' saloon in Vancouver and asked about Folk. Someone in the saloon said that Folk had been sent to Fort Lawton in Seattle. James took a train back to Seattle and found the fort, a rugged outpost on the head of Puget Sound, surrounded by emerald-green forests and wild Pacific waters. James shared her latest findings with Mann, who urged her to telephone Bartlett and update him. James wasn't ready to let Bartlett in just yet though. She needed to see Minnie with her own eyes to verify this was the same person she had known from Fort Leavenworth.

"YOU HAVE FOUND ME TO MAKE TROUBLE"

Back in Tulsa, Bartlett was getting antsy. Mann and James had blown through their travel money, and Mann requested more. He agreed to send it under a pseudonym—Bill Jones. Mann collected another $150 from "Bill Jones" in Seattle. James and Mann went to see a film in Seattle and decided to look for Folk at Fort Lawton the next day.[17] There they learned that Folk's band had been sent from Fort Lawton to Fort Wright in Spokane, Washington. James and Mann went to Spokane intending to meet with a Mrs. Richardson, a friend of Minnie's. James had to be cautious about approaching Minnie out of the blue. There was no telling how she would react when someone from her past approached her, let alone with such an unbelievable story. Richardson might have some insight into Minnie's current state of mind. James took a streetcar to the fort and found a woman near the train station. James asked if she knew a white woman named Mrs. Richardson, a soldier's wife. The woman seemed suspicious. She wanted to know why James was looking for her.

James told the woman she was really looking for a Minnie Atkins or Minnie Folk, a Native American woman with a mysterious boy named Tommy. "What are you hunting Minnie for?" the woman asked.

James concocted a story about being a government officer wanting to enroll Minnie Atkins in the Muscogee Nation so that she could receive payments due from Washington, DC. The woman examined James's face and voice closely.

"This is Sadie?" the woman said, her voice trailing off.

For once, Sadie James was at a loss for words. Now they recognized each other.

"How the hell did you find me?" Minnie Atkins Folk said.[18]

James told her she had been hunting her from small town Oklahoma to the streets of Seattle, from Fort Leavenworth to Portland.

"Well," Minnie said. "What do you want with me?"

Sadie stood by her lie. "I am a government officer working for the government," she said. "I am hunting people to enroll. You know in 1895 when you went to get your money you enrolled Minnie Atkins, Thomas Atkins, Alice Atkins, Charley and Harvey Harrison. I have found three of your children and the two principal ones that I am hunting for. I can't find Thomas and Alice."

Minnie needed to sit down. James's statement about Thomas hit her hard. She did not know how to process that name and hung her head. "Thomas Atkins was my father. He had been dead seventeen years when I drew that money."

Someone had put the name Thomas Atkins down on the Creek census of 1895, she said, but it wasn't her. Minnie figured the name referred to her father. Rather than point out the mistake, she said she saw an opportunity and took it. Minnie had never intended to defraud the government, but given the chaos of Indian Territory at the time, and the widespread swindling the new class of white people engaged in, she figured she should take the money. She had regretted it for years.

"Where is Alice?" James asked. It is possible she truly didn't know that the baby girl had died years ago, but it is more likely that she was testing Minnie to see how far she had gone in distancing herself from her old life.

The question seemed even more painful than the one about Thomas. "Sadie, don't ask," Minnie said. "She has been dead too long and I don't want to know."

"Well, it don't make any difference about Alice because she wasn't allotted, but Thomas was and his land is valuable."

"I have been hiding from the government for nineteen years for the crime that I committed for drawing that money," Minnie said. "Now you have found me to make trouble."

James told her to forget about the extra payment. That was small change. Now Minnie needed to tell a man named Hugh Bartlett that she had had a son named Tommy Atkins. Bartlett would ask her to sign some papers and then he would give Minnie $2,000 for a deed. It would be simple.

Minnie pondered the offer. If she claimed that she'd had a child named Tommy, she would have to say what became of the boy. Was he dead? How did he die? Who was the father? There would be many questions, all of which made her extremely anxious.

James tried to put her at ease by telling her that she already had the details figured out. Minnie would tell Bartlett that she had given her baby to Granny Letcher. Letcher had died in the early 1900s but James had known her well; she claimed her as a grandmother, not by blood but by kinship. James had kept up with a lot of Black folks who had grown up around Letcher's house, and she could get them to go along with the story. The most believable scenario was for Minnie to have given birth to a Black child at Granny Letcher's, since there had been a few Black children born in 1885 who could be construed as Tommy.

Minnie balked at this suggestion. She wanted to make "a white case" out of it. James tried to get her to reconsider: the baby needed to be Black, or at least mulatto, in order for their story to work. There had been few, if any, white children around Granny Letcher's. Minnie asked for some writing paper.

"Let me put that down," she said.

Minnie jotted down some names, places, and the numbers 185. Sadie was unimpressed. "Hell, that ain't no way to put down 1885," James said.

James wrote out the essential plot points for Minnie, then headed back to Seattle, pondering her next move with Mann and Bartlett.

James still had not located Harry Folk, and it was essential that she get his cooperation in the plan. James wanted to talk to the army bandleader on her own before she told Bartlett that she had found Minnie. Folk had been sent back to Fort Lawton, and that's where James finally found him. He seemed to be expecting her. She once again put on her front as a federal Indian agent.

James had no idea what Folk knew about Minnie's past. He did not seem to know about her boys, but did he know that she was a former Muscogee citizen who had been stricken from the tribe's rolls? That she had been married to Charles Peterkin in Fort Logan? It was entirely possible that Minnie had lied to her husband about her entire background. If Sadie revealed too much to him too soon, he could react emotionally, flip on Minnie, and refuse to go along with the Tommy story. She asked him some probing questions and found out that Folk knew very little indeed about his wife's past.

James went back to Minnie with a hard truth and the difficult choice she would soon have to make.

"Minnie," James said, "in thinking over this thing last night, I find out that Harry will have to know about these children, for you to get this money when the white man I am working for comes to pay you the money."

"My god, Sadie," Minnie said. "I can't tell him."

"Let me tell him."

Minnie called Folk during his band practice. She needed him to come home and talk to the mysterious woman who had met him earlier at Fort Lawton. As James and Minnie waited for Folk to arrive, Minnie paced around nervously.

"God, Sadie, Harry will quit me," Minnie said.

"No, he won't," Sadie said. "You know how a white man is about money."

"DO YOU KNOW YOUR WIFE?"

Folk walked in and sat at a small square table in the modest living room. James turned to Folk. "Mr. Folk," she said. "Do you know your wife?"

"No," Folk said, his suspicions clearly already aroused. "I think I do not know my wife."

James began to narrate an amended version of Minnie's past, one that would serve Bartlett's purposes. Most of James's version was true: She and Minnie had met in 1884 in Fort Leavenworth, where they'd both worked as domestic servants. They hung around Granny Letcher's place, and Minnie got pregnant. She told him about Minnie's two dead children, Robert Lee and Alice. Then she told him about Minnie's previous marriage to Charles Peterkin, followed by a sojourn in Colorado. The relationship with Peterkin had resulted in two boys, Charley and Harvey Harrison, who were still living back in Oklahoma.

Folk was speechless.

Minnie put her head on the table. Then James brought up the phantom child.

"She has got a child that I am hunting, that she is going to make some money off of," Sadie said to Folk, ". . . a boy that she had at Leavenworth."

Minnie raised her head from the table. "Harry," she said, "will you forgive me for deceiving you all this time?"

Harry remained standing, motionless.

Minnie desperately sought some kind of reaction from her husband. Finally, he looked at Minnie and said, "Minnie, why didn't you tell me about those children?"

"Well," Minnie said, "you never asked."

FRANK LONG PICKS UP THE TRAIL OF SADIE JAMES

The tension had broken. James had been right about how a white man would react at the prospect of instant money. The opportunity to profit from one of these children made Folk forget about everything else. He went back to drill practice with the army band, and Minnie asked James for news about her family—her boys, her sister. Sadie said that the boys were thriving but that she had noticed something odd about them as they grew up.

"There is so much difference between the color of these children," James said. "One looks like a white man, and the other looks like an Indian."

Minnie explained that their fathers were two different men. Charley had been named after Charles Peterkin, the common-law spouse who had deserted her around 1889. Harvey was the son of the Fort Logan butcher, Harris or Harrison, who was part Mexican.

Then James revealed to Minnie a potential hiccup in her Tommy Atkins plan that they would have to work around. Minnie would not be the only person claiming to be the boy's mother. Her younger sister, Nancy, had already gone to county court to claim Tommy as her late son and herself as the heir to his estate. Nancy had initially won the estate in court, but the much more savvy oilmen she had been up against had appealed, knowing that Nancy's claim held little water.

Minnie confessed to Sadie that in or around 1903, when she and Harry were temporarily stationed in Montana, before anyone knew about the oil on the allotment, she had received a letter from one of her half sisters, Kate Holden. In the letter, Holden had told her of agents from the Dawes Commission trying to locate Minnie to give her a deed to land allotted to a child named Tommy Atkins. Holden wrote that the authorities assumed Tommy was dead but that he had died following the all-important date of April 1, 1899—the cutoff for deceased Muscogee citizens to receive an allotment. When Minnie told

Folk about the letter, they both assumed it was some sort of fraud—some scheme to lure Minnie back to Indian Territory, where she would be prosecuted for taking that extra payment. Folk put the letter in a stove and burned it. As we know, the Dawes Commission allotted the child anyway, but then lost track of all of his papers.

Folk, back at the fort practicing with his band, told no one about the mysterious woman who had visited him and his wife. There was talk of US entry into the Great War in Europe, and Folk's regiment might be called up. Folk had been on two deployments already, to Cuba and to the Philippines. Nearing the age of forty, he was no longer a spry young man. The thought of an early retirement funded by his wife's lost child may have appealed to him. As the days passed and Minnie and James continued to make their plans, Folk expressed no objections.

The big problem with the plan at this point was that Minnie continued to be adamant that her fictitious child be white. He could not be Black.

Sadie urged her to reconsider. If Minnie claimed that her child had been white, or even Native American, her story would sound implausible. Minnie refused, saying she could not go before the world claiming that her Tommy was Black, using a racial slur common at the time.

James obligingly found a witness, George Crilley, who was willing to remember Minnie with a "nearly white" baby sometime in 1885, possibly matching the timeline Minnie would need to make the story biologically possible. Then she found another white man who was willing to make the same assertions, although he insisted on calling Minnie "Indian Mary." Finally, James found a witness at Leavenworth, Mattie Cobb, who would attest to Minnie's version of Tommy. Page's team characterized her as a white person "of good character," albeit one with a shady family history. Cobb, along with the livery driver, Crilley, would provide the corroborating details that Minnie and Page wanted.

After James brought Folk into the plan, news traveled quickly. James soon noticed a pair of men trailing her. Her main worry was that they were federal agents who knew that she was impersonating someone from the government. If they were just private detectives working for Page or some other oilman, she knew how to outplay them. But if they were feds, she could be arrested at any time. She was determined to ditch them, first slipping down to a beach and then to a streetcar back to the fort. They were still there. She met with the Folks anyway.

After the meeting, James snuck out of Fort Lawton, caught a streetcar back to her rooming house, and went upstairs. Looking out her window, she saw the two men standing there outside the door next to a private car. All night they remained outside the rooming house. James feared they would arrest her at any minute. While she waited inside, a telegram arrived from Portland. It was from Bettie Mann saying that "Bill Jones" (Bartlett) had everything arranged and he was on his way to Seattle.

Again, she snuck out of the back door of the rooming house and caught a streetcar to the fort. She wanted to show the telegram to Folk and calm his nerves. But to her surprise, as she approached the Folks' house, she spotted the two men on the porch. Before they could notice her, she went to the building where Folk practiced with his band. By this point, people around the fort were beginning to wonder who this supposed Indian agent was, and why she was so keen to talk to Folk.

When James showed Folk the telegram, he said the timing of Bartlett's visit was terrible. His band had just received orders to travel east to play for a tribe he referred to as the Pot Black Indians in Montana. However, Folk said that Minnie was prepared to sign the deed for $2,000. Captain McNab volunteered to keep watch over Minnie as she signed "Bill Jones's" land transfer documents and collected her payment. Everyone around Minnie was scared she might be kidnapped, a common occurrence among Native Americans with money.

James, meanwhile, was forming a new plan of her own. If Minnie was willing to sell Tommy's land for $2,000, maybe James could team up with Bettie Mann to buy Minnie's land themselves, using the $2,000 that Bartlett had promised them. Nothing in their agreement with Bartlett had stipulated that Minnie had to sign a deed in order for them to get paid. By locating the real Minnie Atkins, they'd already met their end of the bargain.

James went to Mann's hotel to discuss her new scheme. It would mean double-crossing Bartlett and provoking his ire. But if they could secure a clean title, they could then flip it to another oil concern for at least ten, twenty, even fifty times what they'd paid Minnie for it. The more Sadie James understood the machinations of Charles Page, the more she saw an opportunity to conspire with him. She knew Page would pay more than Bartlett for the deed. But his secretary and fixer, Frank Long, played hardball. He might find a way to stiff them.

As James walked down a long, dark hallway to Mann's hotel room, she noticed a vaguely familiar figure: a middle-aged white man she knew from Oklahoma but could not place. The man was also going to Bettie Mann's room. She waited in the hallway as he went in and then left shortly afterward.

When James went in, Mann referred to the person who'd just left as a "beau," but James suspected something else was going on. There was no way that man was Bettie's boyfriend. Mann wanted James to stay with her until Bartlett's train arrived, but James understood this as some sort of maneuver to keep her away from Minnie. Her idea to conspire with Bettie to get the deed now seemed too risky. She decided to leave the hotel and get back to the fort—she thought she had better get to Minnie before Mann and Bartlett did.

When James looped around to Minnie's house, she saw the same two men on the porch, talking to Minnie, who was dressed all in white. As James approached, one of the men asked her for directions to somewhere in Seattle.

Sadie had had enough of the cat and mouse game. She looked him in the eye. "Goddamn you, you are trailing me."

The other man turned to his accomplice. "What do you think?" he asked. "This woman thinks we're trailing her."

"Oh no," the first one said. "We're not."

Unbeknownst to James, one of these men was, in fact, Frank Long, who had ingratiated himself with Folk's commanding officer, Captain McNab. Accompanying Long was the attorney E. C. Hanford. With Bartlett still on the train to Seattle and Folk now with his band in Montana, Long and Hanford had secretly worked out a deal with McNab, whom they had located by trailing James. Captain McNab would act as Minnie's trustee, and no one would be allowed to talk to Minnie unless they had McNab's permission. Long and Hanford had also figured out that James was no government agent. It was possible they'd have her arrested. Rather than confront the two men then and there, James went back to her hotel and worked on another plan.

When she returned to the fort the next day, she found a young soldier guarding the entrance to Minnie and Harry's house. The soldier tried to block her, but Minnie ushered her in.

Minnie told James that McNab wanted her to do something she did not want to do. "Haven't you got sense enough to protect yourself?" James asked Minnie.

She was probably warning Minnie against a possible kidnapping. "Yes," Minnie said. "But I'm still afraid of him."

Minnie wanted Sadie to stay with her, but Sadie was expecting a telegram from Bartlett—or "Bill Jones"—at any moment. The telegram would advise her when Bartlett's train would arrive in Seattle, and she needed to meet him when it came in. James rushed to the telegraph office but found nothing for her. She telegrammed Bartlett's wife, Eve Maude, to say she was in desperate need of money—that she needed to hire armed guards to protect Minnie, because she had fallen under the influence of some dangerous people.

James understood that if she backed out now, she would walk away with nothing. But she was the one who had found Minnie. Perhaps she felt some loyalty to her friend from thirty years prior, or maybe she simply wanted to collect for all her troubles. In any case, Sadie James would not back down. She knew that there was no way Page's team could hold together all the conflicting testimonies at Leavenworth without her help.

"IT'S ALL A BUSINESS MATTER": FRANK LONG REWRITES TOMMY'S LIFE

Someone—probably Frank Long—wrote out a new chronicle of the brief life of Tommy Atkins for Minnie to memorize. Here were the updated facts, as reconstructed by Long: The child had been born May 31 or June 1, 1885, in a barn behind Granny Letcher's place. The mother had been Minnie Atkins, and the father had been a white man, whose identity was unknown, given Minnie's promiscuity. Tommy died in 1899, but his body had never been discovered. According to law, the absence of a body did not make Tommy legally dead until twelve years later, meaning that the legal date of his death fell after the April 1, 1899, cutoff, entitling him to an allotment. This detail was very important. Given that Tommy's only known parent was Minnie

Atkins, she had sole heirship of the boy's estate. Long had typed this narrative and gave it to Minnie to sign.

Sadie James did not like the looks of this story.

"Don't let Minnie sign these papers," James said to Captain Mc-Nab. She thought this version had too many holes in it. She wanted Minnie's Tommy to have as much legitimacy as possible. She thought that a much more convincing Tommy would be mixed Black and Native American, not white. No white people hung around Granny Letcher's, so a white-passing baby would have attracted much more notice than the evidence suggested.

McNab said that Bettie Mann had told him and Minnie that Sadie had already been paid for locating Minnie, and now she was just causing trouble. James realized that Mann had backstabbed her.

"I see I had been trapped," Sadie later said.[19]

Sadie prevailed upon McNab to hear her out. She had not been paid. She was acting in the best interests of Minnie; if Minnie was caught in a lie, Sadie would go down with her. Minnie also wanted the statement changed—she wanted to say that Tommy had lived only a few months, certainly not until 1899. If they adopted Minnie's version of Tommy, however, his date of death wouldn't meet the threshold for allotment. Long wanted to take Minnie to Spokane in the evening to work on the statement and sign it. "Don't let her leave with Long for Spokane tonight," James said to McNab.

James then took a streetcar to Bettie Mann's hotel. Mann had lied to McNab and Minnie about James's having been paid already, and now she realized Mann must be trying to squeeze her out. Perhaps Frank Long had offered Bettie more money than Bartlett had.

James opened the door to Mann's hotel room, ready to berate Bettie for her treachery. But as she went to close the door, she realized Long was standing there.

James began fuming. "You pulled a nice trick on me," she said.

"Hello, Sadie," Long said.

"God damn you," James said. "What did you go out there and tell that lie on me?"

"It is all a business matter," Long replied. Rather than squeeze James out, Long had a new proposition. He and Page would pay her more than what Bartlett was offering—$3,000 to work with Bettie on a new job for them. They would have to, in Sadie's words, "steal

Minnie"—to force her to go back to Oklahoma. It wasn't enough to have her simply sign a statement about Tommy Atkins. She needed to be closely guarded in Sand Springs. And Charles Page had the perfect place for her—a lovely stucco house right across the street from his mansion on Main Street. James would also have to provide witnesses at Leavenworth backing up their story about Tommy.

James refused to kidnap Minnie. She was still angry at Mann for teaming up with Long. Without a written contract, James did not trust anyone. Bettie pulled Sadie aside and whispered to her that Bartlett's pockets were not as deep as Page's. Compared to Page, Bartlett was just a rich rancher with a few pools of oil. When Page wanted something badly enough, he would pay a handsome sum for it. Mann said that they should ditch Bartlett and follow Long.

James pondered her options. She was broke. She had nowhere to go. If she didn't go along with Long, he might have her arrested. Her gambit of impersonating a federal officer was a felony, with a maximum sentence of three years in prison. Stalling for time, she went out and wired Bartlett again asking for $100. She was annoyed at Bartlett for ignoring her requests for money. She began to reconsider Long's offer. She had no loyalty to Bartlett. Long could be cunning and ruthless, but with $3,000, she could restart her roadhouse and be done with all the intrigue. At some point, Tulsa authorities had finally shut down the Bucket of Blood. Sadie's place had been favored by influential bootleggers like Bill Creekmore, but her involvement in the Atkins case had taken her away from managing the place.

Finally, she got a telegram from "Bill Jones." He was almost to Seattle and had the money as promised. Sadie and Bettie went to the train station and waited.

"Hello, girls," Bartlett said, stepping onto the platform.

James ripped into him about not answering her telegrams. He said he had lost count of all the telegrams she'd sent and their contradictory messages. He looked at Mann. Had she found Minnie? As the women filled him in, Bartlett seemed amused to learn that Sadie, not Bettie, had been the one to finally track down the elusive Minnie Atkins. He proposed a coffee at the hotel before setting out to see Minnie. "They've got her locked up," Sadie said. "You won't have time to get the coffee."

Bartlett gave Mann his suitcase and she took it to her hotel. He and James then took a streetcar to Fort Lawton. On the ride, Bartlett took her telegrams out of his briefcase to demonstrate their madness. James recognized the first one—her initial request for money—but not the second one, which said, "Don't pay no attention to the first telegram—mistake, Sadie James."

James leafed through the other telegrams. For each telegram that she had sent, someone had followed up with another telling Bartlett to disregard the previous. James realized that either Frank Long or Bettie Mann had sent the follow-up telegrams to undermine her, keeping her in the dark about Long's real plan for Minnie. Long needed to buy time for Minnie to fully understand the new version of what happened to Tommy.

Bartlett asked James for an update in the case, so she spun him a tale. She said there was a woman in Los Angeles, one Mary Hamilton, who had photos of Tommy as a boy, and also knew him as an adult in Los Angeles. Suddenly, Bartlett was in a hurry to find Mary Hamilton, and then track down this living Tommy. First, he wanted to talk to Minnie.

Bartlett introduced himself to McNab and asked to see Minnie. She came down and sat in front of Bartlett. He asked her if she was Minnie Atkins. Minnie said yes. Bartlett asked if she was the mother of Tommy. Now McNab stepped in to answer for her. Yes, he said, Minnie was the mother of the boy. Bartlett ask some more questions about Tommy, and Minnie went quiet. "You know how these Indians are sulky and won't talk," McNab said. "When Minnie gets on them spells, you can't do anything with her."[20]

Bartlett then told McNab a version of how he obtained the deed on the land. He had subsequently leased the land to the Gypsy Oil Company Tulsa, and was in Seattle representing Gypsy's business interests. McNab explained that Minnie had already sold her royalties to Long and Page. Bartlett did not share what James had told him—that Tommy was alive and living in Los Angeles. Bartlett wanted to send James and Mann to Denver, to get Mary Hamilton and her photos of Tommy ready so that they could find the real Tommy.

All of this madness appears to have been cooked up by James, who was probably stringing Bartlett along to see if she could get more money out of him. Despite Mann's treachery, James knew that she still held a strong hand. Any story that had Tommy Atkins born at Leavenworth in 1885 would need witnesses from Granny Letcher's place. With all of Sadie's connections among the Black folks in Leavenworth, she had the power to sabotage the entire story if she chose to.

Meanwhile, the US probate attorney Frank Montgomery and various Pinkerton agents had been following Mann and James around Seattle. Montgomery had failed to secure Minnie's signed confession that she had no child named Tommy. This failure strengthened his resolve to expose the conspiracies of lies brewing around Minnie. Montgomery had talked over the matter with Allen and other officials in the US attorney's office. Secretary of the Interior Lane had become convinced that the evidence around Tommy Atkins was dubious. Montgomery was charged with getting Minnie Atkins away from Page's team and having her sign an affidavit that there was no Tommy.

At Fort Lawton, Minnie was distraught and seemed to be changing her allegiances by the hour. Her old friend from Carlisle, Bettie Mann, had proved to be a professional liar in the service of whatever oilman paid the most. Minnie had had enough. She had telephoned Page to say she would retract her retraction. She wanted to see Montgomery again and affirm her original confession that Tommy was a fiction.

"I AM STILL THE MOTHER OF TOMMY ATKINS!": MINNIE ON THE BRINK

Captain McNab had now found himself in the middle of a war he had no idea how to fight. His training had been in the art of armed combat with foreign adversaries or hostile Native Americans. This battle was between rival oilmen, government attorneys, two-timing Pinkerton agents, a savvy Black woman from Oklahoma, and his soldier's wife. At some point they all had to collide.

Sadie James may not have inherited her mother's prophetic powers, but she believed that something beyond the realm of plain human perception guided her—a sort of mind control. She characterized it as a "shadow" that she hung over Minnie—a "mystic cord" that bound them. She could use the shadow to influence Minnie's judgment.

James decided to use her power over Minnie one day at Fort Lawton, when the house was swarming with people, including Hanford, Montgomery, and Robinson, the Pinkerton agent. James believed

Hanford was going to force Minnie into signing something she would regret, and that she, Sadie, had to act. Minnie suddenly took Sadie's hand and made to run out of the house.

Hanford grabbed them and broke them apart. "Minnie, you must not talk to Sadie," Hanford said.

Hanford roughed them both up. Minnie let loose on everyone. "You are a bunch of crooks," she said.

She yelled at them all to leave, but no one budged. "I am still the mother of Tommy Atkins!" she cried. This caught the attention of Montgomery, who had been in another room. Montgomery came in and Minnie directed her ire at him, calling him a crook.

Hanford tried to calm down the situation and get everyone to leave. He ushered the men out of the house.

James hung back to talk to Minnie. Minnie said something about hoping that James would stay out of the penitentiary, but as she responded, Hanford pushed her out of the way.

James barely moved. Hanford grabbed her and tried to drag her out of the hallway. Hanford was an alum of West Point, a soldier with impeccable credentials. But he was no match for Sadie in a street fight. She took her purse and struck Hanford on the head. A brawl was on, and no one intervened. When it was over, Hanford had a broken nose, a shattered jaw, and several loose teeth.[21] Hanford learned an important lesson that countless patrons of the Bucket of Blood had taken to heart: Sadie James was not to be trifled with.

For Bartlett, however, the real Tommy was still out there somewhere, far from the spectacle of Pinkerton agents, high-powered attorneys, and army men swarming around Minnie Atkins. Bartlett went back to his family's ranch in Colorado. Minnie agreed to go back to Sand Springs with Long.

James then double-crossed Bartlett herself, working on a scheme to produce false witnesses for Page and Long. She walked the streets of Leavenworth, calling on her old friends. Sam Nash had a vague recollection of a kid named Tommy who had been around Granny's in the late 1880s, but once he understood that James wanted him to participate in a fraud, he balked. He did not want any trouble with the law. There were people like Louis Brown and Will Parker who recalled bits and pieces of a story regarding "Indian Minnie" and a boy named Tommy. One witness remembered a Black Catholic family taking Tommy in for a while. Sadie went to talk to the priest, Father Shortey, about this Tommy Atkins. She doled out money to these witnesses, who would either submit depositions or appear in person to testify at the Muskogee trial.

James recounted all the witnesses in Leavenworth, recalling how she worked with each one to land on the same story of Tommy. All of it, she said during the federal trial, had been masterminded by Frank Long, with the tacit approval of Charles Page. C. B. Stuart raised an objection. He was growing more and more frustrated with James's wandering narratives and advised the government attorneys to rein her in. Two-thirds of what she said was immaterial, hearsay, or narrative that did not address counsel's questions. "We will let this go," Stuart said to the federal lawyers, "but without attempting to be patronizing at all, I do suggest that you let her answer questions that you ask."

Judge Campbell seemed utterly uninterested in Stuart's objections. He, like the legions of reporters and oilmen in the room, wanted to follow Sadie James on her journeys, even if she might be leading them on a shaggy dog story.

While some of Sadie's stories seemed to flow like unmoored rafts into a vast sea of characters no one could keep straight, her story about a certain Mrs. Mary Hamilton caught everyone's attention. Hamilton—the friend of Minnie's whom Sadie had gone to see in Denver, who claimed to have the only known photo of young Tommy—was one of the only people who had known Minnie at both Carlisle and Leavenworth. Hamilton gave James the photo, and the two of them set out for Los Angeles. They visited Hamilton's daughter and James roamed the city, looking for the perfect Tommy Atkins: someone born in late May or early June in 1885, named Thomas or Tommy Atkins, and of an appearance that could be perceived as racially "mixed"— either white and Native American or Black and Native American. Perhaps most important, James's man needed to be skilled enough in the art of deception to stand in as the missing Tommy Atkins.

Unimpressed with the local talent in Los Angeles, James went next to San Francisco to see if a plausible Tommy might be found there. In the meantime, she telegraphed Bartlett, feeding him a cover story that she was on the trail of the *real* Tommy Atkins, who had been spotted leaving San Francisco for Portland. After San Francisco, James continued on to Butte, Montana, then back to Portland, still in search of the perfect Tommy.

In Portland she received a telegram that finally put an ounce of fear into her unshakable constitution. The telegram announced that Hugh Bartlett was at a hotel in Portland and that he needed to see her at once. It turned out that Bartlett had become suspicious of his secret agent and had hired two detectives to follow her trails and leads. They had come no closer to Tommy Atkins than James had, but as they all convened in Portland, they demanded to see Mrs. Hamilton's photo of the child. James let Bartlett's detectives examine the photo but not take it. Knowing that Bartlett, Long, and the federal government all had agents trailing her, she needed to be very cautious.

One of these agents, a man named Mr. Crawley, approached James. She had never seen him before and he refused to say whom he was working for. However, he had an interesting proposition of his own: if James would sign a statement saying that she had never seen baby Tommy since he turned two years old, Crawley would pay her $2,000. There was one catch: she had to completely leave Seattle and have nothing more to do with the case.[22]

Crawley would make it easy for James. He had the statement written out and ready for her signature. "All I had to do was sign my name," she said.

She didn't have to think long about the proposition. She told the court that she said to Crawley: "Ain't nobody on earth going to get me to swear Minnie Atkins ever had a son named Tommy Atkins when I know she didn't, but I said I'm going to make some money out of this case anyhow."[23]

She left Seattle immediately. She went to Portland, then to Leavenworth, then back to Tulsa, where she attempted to collect $400 from Page. Page said that he was running the entire operation through Frank Long, and that she should talk to him. Long made some excuse about not paying Sadie the $400.

"If he didn't pay me," James told the court, "I would blow that case up."[24]

With no money from Page forthcoming, James knocked on another familiar door, that of Bartlett's Gypsy Oil Company. Bartlett still owed her $600 of the fee he'd promised her for locating Minnie Atkins. She thought that Gypsy might pay her directly. She was surprised to find Crawley, the mysterious man from Seattle, at the Gypsy building. He had apparently been working for Gypsy and conducting his own investigation into Tommy Atkins. Crawley had gone after a totally different Atkins boy—one who seemed to have gone to Boston, Massachusetts, on a trip. Crawley wanted to confirm his theory with James.

"Do you think he is in Boston?" Crawley asked her.

"Yes sir," she said. One can imagine her suppressing a smile. The Boston Tommy Atkins was a ruse that Sadie and Dennis Jones, the Black attorney in Leavenworth, had worked up. For the time being, it seemed to distract Crawley, who took off for Boston.

James called her lawyer, C. S. Walker—the same lawyer who had successfully defended her against murder charges in 1913—to help her collect the remaining $600 that Page owed her.

James wanted to show Walker the contract she had made with Charles Page. Because she was afraid someone would destroy it, she insisted on keeping it at the First National Bank, and so the pair went there. Page's bank was Exchange National, not First National. Still, she was afraid he would somehow have the contract destroyed from inside the bank. Sadie James had seen stranger things happen. And she knew Charles Page in a way that few people did.

"ALWAYS AT NIGHT. LATE AT NIGHT": SADIE'S INTIMATE FRIEND, MR. PAGE

Sadie James knew Charles Page in a way that was not fit for print, not even in the pages of his tormentor, the *Tulsa World*. The *World* had intimated something about Sadie and Page's relationship on June 10, 1917. The headline read "Sadie Confesses Page Relations" and followed the salacious comment with a subhead, "Negress Tells of Clandestine Visits to Dark Office and Frameup."[25]

R. C. Allen did not want James to divulge her intimate relations with Page. He tried to put a stop to it in court. "Understand," Allen said, "that our objection to this line of testimony is going to each and every question for the reason that it is incompetent, irrelevant, an immaterial, and improper cross examination of this witness."[26]

Page's lawyers must have been desperate, as they were the ones who questioned James about Page's late-night visits to her home. Stuart had tried to get James to contradict herself, to no avail. The lawyers tried to find other people who would throw doubt on the veracity of James's statements about buying off witnesses. But they mostly confirmed her stories. This left one option open—what if Sadie James was not only a shady character of the Tulsa underworld, but also a spurned lover? Perhaps the payments from Page to James were not to buy off witnesses in Leavenworth, but exchanges for sexual favors.

Much to the surprise of everyone in the courtroom, James testified that Page had begun frequenting her house at 504 East Archer Street in late August of 1914.[27] Each time, before he departed, he would leave her ten or twenty dollars. Then, later in the fall, he wrote her a check for fifty dollars, which she cashed at his bank. The money had come from Page himself, she said. "I don't mean the Gem Company, now—by Mr. Page himself, out of his pocket to me."

This was not oil business, in other words, but a transaction of a more personal nature.

Stuart had to make sure Judge Campbell understood what was really going on beyond the euphemisms. He asked Sadie if this "business" related to the Tommy Atkins case.

A: Not relating to this case, no sir.
Q: What was the other matter?
A: I don't think you want it answered.
Q: Answer the question, Sadie.

Sadie referred vaguely to her "intimacy" with Page, not only at her house at 504 East Archer Street but later at his office. She visited him there late at night from August to November of 1914. Overall, they would meet three to four times a week.

Q: You are familiar with those offices, are you not?
A: Mr. Page would sit on this side, in that big chair and I would talk to Mr. Page.
Q: Laughing and talking with Mr. Page?
A: Yes, sir, I am his friend talking.

Q: Just visit with him there in the office?

A: No, talking of our secrets. We were not doing anything in the daytime, you understand that?

Q: Yes, I understand. And you talked about it openly. You visited before other people? Right there in the office where they were passing back and forth?

A: Oh, yes. You would have to go out that door; that was a good little piece for Mr. Page's table where we were sitting. We would be sitting there and talking. I didn't want to tell that and you brought that out.

Q: How often did you say that you were up there at ten o'clock at night?

A: Why, I don't know; really I can't tell how many times I have met Mr. Page in that three months—

Q: A good many times?

A: Yes, I met a good many times. Just I—

Q: And always at night?

A: Now, what could we do in the daytime?

Q: Answer my question.

A: Always at night, when I met him, yes. Late at night.

Q: Anybody else there?

A: Nobody else there, no, sir; nights when I would meet him, no, sir.

Q: The lights out?

A: The lights would be out and you would think the offices were closed—locked up; nobody up there, yes, sir.

Again, James paused to reflect on the implications of what she was saying. "I am sorry to say this though," she said. "I don't care so much about myself but I wouldn't tell it on him, because he did nothing to me—not a thing he did to me."

She remembered their relationship with some fondness. He never came to her on a Sunday, nor she to him. That was the only day of the week that was out of the question. Sunday he spent with his "kids" at the home. There were other matters as well. "I was Mr. Page's friend, if you want me to tell it," James said.

"I understand," Stuart said. "You claim to be very intimate friends."

"I have been," James said. "I guess I won't be anymore."[28]

Stuart returned to the question of money, perhaps to demonstrate that James would do or say anything to get paid.

She did not disappoint.

Q: He kept you pretty well, didn't he?

A: No, I knew what a colored woman could get out of a white man, and I didn't ask him for no big amount of money, you see. I didn't do that. You are pulling this out of me; I certainly hate it, though.

Q: So, altogether, you had a good deal of money from Mr. Page?

A: You never did see a white man give a negro woman that much money, did you?

Stuart pushed James to clarify the timeline from August to November 1914. He was trying to imply that Page had stopped paying James for her personal services, and so she went to Allen to get back at him. James saw right through the strategy. She noted that bringing up their sexual relationship could destroy Page's reputation.

"You are bringing it out on me and disgracing him yourself," she said.[29]

James understood much about how elite society operated, but she did not fathom the power of Tulsa to whitewash its misdeeds and reshape cultural memory. During the trials, every newspaper except the *Tulsa World* omitted James's testimony about her relationship with Page.

And even the *Tulsa World*, the thorn in Page's side, tiptoed around the sex work, settling for innuendo about her "services" during "clandestine visits to a dark office." The newspaper admitted that much of the rest of the testimony was "not fit to print."[30]

Until this point Charles Page had appeared in public as the more gracious half of the Page and Josey duo of Gem Oil Company. While Josey cursed Allen's name in the lobby of the Hotel Tulsa, Page preferred to show off his own magnanimousness at the Sand Springs Home. He had several newspapers willing to print sanguine stories about his "kids."

Despite the media suppression of James's damning revelations, Page was being exposed. Allen's attack on Page during the federal trial brought out a side of the man the public almost never saw. Page's allies lashed out at his enemies, threatening to sue the *Tulsa World* for libel. An editorial writer for the *World* wrote that their employees' only fear was that Page "will hire some thug to murder them."

Mayor Charles Hubbard, once a Page ally, was now in the man's crosshairs. "Mr. Page started out to bluff me, then he tried to bribe me and now he is trying the blackmail methods he has so often used in his business deals," Hubbard said. "I haven't a million or two of the money stolen from incompetent Indians or the government to run even one blackmailing newspaper, but if I can't get any audience from any other way, I'll make speeches from the street corners or get out hand bills until the folks know about the crooked work of Mr. Charles Page."[31]

— CHAPTER 17 —

"ANYTHING TO GET THE COIN"

The Aftermath of the Trials,
and the Death of Minnie Atkins

A llen and the federal government had banked on Sadie James's ability to name names and tell the unvarnished truth. There were plenty of other witnesses who noted inconsistencies in Minnie's story, of course, but it was James who could detail all the points of the conspiracy, going all the way back to 1884 in Fort Leavenworth. And she had kept the receipts, including checks to her from Page himself.

In the end, Judge Campbell had to balance two conflicting versions of the truth. One emanated from a Black woman who ran a roadhouse of prostitution, gambling, and bootlegged whiskey. The other came from a white citizen, among the richest and most generous men in the state, a philanthropist who gave his money to widows and orphans.

On May 13, 1918, Judge Campbell gave his ruling. To overturn the Dawes Commission's work would take incontrovertible evidence of a fraud. There were contradictions, vagaries, and perhaps, perjury, in the case. No one had been able to establish, without a reasonable doubt, their version of the truth. Given that inconclusive situation, the status quo had to stand. Tommy Atkins, Creek #7913, had been a real person with one living heir, Minnie Atkins.

There was still no guarantee that Judge Campbell's decision would be upheld. The US attorney general authorized an appeal. The government immediately appealed the Muskogee decision, and now it was headed for the United States Court of Appeals for the Eighth Circuit, in St. Louis. Despite the appeal, Page felt confident. Between R. C. Allen, the Bureau of Indian Affairs, and the US attorney's office, his operations in the Sand Springs Home had been subjected to intense scrutiny for the past several years and thus far had emerged unscathed.

"THIS WATER WILL BE FOR SALE":
PAGE MOVES ON TULSA'S WATER SUPPLY

Page was a restless man, and his victory in the Atkins case spurred him into action on his plan to control Tulsa's water supply. Tulsa's subpar water had been a major obstacle to its growth as the Oil Capital of the World. The tap water came from the muddy Arkansas River, unfit for drinking and not even really suitable for bathing. Tulsa residents bought their water in five-gallon jugs for twenty-five cents apiece. This purified water came from the Sand Springs Bottling Company, located west of downtown, where many of Page's industries were springing up. Page proposed to dam Shell Creek, on the border of Osage and Tulsa Counties, to create a new reservoir for the city, to be called Shell Lake.

In 1918, Tulsa's new waterworks engineer, William Rea Holway, a young graduate of MIT, devised a rival plan to build a pipeline carrying water from eastern Oklahoma's Spavinaw Lake to Tulsa. The lake lay in the Ozark foothills, and the elevation of the foothills was such that the pipeline could rely on gravity to propel the water to the city. In terms of engineering and cost, it was a brilliant plan. The intelligent young man from Massachusetts had devised a way for Tulsa to have clean drinking and bathing water starting as early as 1923.

But this was Tulsa, not Massachusetts. In 1919, as Holway lobbied the city to adopt his plan, the city was churning with larger racial and political turmoil. There was the obvious tension between white and Black Tulsa, a ticking time bomb that would soon explode. Political divisions broke down not between Republicans and Democrats but between radicals and white supremacists. The Wobblies had made strides organizing laborers in the oil fields. Even more radical leftist organizations like the Working Class Union had support around Tulsa. They employed violent methods to carry out their anti-capitalist agenda, planting dynamite, robbing banks, and using whips to beat people they deemed scabs. If the radical left employed some violence, the Ku Klux Klan overwhelmed the city and state with more violence.

Finally, there was the tension between the editor of the *Tulsa World*, Eugene Lorton, and Charles Page. Lorton supported Holway's pipeline plan, but Page used everything at his disposal to get Tulsa to implement his Shell Creek plan. Several state officials seemed to side with Page's plan—it was cheaper and the water source was closer. As soon as Judge

Campbell decided the Atkins case in Page's favor, the ever-confident Page went ahead and began construction on the Shell Creek dam before his plan had even been formally approved by the city.

The plan would require control of land held by two Muscogee citizens in Tulsa County. The Sand Springs Home purchased an option to build on the land from one. For the other, owned by a full-blood allottee, Long found a guardian who could make decisions for the "incompetent Indian."

The next order of business was taking control of the planned site of the reservoir. The site was composed of allotments belonging to citizens of the Osage Nation. Still, Long felt confident that with the help of C. B. Stuart, they could condemn the lands as a legal maneuver. That would then authorize the Sand Springs Home to build a dam on Shell Creek and create Shell Lake.

A bigger problem was the nature of the Sand Springs Home, which was not explicitly authorized to provide public services such as a municipal water supply. To get around this, Long created the Sand Springs Power, Light and Water Company, and obtained a charter authorizing the company to engage in the water pipeline and reservoir business. Page had been selling bottled water to Tulsa for many years, but it wasn't enough. He wanted to control the water supply itself and intended to do so through the Shell Creek project.

In the middle of the intense battle between the proponents of the Shell Creek and Spavinaw plans, a familiar name made the headlines once again. On May 24, 1919, Minnie Atkins Folk died at the Sand Springs Hospital. The hospital listed "acute endocarditis" as the cause. In some respects, Minnie's death was a surprise. She had not reported any chronic physical illnesses or health concerns throughout the Tommy Atkins investigation. The matter of what we today call mental health, however, was another matter entirely. One newspaper claimed that she died following a "nervous breakdown."[1] Minnie had changed her version of events several times before. With the US attorney general contemplating another lawsuit, Minnie's continued presence around Sand Springs was a major inconvenience. Harry Folk wrote anxious letters to Page's team—Long, Sam Brown, and Page himself—worrying about the money, new lawsuits, and the constraints on his movements. He periodically sent checks to "Uncle Sam Brown" as a token of "friendship."

A cloud of suspicion hovered over Minnie's death as it was reported in the *Tulsa World*:

Of those who have an interest in the Atkins case, all save friends of Charles Page expressed the utmost surprise yesterday when told that Minnie Atkins was dead.

For some time past, it is said, she has been living in a house midway between Tulsa and Sand Springs which Page fitted up for her, and she was virtually isolated there, although her husband who is a soldier is said to have returned recently on a furlough and he's been spending several days at the house. He is reported to have been at her bedside when death came yesterday morning. Few people knew that she had taken ill and had been removed to the Sand Springs hospital.[2]

Less than a month after Minnie's death, in June 1919, the Sand Springs Home amended its articles of incorporation to include in its purposes to "acquire, hold, manage and operate canals, reservoirs, dams, dishes, flumes, aqueducts, pipes, water and electric lines, machinery and other property for the general purposes herein stated." The Oklahoma Corporation Commission allowed this change, but the *Tulsa World* denounced it as nothing more than a "tax dodge" and a "pseudo-philanthropy."[3]

Exchange National Bank, an institution that liked to refer to itself as the "Oil Bank of America," would help Page finance this ambitious plan. Although Exchange National seemed to represent Tulsa's success in financing oil drilling operations, it was beset by scandal after scandal. In the early 1930s, many of its bankers, including Harry and Earl Sinclair, were indicted for embezzling funds from its many trusts. Harry Sinclair had been in the crosshairs of the Teapot Dome Scandal, and his shady practices led to the eventual dissolution of Exchange National in 1934.

After the embezzlement scandal, Exchange National Bank rebranded itself as the National Bank of Tulsa. This bank became known as Bank of Oklahoma in 1975, and it continues to be the state's most important financial institution. Today, Bank of Oklahoma is run by billionaire philanthropist George Kaiser, the richest and most celebrated public figure in Tulsa. Kaiser has a stated goal of donating almost all his wealth to philanthropic causes. One of Kaiser's many nonprofits is the Bob Dylan Center in downtown Tulsa, which has collected the entirety of the singer-songwriter's archives. During the renovation of the brick building that houses the Dylan Center, I watched workers sandblast the façade of the building. The operation revealed an inscription: "S.S. Home, 1922."

Tulsa's greatest living philanthropist had acquired a building built by Charles Page in the aftermath of the death of Minnie Atkins, and almost certainly financed in part by the Tommy Atkins oil fortune. In 2022, the Bob Dylan Center opened to the public, with media outlets like the *New York Times* providing coverage of the unlikely new home in Tulsa for Dylan's oeuvre. No one—not the *Times*, the George Kaiser Family Foundation, or the Bob Dylan Center—has ever commented on this peculiar history involving Charles Page and Minnie Atkins. Not that anyone could blame them; the only recorded history of Charles Page and the Sand Springs Home is one of benevolence and good Christian charity.

But as the poet from Duluth is reputed to have said: "Life is more or less a lie, but then again, that's exactly the way we want it to be." Tulsa wanted a lie, and it got one.

Page wanted to expand his reach into public utilities, including water and power, after Minnie's death. Eugene Lorton was outraged: Page had finally gone too far in his ambitions. Lorton, along with a former mayor and some city councilors, opposed Page publicly.

In June 1919, Page wrote to city officials to tell them that the dam would be completed in nine months. Page made it clear that this was not simply a public service, but a business venture. "Now, this water, gentlemen, will be for sale. If Tulsa wants this water, they can go to Spavinaw or any other sea port." If Tulsa continued to grow, Page said, he had the power to dam up Euchee Creek.[4]

A nonpartisan board found that Page's estimates were overly optimistic. Both Page's and Holway's plans were implemented, but when it was all said and done, Holway's plan proved superior. Shell Lake was completed first, in 1919, but struggled to supply even just the small town of Sand Springs with water. Meanwhile, Tulsans approved the largest per capita bond sale in history to fund the Spavinaw project.

Despite Page's continued attacks on the Spavinaw project, the Spavinaw pipeline was completed. As part of the surrounding media hoopla in November 1924, Tulsa officials rigged up a connection to the White House so that President Calvin Coolidge, with the push of a button, started the flow of water, signaling that the president himself was powering the supply of clear, sweet water from Spavinaw to Tulsa. President Coolidge pressed the button, and soon thereafter Governor John Walton of Oklahoma drank Spavinaw water in Tulsa from a golden goblet.

It has been flowing ever since.

In 2020, Apollonia and I forked over the $50 to get a certified copy of Minnie's death certificate in the mail. The person who filled it out had misspelled the cause of death as "encarditis," corrected later to "endocarditis." The certificate listed her father as "Tom Adkins" and her mother as "don't know." Her mother's birthplace was also listed as "don't know." In death, Minnie's race had once again changed. It had been "white" on her marriage certificate; now it was "Indian" on her death certificate. There was something hasty and downright sloppy about the way the death certificate was completed, but that didn't mean she was murdered.

At least, that was what I thought until 2023, when I made a trip to the courthouse in Sapulpa. I wanted to learn more about a lawsuit, *Nathaniel Atkins et al. v. A. G. McMillan, Sand Springs Home, et al.*, which had been filed in 1929 in the Creek County Court by a group of Atkins descendants against the Sand Springs Home.[5] It seemed that by 1929 the entire Tommy Atkins controversy would have blown over. The US economy was on the verge of collapse. The Cushing Oil Field was no longer the heart of the oil industry (although later innovations, such as fracking, would bring more oil to the surface). Many of the principal players were dead: Minnie Atkins, Nancy Atkins, Dick Atkins, Sally Atkins, Charles Page.

But there was one important person still alive: Nathaniel Atkins, son of Dick and Sally Atkins, half brother to Nancy and Minnie. Nathaniel had grown up with Nancy in Wagoner, and during the federal Atkins case he had been a party to his mother's attempt to claim Tommy's land. Nathaniel had long ago sold his own allotment and lived as a laborer in a thriving Black neighborhood in Kansas City. Nathaniel had been following the various lawsuits closely, writing to the Department of the Interior with requests for information throughout.

In 1929, Nathaniel Atkins brought suit against the Sand Springs Home, along with Charley and Harvey Harrison, Harry Folk, Frank B. Long, and the former commissioner of the Five Civilized Tribes, A. G. McMillan. The Associated Press reported that Nathaniel and his surviving siblings had brought "sensational" charges against the Sand Springs Home and the Dawes Commission.[6] They sought immediate possession of Tommy's two allotments and over $4 million in lost royalties. This was not a frivolous attempt to get money; it had an unlikely ally, the attorney Charles West, one of Oklahoma's first attorneys general, by then in private practice.[7]

I went to the courthouse in Sapulpa to see the documents relating to the lawsuit, stored on microfilm in a back room. A day later I had a scanned copy in my email inbox. Many familiar facts about Tommy were recounted in the lawsuit, including the charge that the Dawes Commission had relied on bogus evidence to enroll Tommy as the son of Minnie.* Nathaniel cited Ed Schrimsher's statements that Tommy's name was put on the 1895 census not by John Davis but by Schrimsher himself, after he met with Dick Atkins in a Muskogee butcher shop. The statement of facts was quite familiar at this point.

But there was one bit in there that jumped out at me. Deep into the "sixth cause of action" the following statement was made: "Page, together with other persons unknown to plaintiffs, had conspired to prevent Minnie Atkins from testifying therein and admitting that her

---

* As recounted earlier, Sam Brown's statement that John Davis told him Tommy was Minnie's son was proven false after the federal trial, as Davis had been in prison in Michigan. Minnie's testimony had almost certainly been subject to witness tampering by Page. Original Dawes records had been altered, and a Euchee Town census had been held, and possibly destroyed, by Frank Long. The list of improprieties is long indeed.

claim to the lands of Thomas Atkins was wholly without true basis, *and had caused her death to prevent the truth from coming out* [my emphasis]."

I went back to the *Tulsa World*'s 1919 coverage of Minnie's death. The only people not surprised by her sudden passing, it said, were the people in Page's orbit around Sand Springs. I thought about the many threats hanging over her head—some from her husband, Harry, and some from Frank Long. I thought about the anxiety she had expressed to the detective, Albina Dlabal; Minnie told her she had been afraid that someone might kill her. Someone in Tulsa "would do her up if they could," she had said.

The US attorney general was contemplating an appeal of the federal decision in April 1919, and then another mother of Tommy Atkins arrived from Canada, Sally Atkins (more about her in the next chapter). For Minnie's troubles, her only recompense was a guaranteed $200 a month from Charles Page and her home across the street from the oilman. Otherwise, she had quite little to show for all that she had been through. When Sally Atkins returned to Oklahoma from Canada, Minnie Atkins Folk was fifty-four years old; she was tired, jaded, and resentful that she had ever agreed to take part in the lawsuits. "She was nervous and afraid of everyone in the world," an acquaintance wrote about her. She carried a revolver and had used it to drive away a curiosity seeker.[8] She had even been warned against being alone in the evening. "It is not safe," she said.

Minnie must have known that she would be called to testify in court all over again. Would she tell the whole truth this time? Would she admit that she, Page, and Long had lied about a child's life in order to fit their business plan? There was mounting tension between her and Harry Folk. There was tension between her and her estranged sons, and between her and her supposed supporters around Sand Springs. *Tulsa World* reporters intimated that Minnie was a kept woman in her gracious Sand Springs home, ever under the watch of her neighbor across the street, Charles Page. Whatever force that killed Minnie on May 24, 1919, did not come naturally. If she did die of heart failure, it was induced by overwhelming stress.

The researchers on the Tommy Atkins research team—Gina and Apollonia—came to believe that Minnie was murdered. Her death occurred just as the Osage Reign of Terror began, north of Sand Springs in Osage County.[9] There, white men were killing Native women for their headrights to oil and gas royalties. I thought back on oil historian and veteran Tulsa journalist Ruth Sheldon Knowles's casual remark in the 1950s about the killings in the Tulsa area during the first oil boom. She wrote about one allottee in the Glenn Pool who had been slain in an alley after he contested a deed he had signed under the influence of whiskey. Knowles provided no documentation or even a name regarding this crime, an unusual decision for a writer known for her attention to detail. It wasn't that Knowles was lazy; the violence was simply background noise to the real event: the making of money. "Such deaths occurred every night," Knowles wrote.[10]

Another possibility has haunted me: What if Minnie killed herself? She would not have been the only character in this story to have committed suicide. Probate attorney Frank Montgomery—the man who had extracted a confession from Minnie that she had no son named Tommy—ended his own life in a devastating murder-suicide. In all likelihood, federal judge Ralph Campbell also ended his own life (the official explanation was an accidental gun discharge in his office) in 1921. Nancy Atkins literally went insane and was committed to the state mental hospital, where she died in 1927. Even the simplest explanation for Minnie's death is disturbing: the pressure, intimidation, and anxiety associated with having to lie to protect Page's oil lease just wore her down until her heart failed.

CHAPTER 18

FROM BLOOD QUANTUM
TO LIQUID GOLD

*Sally Atkins and the Erosion
of Black Freedom During
Oklahoma's First Oil Boom*

Nathaniel Atkins's mother, Sally Atkins, died most likely in 1922. (She was alive in 1921 but dead by 1927.) He and his siblings dispersed throughout North America—from farms in western Canada to the suburbs of Los Angeles. Nathaniel found a place for his young family in a vibrant Black neighborhood on the east side of Kansas City, Missouri. He rented a home for $30 a month and raised four sons with his wife, Ethel. He worked as a laborer and rarely, if ever, returned to his family's allotment in the hamlet of Sharp, south of Okmulgee. Kansas City at the time represented opportunity and freedom for Blacks, as well as being a laboratory for big band jazz. He had put the violent tumult of Oklahoma in the rearview mirror.

Nathaniel never forgot his little brother, Thomas. They were approximately a couple of years apart in age. Nathaniel had a special bond with him. The two boys worked and played near the Verdigris River on the outskirts of Wagoner. From an early age, the boys worked tough jobs around the town of Wagoner: clearing brush, carrying firewood, picking cotton. Nathaniel remembered how Thomas, then thirteen or fourteen, had suddenly fallen ill, probably in the early fall of 1898 or 1899. One evening, Thomas returned home feeling nauseated and dizzy. The boy got sicker and sicker with each passing day. His symptoms lined up with those of Bright's disease, which leads to kidney failure.

All the brothers and sisters gathered around Thomas in his final moments. Thomas told another brother, Annanias, that he should take care of the land he was to be allotted. Two days later, the family buried him at a small cemetery for Black Creeks, called Knee-High Cemetery, adjoining the land of their half sister, Chaney Trent. It was a peaceful spot near the Verdigris. Annanias remembered having to scrape together the $35 for the funeral.

Over the years, Nathaniel closely followed the news about the Tommy Atkins allotment and Charles Page. Nathaniel must have found it odd that no one had ever reached out to him to ask about his brother. Hundreds of depositions had been taken about Tommy Atkins, and hundreds of newspaper articles published, but Nathaniel and his brother had been overlooked. The government's case to cancel the allotment had become both a national sensation and a byzantine treatise in federal, state, and Indian law. It had cost $16,000 to reproduce all the transcripts and exhibits.

In 1922, Nathaniel decided to write to the Bureau of Indian Affairs. The more he learned about the Tommy Atkins case, the more convinced he became that Tommy was neither a fiction nor a child of Minnie or Nancy Atkins. He was convinced that the Tommy who had been allotted land had been his late brother.

On November 18, 1922, the Office of Indian Affairs received the following letter from Nathaniel, written with steady but simple looping penmanship.

Dear sir's—

My brother, Tommie Atkins, is dead, and he left his allotment, which is the West half of the northwest quarter Section 4 in the West half of the northeast quarter of Section 5 all in Township 18 N range 7 east in Creek County Oklahoma. This land has been in litigation since 1915, I want to know who is heirs to the land. My mother Sallie Atkins the mother of Tommie Atkins got a decision in the District Court of Creek County on the first day of April 1921, by Judge Lucas [sic] B. Wright. Said Sallie Atkins was the mother of Tommie Atkins which he lived and died in Wagner County. Since that the case was taken to the State Supreme Court

and it was given back to Charlie Page. Now I am trying to find
who is the rightful owner to this decided land.*

*Nathaniel Atkins
2315 Highland
Kansas City, Mo.*[1]

This letter was only the beginning of Nathaniel's quest. For years,
he would continue to write to the Department of the Interior, offering
evidence that everyone had gotten the identity of Tommy wrong. Nathaniel had leads all over Oklahoma. This had culminated in attorney
Charles West's suit against the Sand Springs Home and the commissioner of the Five Civilized Tribes. But that lawsuit was dropped by
West for reasons that are unclear. In any case, the Department of the
Interior took West's charges seriously and the attorney general once
again contemplated taking on the Sand Springs Home.

When Nathaniel started his inquiries, Page was still alive, but after
his death in 1926, he could no longer wield his combination of charm
and intimidation to influence elected officials. The home continued
to operate an array of industrial businesses in Sand Springs and West
Tulsa. Nathaniel's quest eventually drew him into conflict with the
home. By 1930, times were changing. Oklahoma's Indian policies were
widely regarded as catastrophic failures. Washington was considering
an entirely new approach to Indian Country.

That year, Nathaniel's pleadings reached the desk of one of the most
important men in the country, FBI director J. Edgar Hoover. Hoover
approved an investigation into fraud around the Tommy Atkins allotment. It is quite possible that Hoover had no idea that Nathaniel
and his siblings were Black. Had he known that, it is possible Hoover
might have ignored Nathaniel's requests. But Nathaniel and the rest of
Richard's offspring were classified as "Indians by blood" by the Dawes
Commission. As such they held a special relationship with the federal
government, similar to that of wards to a guardian. Even a staunch
conservative like Hoover knew that from 1907 onward, the United
States government had been a terrible substitute for a legal guardian.

---

* For reasons that are not entirely clear to me, rulings from the Oklahoma Supreme
Court and US Supreme Court on this case came down almost simultaneously in 1922.

An FBI agent named E. R. Cushing was assigned to the case. Cushing examined pages of testimony from the Dawes Commission. If the late Tommy Atkins had indeed been the son of Sally and Richard Atkins, Cushing wanted to see verification from Sally herself. Sally was dead—it was unclear when and how she had died—but thankfully, there was a record of her talking about Thomas in 1902.

"THEY ALWAYS CALLED HIM AN INDIAN": RETHINKING THE LIFE OF DICK ATKINS

On a summer day in Okmulgee in 1902, Sally Atkins had stood before Tams Bixby, the acting chairman of the Dawes Commission. Sally, a widow and mother of twelve children, had been born into slavery in Missouri in 1855. She sought to prove to Bixby that her children belonged to Cheyaha Town, a Muscogee Nation tribal town, through their late father, Dick Atkins. Although Dick, a Black man, had been a documented citizen of Cheyaha Town, their children had been unexpectedly kicked off the Muscogee Nation's rolls and had been refused allotment by Dawes. In the eyes of white men like Bixby, Atkins's children were freedpeople, descendants of enslaved people, to be distinguished from Native American citizens "by blood."

Sally claimed that Dick's father had been the well-known full-blood Mvskoke warrior (*tvstenvke*) Thomas Atkins, the father of Minnie and Nancy. Dick, a Black man, had been known among the mixed white-Mvskoke people of Coweta Town as an intruder who had come to Indian Territory claiming to be Thomas's son, after living in bondage in Missouri until Emancipation. In 1896, however, the town king of Cheyaha, Anderson Childers, remembered Dick from his infancy in Coweta and affirmed his citizenship.

Sally maintained that Dick Atkins had indeed been born in the Muscogee Nation in 1845 to the warrior Thomas Atkins and a Black woman named Mary. Mother and child had been carried off to Missouri shortly before the Civil War (probably 1860), where they were in bondage to a man named Havans (sometimes spelled Havens). Mary took Havans's last name but told her son that his father was the legendary Muscogee warrior Thomas Atkins. After Emancipation, Dick and Sally married, and Dick worked odd jobs for former slave holders. Sally told Bixby that "they always called [Dick] an Indian back in Missouri."[2]

If, as Sally claimed, Dick was indeed half Muscogee by blood, then his twelve children were one-quarter blood quantum, entitling them to 160 acres of land apiece—1,920 acres total. They intended to claim land in the heart of Indian Territory's "black belt," where prosperous all-Black towns like Boley and Clearview were emerging. The rise of Black townships gave rise to another conflict between the Black Creeks (*estelvste*) and the newly arrived Blacks from the States, with no connections to Indian Nations.

There were dozens, if not hundreds, of cases like Sally Atkins's before the Dawes Commission, so the final ruling on their citizenship and identity had huge consequences, not only for the families involved but for their descendants down to the present.

Bixby had ruled that *some* of the surviving children of Dick Atkins were, in fact, Indians by blood, and eligible for allotment. It was a curious decision: eight of the children were found to be "recognized citizens of the Creek Nation," while four had their enrollments denied. Three of the four who were denied—Mary, Geneva, and Nancy—could not be directly traced to annuity payments or town censuses. Without a paper trail, the Dawes Commission would not verify their enrollment. There remained a question about little Thomas, however. As we've seen, the question of his enrollment was held for further investigation but no further investigation appears to have happened after 1905 until the discovery of oil in 1912. Meanwhile, most of Dick and Sally's children were able to select homesteads and surplus lands close to their actual home, about eight miles southeast of Okmulgee, near the Deep Fork River.

Sally Atkins appealed in 1905 on behalf of her children who had been denied enrollment. Her lawyer called the Dawes Commission's partial rejection of the family "the rankest sort of injustice."[3] The Muscogee Nation had acknowledged that Dick Atkins had been a Muscogee citizen by blood. His children had every right to citizenship as well. The appeal succeeded. Tams Bixby registered all the children of Sally and Dick with the commission except for one: "Tommie" Atkins, who, Bixby believed, had died prior to April 1, 1899.

Quietly, a few of Sally Atkins's children decided that they would not stay in Oklahoma after statehood. Conditions for all Black people, both freedpeople and State Blacks, quickly deteriorated as land grafting and racial oppression became commonplace. Lynchings at

Okemah, Boynton, and elsewhere set this section of eastern Oklahoma on edge. Sally's half sister, Chaney Trent, found herself kicked off her land in the aftermath of statehood by a woman she had thought was her tenant, Lizzie Miller. Miller had signed a document that Trent had understood to be a lease. In fact, it was a transfer of ownership from Trent to Miller. Trent eventually regained title to her land but only after years of lawsuits.

Sally Atkins emigrated to Canada, another place of false promises and illusory freedom. Unlike many African American migrants to Canada, however, Atkins returned to Oklahoma sometime in 1917, when the state was briefly the nation's leading producer of oil and gas. On April 11, 1919, Sally filed a lawsuit against the Sand Springs Home and Charles Page, claiming that she was the rightful owner of the Tommy Atkins allotment. This was a civil suit filed in Creek County District Court against the Gem Oil Company and the Sand Springs Home. Sally sought $2.5 million in lost royalties, plus additional revenue in rents from the land.

JUDGE WRIGHT HEARS
FROM TOMMY'S THIRD MOTHER

Lucien B. Wright, district judge of Creek County, presided over Sally's case against the Sand Springs Home. Many of the same lawyers from the federal Tommy Atkins trial returned for this new case: Nancy Atkins's team, R. C. Allen, some of Bartlett's lawyers, and another team from the Muskogee Nation. They all joined forces to ask Judge Wright to invalidate Charles Page's claim to Tommy's land and give it to Sally. Unlike the Tommys allegedly born to Minnie and Nancy, there was no question that Dick and Sally's child had once walked the earth in Indian Territory. But when did he die? If Sally could show that he had been living on April 1, 1899, she had a decent chance at claiming a significant slice of Page's fortune.

The *Tulsa World* gave ample coverage to Sally's claims. "Not only can she establish her right to be known as his mother," one article stated, "but she can relate the circumstances of his death, point out his burial place and summon witnesses to prove that she and Tommy . . . were known as mother and son in Wagoner County, where they lived many years ago."[4]

Frank Long was alarmed that Sally Atkins had rematerialized in Oklahoma. He prepared a defense, using Bixby's initial queries about the family in the late 1890s during the Dawes Commission days. "According to my files," Long wrote, "this Richard Atkins came into the Indian Territory in the early 80's from Missouri where he had been known as Richard or 'Dick' Havens. He made some sort of a connection with the Atkins family down there and claimed to be an illegitimate son of old Thomas Atkins."[5]

Although Sally had told the Dawes Commission in 1902 that the last name Havens had come from the slave owner of Dick's mother, Long was not alone in believing that Richard Havens had simply assumed an Indian paternity after the Civil War to get land. The other Richard Atkins, Richard "Lump" Adkins, thought his namesake was not his half brother with a different mother but rather an imposter. It is possible that, for this reason, Richard (Lump) Adkins insisted people spell his last name with a *d* instead of the more common *t* spelling used by his father and by Richard (Dick) Atkins.

If Dick Atkins was an intruder, why would he, of all the possible Native Americans eligible for allotment, have claimed the paternity by way of the warrior Thomas Atkins? Was it his reputation as "a wild sort of fellow" (he'd had relationships with many women) that made him seem like a plausible father to claim? Frank Long did not have an answer for that one. His best guess was that Ellis Childers, along with some of the people associated with the Davis and Jones Mercantile Store in Wagoner, had been in the business of finding "Indians" to register, who would then become pawns in white men's allotment fraud schemes. In other words, it was also possible that someone at the Davis and Jones Mercantile Store cooked up the scheme and Dick Atkins was forced to play along. Considering the near-constant threat of jail time for Black and Indigenous people at this time, it is not hard to imagine Dick Atkins getting pulled into some scheme devised by someone like Ellis Childers, who had demonstrated himself capable of taking financial advantage of a situation that confused outsiders. Childers, the one-time treasurer of the Creek National Council, had made himself some money when the nation's checkbook disappeared from the chief.

The most plausible explanation, however, is the simplest one. Thomas Atkins was very close to Benjamin Marshall, the wealthy slave owner whose slaves had fled for Kansas during the Civil War. Marshall enriched himself by selling many enslaved people to white people in Missouri. To make more enslaved people, he had young men like Thomas Atkins—seventeen or eighteen at the time of Dick's birth—impregnate the women belonging to Marshall.

One of the people enslaved by a Muscogee slaver told a Works Progress Administration oral historian that it was common practice to force pregnancies upon enslaved women by Muscogee men by blood. "The slave man would then be put to work in the fields or some place outside of the home, while the woman was kept at the house, especially if her physical appearance was healthy and strongly built. This colored woman would then bear children for her master, thus resulting in mixed blood. Slave sales were advertised in the newspapers. The newspaper would state that so many slaves were to be sold 'on the stump.'"[6]

Thomas Atkins was not a slave master himself, but considering his family, tribal, and business connections to "Chief" Marshall, it is likely that he participated in this horror of rape and enslavement. Atkins had run down whiskey traders and livestock poachers; he almost certainly ran down runaway slaves as well. Later in life, Atkins married Marshall's daughter, Louiza, who died as the Marshalls followed Confederates to safety in Texas. After Louiza's death, Thomas married her sister, Millie, who also died before the end of the war.

In any case, the question of Dick Atkins's citizenship had been settled when it was affirmed in 1896. The Dawes Rolls had been amended to state that he was Mvskoke by blood, and it was not legally feasible to challenge that, even though many Lower Creeks tried to purge as many people of African descent as possible from the rolls.

With this in mind, Sally laid her case out in Creek County District Court in Sapulpa before Judge Wright. The Tommy Atkins listed on the Creek Rolls—patented by the United States government and now making millions of dollars for Page's Sand Springs Home—had been mistakenly grouped together with Euchee Town, when he should have been grouped with the rest of Dick and Sally's children in Cheyaha Town.

Judge Wright simply needed to recall the encounter between Ed Schrimsher and Dick Atkins in Muskogee at the butcher shop. The pair discussed Sam Brown's role in securing payments for Muscogee citizens for the 1895 payment. Schrimsher told Judge Wright what he had told Judge Campbell in 1917: he urged Sam Brown to put down this Tommy in the same grouping as Minnie and Nancy because they were all "kinfolks." At the time, Schrimsher's testimony had little weight as people believed Sam Brown's version that John Davis had told him Tommy belonged to Minnie. By 1919, it was clear that Brown either had lied or had a fallible memory.

Ed Schrimsher said that Dick Atkins must be kin to Sam Brown, but this was intended as a joke. (The "joke," I suppose, being that Brown, as a blue-eyed "king" of the Euchee who vowed that there was virtually no Euchee of African descent, would not want to be family with a formerly enslaved person like Dick Atkins.) Brown submitted this Thomas in that family grouping of Euchees, despite Schrimsher's testimony. Sally's attorneys argued that officials back in Washington then mistakenly created an enrollment card for a Tommy Atkins of Euchee and of white descent, when really he had been of Coweta Town and of African descent.

At this point, Minnie was dead. Nancy had been ruled legally insane and confined to the state mental hospital, in Norman, Oklahoma, in 1927. Sally's lawyers told Judge Wright that those two women—both of whom had claimed to be Tommy's mother in the federal trial—had been forced to give false testimony and reminded Judge Wright that R. C. Allen and Frank Montgomery had strong evidence that Minnie had committed perjury while changing her narrative of Tommy's life. Minnie had not capriciously changed her story—she had been forced to by Page and Long.

Charles West, Sally's attorney, argued that there was one fact staring everyone right in the face: the only Tommy Atkins born in the mid-1880s in the Muscogee Nation that had existed beyond a reasonable doubt was the child of Dick and Sally.

Judge Wright pointed out that the Dawes Commission had denied Dick and Sally's Thomas the right to citizenship in the Muscogee Nation in 1903; when Sally had appealed, the commission's decision had been upheld by the secretary of the interior in 1905. C. B. Stuart argued that since the Dawes Commission had denied Thomas twice, there was no reason for Judge Wright of Creek County to reverse that decision and he did not have standing to do so. Nevertheless, Judge Wright wanted to hear out Sally's claim. In an echo of the receivership that Judge Campbell had ordered back in 1915, Judge Wright now forced Page to post a bond of $900,000 to continue his drilling operations on Tommy's land while the case went forward.

Frank Long wanted to reiterate the old charge that Dick was simply an intruder impersonating a son of Thomas Atkins. Long wrote to C. B. Stuart, "The very fact that this negro Dick and his family were shunted around, rejected and enrolled, then re-enrolled, must mean that there was a lot of maneuvering, manipulating going on down there."[7] The argument held no legal basis, as the rolls had been fixed. Even those later found to have worked their way on to the rolls had their citizenship in the Five Tribes affirmed.

As Sally's lawsuit proceeded, the entire convoluted story of "the boy with three mothers" had been told many times in the press, but the possibility that Tommy Atkins had been Black added a layer of bitter irony, considering that the Sand Springs Home's charitable work was entirely geared toward white people. Sand Springs was a planned community, and it was planned with segregation in mind.

The Sally Atkins trial provoked Page and his team like no other previous suit. They seemed terrified that Judge Wright might rule in Sally's favor. In a summary of the defense, Long wrote that Page's interests would show "that Euchee town was different from the other towns in the Creek Nation in that the language of the Euchee Indians was different from the Muscogee or Creek language; that with one or two exceptions there were no kinky haired families in Euchee town; that Euchee town was almost wholly free from negro taints."[8]

DARK CLOUDS ARISE AS SALLY PREVAILS

On March 31, 1921, Judge Wright shocked Oklahoma by awarding Sally Atkins nearly $1,960,000 in damages from the Page interests (around $33.5 million in 2024 dollars). This decision very likely made her the richest black woman in the United States.*

Almost as soon as the decision came down, Oklahoma Attorney General S. P. Freeling accused Judge Wright of colluding with Governor James B. A. Robertson to move the Sally Atkins suit to a favorable district, and then accepting a $10,000 payment to rule in Sally's favor.

---

* The Black entrepreneur Madame C. J. Walker was said to be worth around $1 million at the time of her death in 1919.

The Page interests demanded a new trial in May 1921. More salacious rumors were spread through the newspapers, but this time the target was not Page, but Judge Wright. One story claimed that Wright had been drinking bootleg whiskey with his paramour while concocting a plan to steal oil money from an allottee named Lete Kolvin.[9] For a few weeks after the ruling, it looked like Lucien B. Wright was exhibit A in the machinations of Crook County corruption. Judge Wright was arrested after Freeling charged him with taking a bribe.[10]

D. H. Linebaugh, the federal attorney who unsuccessfully tried to cancel the Tommy Atkins allotment, jumped to Wright's defense, as did one of the lawyers for Nancy Atkins. Wright was released on a $10,000 bond and set about gathering evidence that the real crook was Page, not himself. Freeling's charge against Wright named a "John Doe" as the agent of the bribe, and no one stepped forward to verify the charge. Wright said that the only payment he was offered was $5,050, and that was made by an agent of Charles Page. Page, as we've seen, had a long history of doing financial transactions with Oklahoma county judges, so he probably thought little of offering this payment.

Perhaps Wright did not understand that his ruling against Page would unleash the power of the state's top law enforcement official upon him, nor that Page would strike at him personally. Wright had stood up to Charles Page verbally, but by July 1921 he was carrying a pistol, ready to defend himself as he met with Tulsa police in the Hotel Tulsa. Page-allied newspapers went so far as to say that Wright's pistol was evidence that the judge planned to assassinate Page.[11] Attorney General Freeling thought he had a good case against Wright, as other witnesses testified that they had heard him say he "would clean up between $200,000 to $300,000" by reversing the decision on Tommy Atkins.[12] Some of Freeling's witnesses seemed like figures from Central Casting. There was a disreputable woman who claimed that Judge Wright had pulled back the mattress on his bed to reveal a fat stack of cash and had made a phone call during which he yelled, "I am ruined! They know everything!"

The chaos of this entire era is apparent in the headlines of the newspapers. On the same front page of the *Tulsa World* telling of Page's vendetta against Wright, the paper also reported that the sheriff of the city had slept through the city's race massacre on May 31 and June 1.¹³ Murders in Osage County would soon grip the public's attention. By 1922, the Ku Klux Klan was in control of state government and the city of Tulsa. The 1920s are remembered as the heyday of Tulsa's oil boom, the Oil Capital of the World days, but it was also an era of plunder, lawlessness, and brutality perhaps unparalleled in the twentieth century in the United States.

The State of Oklahoma failed to produce evidence to back up its salacious charges against Judge Lucien Wright. Much of this evidence was based on preposterous tales reported in the newspapers that lacked legal weight, and the charges were eventually dropped. Judge Wright had been stunned by the brief scandal. His lawyers found that either Page or Long had hired an Oklahoma City private detective to obtain false testimony. Wright deemed the operation a character assassination, and he sought revenge. Wright named Page and two other oilmen in a $500,000 defamation suit. Wright accused Page of blackmailing him with dirt about his paramour and his proximity to a bootlegger. Judge Wright was far from unimpeachable (he would later be convicted of perjury in a separate case). One did not become district judge of Creek County by walking the straight-and-narrow path. But Page's attacks came out of the Tommy Atkins playbook, involving false testimony, harassment, and libel.

The matter was still unsettled, however. As we've seen, Attorney General A. Mitchell Palmer was in favor of appealing Judge Campbell's decision.¹⁴ The documents in the Tommy Atkins case had cost $20,000 to be reproduced or printed for the circuit court of appeals in 1920. Then, the US Supreme Court agreed to hear the case. Justice McReynolds delivered an anticlimactic ruling on November 20, 1922. The court was not interested in the long trail of deceit and graft after allotment. McReynolds wrote that the Dawes Commission, vested with the power of the US Congress, had the authority to decide who was and was not an Indian. The "mere allegation of nonexistence" was not enough to overturn the Dawes Rolls. If Dawes understood Tommy to be the son of Minnie and living on April 1, 1899, it would be thus. We are only left to ponder the cruel irony of the commission selecting April Fool's Day as the cutoff for determining who would receive such valuable land.

Sally Atkins had produced a tantalizing theory based on the testimony of a few Muscogee citizens who pointed to a mistaken grouping of Tommy Atkins with Euchee Town. Nothing in her theory, however, could be demonstrated as conclusive, especially not a conspiracy involving a man venerated as Oklahoma's greatest philanthropist. For a few months, Sally Atkins had been the richest Black woman in the United States. By the end of 1922, she had disappeared. Records on her are virtually nonexistent after the conclusion of the Oklahoma Supreme Court trial. It is unclear when and where she died.

Sally and Dick's children, however, kept up their struggle to be recognized as the true heirs of Tommy Atkins. This brings us back to Nathaniel Atkins's lawsuit in 1929. He and his siblings were represented by Charles West, a former attorney general of Oklahoma. Although newspaper headlines emphasized the money the plaintiffs sought ($4 million), the real bombshell in my eyes was the allegation of a conspiracy by Charles Page to silence Minnie Atkins's testimony on the case. This piece of the story was quickly suppressed after a United Press report in 1929.

Nathaniel's allegations also brought up the attempted bribery of Creek County Court judge Lucien B. Wright. Page, as with Judge Gubser in Tulsa, had attempted to get Wright in his back pocket with a bribe. Wright had refused the bribe and then issued a judgment unfavorable to Page. In the aftermath of that trial, Wright had been arrested. Oklahoma Attorney General Freeling charged Wright with bribery, but then acquitted him. The entire scandal had been intimately tied into Page's plan to dominate Tulsa's water supply by using his profits in Creek County oil fields to build the Shell Creek project. So much had been riding on Minnie Atkins's maintaining her story about Tommy. She had disavowed the story before. Perhaps when Sally Atkins came back from Canada to open up old wounds, Minnie had decided to come clean. Before she could do so, Minnie was dead.

Nathaniel's attorney, Charles West, said what many people only dared whisper: Minnie Atkins had been killed before she could be forced to testify to the truth under oath. The United Press summed up West's position: "Plaintiffs say that Page, together with other persons had conspired to prevent Minnie Atkins from testifying therein and admitting that her claim to the land of Thomas Atkins was wholly without true basis and caused her death to prevent the truth from coming out." There it was: a former attorney general of Oklahoma accused Charles Page or his allies of murdering Minnie Atkins.[15]

The lawsuit was dropped later in 1929. No one knows why, and there is no explanation in the official record in Creek County. If Page was indeed the primary suspect, he had died by this date. I suspect that a monetary settlement was reached, to keep the good name of the Sand Springs Home intact. The home had a record of settling the many claims against it out of court. During the various Atkins trials, Page's reputation had been tarnished by accusations of fraud, black-mail, perjury, and even conspiracy to commit murder. One only need remember the payments Harry Folk continued to send Sam Brown until the former's death to know that money could quiet almost any-one's conscience. If the home, or anyone connected to it, settled out of court with the heirs of Sally and Richard Atkins, however, that money never replaced the sense of injustice that the descendants felt and continue to feel.

By 1930, the work of repairing the image of Charles Page and silencing the various claimants to the Atkins fortune was well under way. A museum and statue in Page's honor were completed in down-town Sand Springs that year.

The *Tulsa World* halted all attacks after 1926 on the man it had once tried to destroy. As the city prepared to inaugurate the statue and museum, the paper published a revisionist history on Page:

> The Sand Springs Home, probably the most outstanding charitable institution established by Mr. Page, where the benefactor spent many hours of his leisure time in close contact with the small homeless children that enjoyed his beneficence, and where one day, late in December, 1926, his body lay in state while thousands mourned, is to figure in the plans to honor the late Mr. Page. . . . The wheels of industry will be stopped and a civic holiday will be declared in honor of the occasion.[16]

THE FIGHT FOR RECOGNITION CONTINUES

One of Dick Atkins's great-great-great-granddaughters, Rhonda Mc-Fee, told me in the fall of 2023 about her own battle for recognition as a citizen of Muscogee Nation. "I almost gave up," McFee said of her fight to be recognized as Mvskoke by blood. I had come across her name on a Facebook group dedicated to Mvskoke language, culture, and history. She was trying to figure out what her clan and tribal town were. So much history had passed between her ancestors' fight for recognition and her own struggle. She needed information. I asked her if she might be connected to the Atkinses or to Chaney Trent.

I showed her my research on Dick and Sally, and she emailed me a photo of her great-great-grandmother, Mary E. Atkins. Mary was one of the children of Sally and Dick who had been stricken from the rolls and then reinstated by the Dawes Commission. Rhonda now has a citizenship card but is still trying to identify her clan and tribal town.

Sally Atkins, meanwhile, died in obscurity, with even the most basic facts of her passing unknown. Her children worked as laborers and domestic servants in an increasingly urban nation. Oklahoma farmland was consolidated and, as the historian Alaina E. Roberts notes, Black landownership declined.[17] Although oil royalties continued to enrich a lucky few such as Sarah Rector and Jackson Barnett, stories about Black and Native people transformed into millionaires by oil wealth faded from the pages of newspapers. Their estates rarely endured beyond their deaths. Instead, their wealth fell into the hands of guardians, debt collectors, and attorneys.

— CHAPTER 19 —

"BUT INSISTS HE HAS NEVER DIED"

On an unseasonably cold day in April 2023, I walked down Pennsylvania Avenue in Washington, DC, a wind whipping through my jean jacket. The imposing neoclassical Federal architecture seemed designed to intimidate and dehumanize. I had come here to view the "R. C. Allen Investigation" file at the National Archives. I assumed it contained Allen's investigation into the fraud around Tommy Atkins; I knew Allen had compiled a dossier that he had used in his case against Page.

But when I viewed the materials, I was surprised to learn that the "R. C. Allen Investigation" was actually E. B. Linnen's investigation into Allen himself. I'll admit to some disappointment. I had hoped for some bombshell piece of evidence that would reveal, definitively, how Minnie had been forced to lie about Tommy to prove Page's claim to the land. I had also been hoping to find some compelling theory about her death.

I still had one day left in DC, so I asked a staff member at the National Archives and Records Administration (NARA), Rose Buchanan, if there might be anything else involving the cast of characters I was researching. I gave Buchanan the names of the US attorneys who had worked on the Tommy Atkins case: Linebaugh, German, and Montgomery. I waited.

I sat outside the building near the US Navy Memorial and ate a burrito. Among the scenes depicted in bronze bas-relief at the memorial was Theodore Roosevelt's "Great White Fleet," a group of sixteen steam-powered battleships dispatched on a worldwide circumnavigation in 1907, the same year as Oklahoma statehood. The fleet switched over to oil-powered turbines starting in 1916. These ships, powered by oil, much of it from Creek County, established the United States as the world's newest imperial power. America's mastery of oil led to world domination—and to the illusion that other nations could simply follow the American path to prosperity with cheap fuel.

As I sat and waited, I battled conflicting emotions. I realized that I had wanted R. C. Allen to be the good guy in this story, even though I had the critical apparatus to be wary of such labels. Still, there was something compelling about the man. Allen could have looked the other way in the Tommy Atkins case. He could have let Bartlett, Page, and all the other oilmen fight it out. Page had a well-established practice of paying off people who stood in his way. Allen could have parked himself in some Hotel Tulsa suite and taken a bribe from the highest bidder for the Tommy Atkins play. Instead, he fought to prove what I had come to believe was the truth: that Minnie Atkins's claim to be the mother of Tommy Atkins was part of a setup she had been forced into. Minnie had balked several times at the stories Frank Long and Charles Page had cooked up for her. Allen was convinced that, had he more time and support, he could get Minnie to tell the story she originally told Frank Montgomery—that Tommy Atkins was a lie, pure and simple. Instead, Minnie wound up dead.

Did it matter that Allen was in this fight for not entirely altruistic reasons? He most likely had an eye to selling the allotment down the line and enriching himself with a handsome commission. He was no white savior. But do we need our truth-tellers to be saints?

As I ate my burrito and watched some school kids kick a soccer ball around the monument grounds, I wondered if there was anything more to be said about Tommy Atkins. I now believed that Minnie's Tommy was a clerical error that Charles Page and some of the most brilliant legal minds in Oklahoma had converted into a real person. As nefarious as Frank Long seemed to be, his writings revealed a sharp mind, someone who understood the machinations of human greed and exploited them relentlessly. Did it matter that much of this money went to a good purpose at the Sand Springs Home—sheltering and feeding orphans? Of course it mattered, but so did the hospitals, stadiums, and housing for the poor in Colombia created by the drug lord Pablo Escobar. History is littered with scoundrels who did a kindly deed along the way. As Honoré de Balzac writes in *Le Père Goriot*: "Le secret des grandes fortunes sans cause apparente est un crime oublié, parce qu'il a été proprement fait"—"The secret of great fortunes without apparent origin is a crime that has been forgotten because it was properly executed."

Nancy's Tommy had been, in all likelihood, a stillborn baby, a ghost child that caught the attention of a few oilmen. Henry Carter had made for a plausible Tommy when one considered Minnie Atkins's activities around Granny Letcher's place. But Henry's biological mother was almost certainly not Minnie. That left Sally Atkins's Thomas. This was the only Thomas Atkins who had a verifiable story on this earth to go along with a land claim. But the uncertainty around his death date created too much doubt for the US Supreme Court to throw out Page's claim and upset precedents. Anti-Black racism was also a factor. Was the court really going to take a major fortune away from Page and make Sally Atkins the richest Black woman in America?

The justices were rightfully skeptical about the one witness, Ed Schrimsher, who said that Sally and Richard's Tommy should be grouped together with Euchee Town. There were also lingering doubts about the two Richard Atkinses. Was the Black Richard really the son of Thomas Atkins, captain of the Lighthorse? Or was he an intruder caught up in yet another grafting scheme by the Davis and Jones Mercantile Store of Wagoner? Ellis Childers had clearly been a corruptible figure within Muscogee Nation, but the most plausible explanation was that Thomas had fathered Dick, with one of Ben Marshall's enslaved women as the mother.

With all these questions still in my mind, I went back to the National Archives, accepted a box of folders from Rose Buchanan, sat down, and began to read.

The first letter I pulled out of the central classified file was dated May 26, 1927, from Kansas City, Missouri, and was addressed to the secretary of the interior.

> *Dear sir,*
>
> *Almost a year has elapsed since I last wrote you and never have received a reply from you direct. I have some very startling revelations to disclose in this case I would like for you to arrange a trial for me in the Supreme Court in Washington at your earliest convenience. I think it will result to great advantage to both. I*

have found in the Capitol in Oklahoma City that the case never
reached Washington, and the parties have died that have been
usurping my rights. Trusting you will comply with my desire for
a trial.

Very respectfully,
Mrs. Minnie Atkins,
Kansas City, MO

Minnie Atkins, alive and well in Kansas City in 1927!

It seemed like it must have been a joke, some sort of prank, or maybe a long-shot attempt by a namesake to claim a few million dollars. Perhaps it was the Minnie Atkins of Kansas who had signed the initial fraudulent lease in 1912, now trying to claim the land again.

Charles Burke, the commissioner of the Bureau of Indian Affairs, wrote back to Mrs. Atkins on July 21, 1927:

From examination of your above-mentioned letters, it seems clear
that you are not the Minnie Folk, nee Atkins, referred to in the
above-mentioned court decisions. This office can afford you no
relief or assistance in the matter of your claim.

Sincerely yours,
Chas. H Burke

Shortly after sending this letter, Commissioner Burke resigned from his post. A new era in Native American policy was on the horizon. Burke would be the last of the strident assimilationists to advocate for tribal termination. His replacement, Charles Rhoads, began to adopt reforms that had been suggested years earlier. In June 1934, the Indian Reorganization Act spurred a revival of tribal sovereignty, Indian arts, and language revitalization under the leadership of the vaunted reformer John Collier, appointed by President Franklin Roosevelt to head the Bureau of Indian Affairs. Things were changing dramatically in Indian Country, but one thing did not change: the persistence of the ghosts of Tommy Atkins.

On November 17, 1937, the Bureau of Indian Affairs received another astonishing letter, this one from Orin Jordan, the county attorney of Mitchell County, Kansas. Jordan wrote that he had been approached by a man in distress who claimed that some powerful oilmen were out to kill him. The man had many documents showing that he had been born under the name Thomas Atkins in Leavenworth in 1885.

Jordan wrote that he had researched two court cases: *United States v. Minnie Atkins*, Equity 2131, along with *Nancy Atkins v. United States*. Jordan interviewed the man in distress and came to believe that he was indeed Tommy Atkins, Creek Indian #7913.

"Mr. Atkins," Jordan wrote, "had papers showing that he was born in 1885 at Leavenworth, Kansas; *but insists that he has never died* [emphasis added]."

Jordan received no reply from Washington. On December 6, he wrote to Collier, "This man insists that he is in fear of bodily harm because the owners of the oil lease are trying to do away with him."[1]

Jordan was not the only person writing to Collier with requests for information about Tommy Atkins. On August 23, 1939, the assistant district attorney for Philadelphia, Harry Felix, wrote that he had been approached by a man claiming to be Thomas Atkins, "a member of the Five Civilized Tribes entered on the Creek Nation roll as 7913." He asked Collier to look into the case: "Can you tell me if you have any information about this man and his bona fides?"[2]

Around the same time, thousands of miles away in Los Angeles, a California congressman, Jerry Voorhis, had been contacted by a man named Gulick who was investigating a potential employee, Thomas Atkins, for "a position of responsibility and trust." Gulick thought the man seemed trustworthy and was inclined to recommend him for employment. But Gulick had one reservation, which he laid out to Representative Voorhis in a letter dated August 28, 1937: Atkins claimed to be the heir of oil-rich land in Oklahoma.

"Atkins claims that during the World War he was a member of the Lost Battalion and also that he is one-half Creek Indian," Voorhis wrote. Mr. Atkins had shown Gulick an allotment deed as proof. Gulick did a little research on his own. Could this be the real Tommy, the one named in all those lawsuits from 1914 to 1929? The question seemed important enough that Gulick wanted to enlist the help of Congressman Voorhis. The case caught Voorhis's attention. He wrote to the Interior Department in 1937, forwarding Gulick's request to "provide photostatic copies of the original [allotment deed] with the Department of the Interior seal for U.S. Indian Service. If the above deeds and service record of the above Thomas Atkins could be verified by your office, it would greatly assist me in my investigation."[3]

Also in the documents was a handwritten letter from 1923 addressed to the Bureau of Indian Affairs from a man in Wewoka, Oklahoma. He explained that there had been "some crooked work don [sic] and my lawyers have refused to talk to me." This man lived on a farm in Seminole County and requested that someone from the Indian Office come visit him so he could explain everything. The letter was signed, "Respectfully yours, Tommy Atkins, Creek Rolle [sic] no 7913."

Another Tommy Atkins surfaced on Broadway in New York. There was a Minnie Atkins in Oilton, Oklahoma. There was a Minnie Burgess in Texas who in the 1940s claimed that she had been born Minnie Atkins and had been adopted by a white family after attending the Carlisle Indian Industrial School. This Minnie wrote repeatedly to Carlisle, hoping to retrieve records of her attendance there. All of this was part of a central classified file on all things Tommy Atkins. Most of these claimants received some sort of reply from the government, but after the FBI's investigation, no government agency seems to have taken the claims seriously.

One day, my mother-in-law, Lenore Dolin, sent me a photo from her local supermarket: Tommy Atkins mangoes were on sale in California. Tommy Atkins mangoes were not valued for their sweetness, but, according to Wikipedia, they have a "very long shelf life and tolerance of handling and transportation with little or no bruising or degradation."

A research librarian at the University of Tulsa was working on an exhibit about World War I when I visited in 2021 to consult its holdings on Alice Robertson, Minnie's old teacher.

"You know who Tommy Atkins was in the Great War?" he asked me.

I had no idea.

"Tommy Atkins" was slang for a common soldier in the British army, he said. Like a British GI Joe. Tommy Atkins became popular slang during World War I to describe a generic enlisted man.

A nobody, an everybody.

"A FICTITIOUS PERSON"

In 1923, Charles Peterkin—Minnie's first love interest from Leaven-worth, now a retired soldier living in Somerville, Massachusetts—wrote to Commissioner Burke. He referenced the Sally Atkins case, which had concluded a year prior, and then something about the US Supreme Court ruling in favor of his now-deceased common law ex-wife. He had been deposed about the case years before. At the time, he had said he knew nothing about a Tommy Atkins, throwing more doubt on Minnie's story. Now he was just as confused as everyone else. "Was Minnie Atkins decided as the mother of Tommy Atkins?" he asked Commissioner Burke. Peterkin never received a response from the government.

The paper ghosts of Tommy Atkins haunted the nation, from small towns in Kansas to Los Angeles and New York. Rumors of Tommy's un-demise bedeviled the Bureau of Indian Affairs, the FBI, the Sand Springs Home, and various lease hounds during the Depression. The government had tried repeatedly to demonstrate that the enrollment of Tommy was based on a fraud—that the only proper thing to do was to cancel his enrollment and return his two eighty-acre tracts of land in Creek County to the Muscogee Nation. But the 1922 Supreme Court ruling had vanquished that possibility.

The last attorney general to seriously consider re-prosecuting the case was A. Mitchell Palmer. Palmer is mostly remembered for his repression of radicals under the Woodrow Wilson administration, and he never pretended to be a "friend of the Indian." But when news of Charles Page's US Supreme Court victory in the Tommy Atkins case crossed his desk in 1922, he was resolute in challenging the power-ful oilman and philanthropist. Palmer wrote to the secretary of the interior that, despite all the court rulings, "the evidence is clear and convincing that Tommy Atkins, the Indian who was enrolled, was a fictitious person."[4]

He wanted to appeal yet again, but the US Supreme Court had issued its ruling—there was no higher court to hear another appeal. The Supreme Court had taken little time considering the case. The court considered only whether the finding of the Dawes Commission should be impeached due to fraud. The court found no clear evidence of fraud in Tommy's case, and absent this, the Dawes Commission needed to be respected as the authority of who was and was not an Indian. Minnie Atkins, now dead, could finally "quiet title" her land.

In the end, myth triumphed over reality. No amount of evidence, no volume of letters from government agents would change the prevailing social and economic order in Oklahoma. The last surviving original allottees passed from this earth in the 1990s, just as I was becoming aware of what it meant to grow up in a place that had once staked its identity on being the Oil Capital of the World. I was shocked to learn that an Indian burial ground actually backed up to my mother's house in quiet Maple Ridge. The world was shocked, in 2020, to learn that there were mass graves in the shadow of downtown Tulsa from the 1921 Race Massacre. The crime had been almost perfectly executed. Almost.

During the second half of the twentieth century, Tulsa city leaders labored to brand my hometown as a friendly mid-market consumer testing site in the American heartland. When it came to history and identity, we were a business-friendly, low-tax city with good airline connections to Dallas, lots of churches, and cheap real estate. The violence, mayhem, and state-sponsored dispossession of Native and Black people was mostly over. The Bucket of Blood was long gone. Charles Page was just some mustachioed, rotund guy cast in bronze on a pedestal, remembered as one of the state's most generous men. He was inaugurated into the Tulsa Hall of Fame during its first round of inductees, in 1987.

The custodians of collective memory endeavored to clean up the mess of Oklahoma's post-statehood history. The Osage Reign of Terror, the preponderance of the Ku Klux Klan in state government, widespread lynching, the 1921 Race Massacre, the crimes documented in this book—all of it needed to be tidied up and tucked away in archives where no one would bother to look. But ghosts have funny ways of haunting us. They are not necessarily apparitions in the night, tormenting us about the dead. They need not be demons torturing our souls. Sometimes ghosts register as faint voices from the past, telling us stories in whispers.

We can only ignore these voices for so long. The passage of time has not healed the wounds here. It has only deepened those wounds, passing them on to other generations in Crook County and beyond.

TAKE ME BACK TO TULSA

In August 2023, I presented what I knew about Charles Page's involvement in the Tommy Atkins episode at the Will Rogers Memorial Museum outside Tulsa. As I spoke, I noticed an elderly woman near the front row shaking her head slightly. Her eyes gradually welled up with tears. She approached me after the talk. "I grew up around the home," she said quietly. "That's what it was—a home. We never said orphanage."

I told her I was sorry if I offended her, but the historical record of the Sand Springs Home had another side that needed to be told. She shook her head again. "Just a little critique," she said. "Never say 'orphanage' when you're talking about the Sand Springs Home," she said.

She had a point. In a typical orphanage, the goal is to place children with families that can give them a permanent home. That was not the case in Sand Springs. Once the children were placed under the guardianship of the Sand Springs Home, they could not be adopted out. They remained there until Charles Page or the home superintendent decided they were fit to move out and sustain themselves on their own.

As the children grew up in the home, Page placed them with employers along the Sand Springs Line. Many people from the home worked at Commander Mills, a textile plant that churned out 185 miles of cotton bed linens per week. Some children worked at the amusement park, the zoo, or one of the home's farms. They bottled the water that was essential for Tulsa before it had a reliable source of drinking water. Boys and men worked on the Sand Springs Railway, in a steel plant, even in a chandelier factory. All these industries were owned, at least partially, by the Sand Springs Home. Page and Frank Long corresponded about these industries, about how to develop the maximum productivity from the workers. Long worried about investigations from the Oklahoma Labor Commission. He conceded that they had to give the girls and women one day off a week to do shopping and laundry. It seems that Page need not have worried too much, as the second governor of Oklahoma, Lee Cruce, was also one of his attorneys, but there were pesky reporters from the *Tulsa World* to contend with.

As I started to release some of my findings on social media, I heard a rumor going around Tulsa that Page had put Muscogee children into the Sand Springs Home so that he could become their guardian and then pillage their estates. This did not seem quite right to me. Mixing Indian estates into the home's affairs would have invited federal investigators into the books of the Sand Springs Home. It would have also violated some unwritten racial taboos in this segregated city.

Still, I wanted to research the possibility further. I asked a Sand Springs journalist for help in trying to clear up some of the enigmas about the operation of the home. I'd followed the journalist on social media and they had taken some brave stands that were unpopular in the small town. This journalist replied to my Facebook message with a clear message: If you're going to throw stones at that bronze statue, don't expect me to give you the rocks. My friend Lisa, a native of Sand Springs, was right: Page was a secular saint, and to question the mainstream narrative was a form of heresy that could get me into trouble.

One could chalk up this ignorance to small-town, parochial thinking. Sand Springs, after all, is an overwhelmingly white, mostly conservative town of around twenty thousand people. But Page's reputation was solidified in nearby Tulsa, a place that has always believed itself to be more worldly and enlightened than the rest of Oklahoma. It was Tulsa that placed Charles Page in its inaugural Hall of Fame class of 1987. Tulsa named the main road connecting its downtown to Sand Springs Charles Page Boulevard, despite what Eugene Lorton had revealed about him in the 1910s and 1920s. It was this Charles Page that came on my hotel television in 2019 in an ad for BancFirst.

The *Tulsa World*, apparently ignoring its own archives from a century past, continues the mythologizing of Charles Page in occasional tributes, including a lengthy one in 2010, on the occasion of his 150th birthday. "Charles Page is and always will be the Father of Sand Springs," wrote one Sandite in the pages of the *World*: "Every time I pass the statue of Charles Page and see the grand building that is now our Museum, I am thankful for Charles Page and his sincere caring for children," wrote another Sand Springs resident.

But not everyone trusts this mainstream narrative. "I will not allow his bones to rest peacefully," a Muscogee descendant, Darla Ashton, told me. Her great-grandfather's allotment had been divided up by the Sand Springs Home and then sold off to help create Keystone Lake, a reservoir west of Tulsa. A later judgment ruled that the home had illegally portioned restricted Indian lands. Ashton is a descendant of the Naharkey family. Her grandmother was still considered "incompetent" by Tulsa courts into the 1970s. Ashton wanted justice, not revenge. She has tried to have a landmark near the Emarthla and Naharkey allotments on Tulsa's Turkey Mountain named in honor of the original Muscogee tribal town that created modern Tulsa. She continues to be ignored.

After Apollonia and I drove out to Tommy's allotment, we found that Minnie Atkins's house still stood, just about a mile north of the Sand Springs Museum. We contemplated knocking on the door. It was unlikely that meeting the people living there would yield anything interesting, but the residents might find it interesting to know their house was once ground zero for national scandal and the most litigated oil lease in the state's history. As we started up the path, Apollonia noticed that the cars in the driveway had license plates issued by the Osage Nation.

Apollonia told me to go back to the car. The people living there were Native Americans, but not Muscogees. David Grann's book *Killers of the Flower Moon*, about the reign of terror in Osage County, had been on everyone's reading lists in those days. Grann revealed how Osage citizens were killed to obtain their headrights to oil and gas royalties. I went back to the car and watched as Apollonia knocked on the door. She left a note, with a few words in Mvskoke, saying she was a Native American woman who had come across some interesting research on the house's original owner.

A few hours later, the resident of Minnie's old house called Apollonia. She told her not to come knocking again. "I have a shotgun and I'm not afraid to use it," the woman said. Then she said that she had learned to be extremely wary of strangers. Because Apollonia was a Native American woman, she wanted to hear about our research about Minnie Atkins. But she needed to be careful about it. This history wasn't dead and given the hostility of the current governor to Indigenous sovereignty, it wasn't even past. The woman held an advanced degree from Yale University and had been involved in Osage Nation politics. She'd never heard of the Tommy Atkins story, but she was not surprised at all that it had occurred here in Sand Springs.

On that same trip, a geologist friend, Shane Matson, took me around in his oil field truck on some back roads of the Glenn Pool, on the border of Tulsa and Creek Counties. Shane still operates oil wells on the land. He pointed to a cluster of trees on the prairie. There was a cemetery over there, but he knew nothing about the people buried at the site. I pushed back some weeds and saw a name: Poloke. I later found that the allotment had yielded little oil, but it did yield millions of cubic feet of gas. A farmer had made the mistake of lighting a match in his cornfield near the Poloke land in the early 1900s. The flame was visible from miles away. The farmer was dead in an instant. Poloke, another ghost whose presence had almost been erased in the aftermath of statehood.

Shane had hired a man to look after his modest drilling operations, and we met him in a trailer just as a thunderstorm approached. We cracked open some beers, and the roughneck asked me what I was doing, kicking around this old oil field whose heyday had passed over a century ago. I told him that so many of the Muscogee allottees' stories were mysteries, and that one had caught my attention. We talked about the Poloke cemetery off in the weeds, a mile away, and how so little was known about the people buried there, away from any public road. I mentioned the name Charles Page.

This rugged oil field worker, the model of a laconic, tough, beer-drinking Okie, leaped up from the lawn chair beside the pickup truck. He muttered something about his mother. His face went white. Shane asked him what had spooked him. The man said that something about the name Charles Page startled him. His mother had grown up in the Sand Springs Home and it was not the idyllic place everyone understood it to be. I wanted the man to tell me more about his mother's experience at the home, but he was not in the mood. The storm was closing in. I didn't push him; besides, I had already been haunted enough by the heap of grave markers and tombstones in a neglected corner of prairie grass.

When I got home that night, I looked up more recent stories about the Sand Springs Home. In the 1940s, after all the Tommy Atkins claimants had finally died and postwar recovery came to Page's model town, the story was mostly positive: Christmas celebrations, Charles Page High School graduates moving on to a bright future, improvements to the widows' colony. There had been some labor troubles, some accusations of tax dodging, but most of the stories about life in Charles Page's model town were positive. Charles Page High School was the site of a bitter fight over desegregation in the 1960s. There was some discussion about Page's attempt to resettle victims of the Tulsa Race Massacre of 1921 in a segregated area of town called Southside Addition. Some people tried to understand this act as yet another example of Page's benevolence, but after reading about Page's involvement with Sadie James, I knew there had to be more to the story. There was also a very disturbing story about a rape by a superintendent of the home in 1969.*

Perhaps the home had been a peaceful refuge for hundreds of children after the Atkins trials ended. But that was not the entire story. Turning over rocks in the Tommy Atkins case had led from one uncomfortable truth to another. I never set out to take down Charles Page or any other venerable man from Tulsa's heyday as the Oil Capital of the World. After all, in one way or another these people were all tied to my own family's history. The first Russell Cobb helped establish All Souls Unitarian Church with Richard Lloyd Jones, the editor of the *Tulsa Tribune* and a stalwart ally of Charles Page. That church has become a bastion of liberalism in Tulsa, but the truth was clear: it had been founded by an editor who race-baited white Tulsa into a pogrom of the city's Black population. The more I looked at the web of connections among Tulsa's oilmen, the more connections I saw, from the church to the country club to my childhood home in Sunset Terrace, built on

---

* The superintendent of the home in 1969 was Rev. Floyd D. Sutterfield, also a pastor for the True Baptist Church of Sand Springs. On September 30, 1969, a fourteen-year-old girl living at the home was taken from a hospital to the dormitory of the orphanage. Judge Bussey stated that the girl "left the house sometime that afternoon and the defendant [Sutterfield] called her upstairs. She further testified that upon going upstairs, the defendant pushed her down on a bed, and had intercourse with her. She testified that the defendant had other acts of intercourse with her prior to this time. On cross-examination, she testified that the defendant had always been nice to her, and that she at first had denied the defendant's having intercourse with her, when one Betty Lou Cranston questioned her about it." *Sutterfield v. State*, Oklahoma Court of Criminal Appeals, case number A-16628, October 20, 1971.

the family cemetery of Tuckabache. There's a Hollywood horror film trope about a suburban subdivision built on an ancient Indian burial ground, but my boyhood home backed up to a quite modern Muscogee family cemetery. That cemetery had been dug up to make way for the quaint bungalows like mine on Twenty-Seventh Place and Cincinnati Avenue during the Oil Capital heyday. It's enough to drive a perfectly rational person to believe in curses.

My people—white oilmen—had covered up so much, starting with nearly seventy-five years of official silence about the 1921 Tulsa Race Massacre. My mother was the manager of a university bookstore in the middle of the neighborhood—Greenwood—razed by a white mob. During the 1990s, I never heard anyone speak of this event, and it certainly was not discussed in my elite private school. The 1921 massacre, I have come to believe, was but one atrocity among other acts designed to impose a white, petro-Christian supremacy on a land with a rich history of Indigenous, Black, and mixed-race identities, religions, and political organizations. What came before this era of violence was no golden age; as I've documented here, there was plenty of corruption, exploitation, and hypocrisy during Indian Territory days. But that era represented a time and place in which people of color held enough land, wealth, and political power to experiment in self-determination.

For so long, "dead Indians" in land titles and oil leases were vague inconveniences. As I researched and wrote this book, the past was coming into focus, almost like fine-tuning a microscope on a leaf of a tree. At first it was a vague story of land theft, oil money, and difficult-to-pronounce Indigenous names. Those names started to acquire vitality and detail. After a while, these were not dead Indians but people who had lived complicated lives during a period in which a modern industrialized society implanted itself in a land only recently dominated by tribal laws and customs. As the lives of people like Sadie James, Minnie Atkins, Bettie Mann, and Sam Brown started to take shape, I wanted to share their stories. I talked about my research on social media and found a small community of people who also wanted to know this shadow history of the Oil Capital of the World.

It was a hell of a time to seek a redress of past wrongs. In May 2021, Oklahoma governor Kevin Stitt signed into law House Bill 1775, which aimed to control how history was taught in the state's schools. Among other things, it was now illegal to teach anything that would make an "individual . . . feel discomfort, guilt, anguish or any other form of psychological distress on account of their race or sex." At the same time, the eastern half of the state was still trying to figure out what it meant that the US Supreme Court, in *McGirt v. Oklahoma* (2020), had upheld the region's status as Indian Country. The city of Tulsa welcomed President Joe Biden to town in June 2021 to commemorate the centennial of the 1921 Race Massacre, while still refusing reparations to the three living survivors of that tragedy. There was talk of reconciliation, but how could such a thing be accomplished without even the largely symbolic gesture of paying reparations to the three survivors of premeditated racial violence?

Meanwhile, I was still trying to sort out the affairs of my mother's estate in the middle of a pandemic. I inherited my boyhood home when my mother died in May 2019. After a tenant moved out a couple of years later, I was unsure about what to do with this property and another I had inherited from my grandmother and was partially raised in. Should I sell the properties and move on? I thought that, after a lifetime in which a gravitational force always drew me back to Tulsa, I might now begin to put the place in the rearview mirror. Maybe selling the two cottages would break the curse.

It would have been a good time to cut my ties to the place and move on with life in Canada. But I, too, was haunted by the ghosts of Crook County. When I discovered that a chapter of the Tommy Atkins story unfolded in my adopted hometown of Edmonton, I knew I had to write this book. It was in Edmonton—of all places—that Oklahoma oilmen opposed to Page, along with a Pinkerton agent, caught up with Sally Atkins in 1919. This was the origin story of Sally's lawsuit against the Sand Springs Home that wound up in the Supreme Court in 1922.

Some of Sally's descendants still live in Alberta, including Brandy Fredrickson, a city councilor in Drayton Valley, a small town southwest of Edmonton; Bobbi West in Atlanta, Georgia; Vivian Webb in Wichita, Kansas; and Rhonda McFee in Tulsa, Oklahoma. They want to know if their relative was the millionaire boy with three mothers.

The web of kinship to Tommy Atkins includes people of African descent in Canada, Kansas, and Georgia; it includes white-passing people in Texas and California; it includes Muscogee citizens in Oklahoma of all races. Despite nearly a century in which the story of this boy and his fortune was scrubbed from the official history of the Oil Capital of the World, the history was carried within dozens—if not hundreds—of descendants. Even after six years of working on this story, I cannot solve this mystery in a tidy way. I am certainly in no position to say who deserves the tens of millions of dollars in oil money that came from the allotment of Creek Indian #7913. But Tommy's descendants, at the very least, deserve the truth, as best as we can know it.

In fact, we all deserve that, no matter how uncomfortable it might make us feel.

ACKNOWLEDGMENTS

It seems customary to thank an author's family at the end of an acknowledgments section, but I'm putting my wife, Dr. Rachel Hertz Cobb, first and foremost. My sounding board, editor, audience for rants and dad jokes, Rachel heard it all as the research and writing took shape. She also held down the fort at home when I ran off to various archives for weeks at a time, making sure August and Henry Cobb were taken care of. My children often wandered over to my desk, asking if I was obsessing over that Tommy Atkins guy again, when it was a beautiful day to do anything other than squint at scanned documents from 1915. Almost invariably, I *was* obsessing over Tommy. Now that this wild and woolly story is in the bag, maybe these kids will catch the history bug. A step toward making the world a better place is understanding how it got this way in the first place. This book is dedicated to you, my loves.

As I wrapped up my last book in 2019, I asked questions about the enigmatic Tommy Atkins with a small group of Tulsans who had been part of an informal research cohort. Two of those people, Apollonia Piña and Gina Covington, followed me down the Tommy Atkins rabbit hole. Apollonia and Gina were early sleuths on the case, turning over rocks and pulling documents that had not been examined for a century. As we began the journey, Apollonia and I enlisted the help of Allison Herrera, an audio producer, to create a podcast. We went on hasty field trips around the Muscogee Nation, and although the podcast never panned out, Allison organized a bike tour that helped people visualize all the major scenes and characters.

At this early stage of the research, I met an array of intelligent people that filled in my many knowledge gaps about Indian Territory, allotment, Indigenous identity, and oil exploration. RaeLynn Butler, Jason Salsman, Gano Perez, and Turner Hunt at the Muscogee Nation all helped me reorient my thinking to see this tumultuous chapter of history from an Indigenous perspective. Veronica Pipestem guided me around the Creek Council House and later helped me research materials at Tulsa's Gilcrease Museum. Wilson Pipestem, Graham Lee Brewer, and Chief Jim Gray provided some broader insights about Oklahoma and Indian Country that got me questioning the entire meta-narrative of Tulsa as the Oil Capital of the World. Consultations with Dr. Betty Gerber helped me—I hope—understand the ways Muscogee tribal towns worked. Dr. Richard Grounds of the Yuchi Language Project provided some leads about the enigmas of S. W. Brown, Sr. and Jr.

Talking to the descendants of Muscogee allottees in the Tulsa area brought home the reality that history lives within us, whether we acknowledge it or not. Those conversations with Darla Ashton, Tatianna Duncan, Rhonda McFee, Vivian Webb, and others were not always easy, but this book would not be the same without that living connection to history. A shout-out to some true Tulsans who have persisted in shining lights in the darkness involving the city's past and future: Aaron Griffith, Marlin Lavanhar, Lindsey Claire Smith, Michael Wallis, the late Reverend Carlton Pearson, Michael Mason, Jane Beckwith, Whitney Chapman, and Randy Krehbiel. Without a network of brilliant artists, historians, and writers around Tulsa's Center for Public Secrets and the defunct This Land Press, I'm not sure who my audience is. Stuart Hetherwood helped bring the art and images in this book to life. Stuart's eye for detail and his ability to visualize Tulsa history were instrumental in the completion of the book.

Teaching at the Center for Poets and Writers at OSU–Tulsa in the spring of 2023 helped me refine my craft and methods with some wonderful people, including Dana Schuler Drummond, Doug Drummond, the poet Zhenya Yevtushenko, Ashley Daly, Arena Mueller, Kathe Crapster, and Carol Rose Little. In particular, I want to honor Darla Ashton, the granddaughter of Millie Naharkey, whose family suffered so much during Tulsa's oil boom. Thank you, Erin Turner, for inviting me back to Tulsa to talk about Charles Page and for the opportunity to connect with artists involved in difficult but honest conversations about appropriation, history, and reconciliation. Dr. Neville Hoad, an honorary Tulsan and fellow Longhorn by way of South Africa, saw the value in this work and helped me see how it intersected with the broader phenomenon of racial capitalism. Neville is also just an all-around mensch. The irrepressible writer Mark Singer has been an inspiration and a mentor.

I am Russell Cobb IV, but I did not follow the preceding three generations of Russell Cobbs into the oil business. I knew very little about petroleum: how it was formed, how it is extracted, the laws governing its ownership. I am indebted to Shane Matson, a petroleum geologist, for showing me the ropes and driving me around the fairways of Oklahoma oil fields. I would also like to thank the Cherokee geologists who told me Creek County is still known as "Crook County" in the business.

Although I am not a historian by academic training, I have had the remarkable privilege of working with historians and learning the craft of history writing from some brilliant people, especially Dr. Brian Hosmer. A key piece of this research came together over the summer of 2021, when I had a Masterson Fellowship at the Western History Collections at the University of Oklahoma. Dr. Todd Fuller helped me locate materials, contextualize the collections, and provide all the support a researcher could ever want. My sojourns to OU would have been a disaster without the help of Dr. Joy Pendley and her whole family. My Tulsa fam also helped out with a bed, a meal, a drink, and endless nights of storytelling: Apollonia, Bob Blakemore, Lisa Stephenson Blakemore, and Sunny Mills.

I am indebted to the work of several librarians across two countries and several states. In particular, I want to thank Rose Buchanan at the National Archives, who located the FBI investigation into the allegations that Tommy Atkins's siblings made against the Dawes Commission and the Sand Springs Home. I gave Rose a few random names, and before I knew it, I was looking at files signed by the likes of J. Edgar Hoover and Woodrow Wilson. Everyone at the Oklahoma History Center was helpful, and the center was a delight to visit. The late Marc Carlson at the University of Tulsa Special Collections helped me establish the Alice Robertson connection to this story and encouraged this work, even as it became clear that it might upset some powerful people.

At the University of Alberta, my home university, the library provided some essential support. Celine Gareau-Brennan helped me find some indispensable materials. I have been lucky enough to work with people who have not only tolerated my deviation from my initial field of scholarship (twentieth-century Latin American literature) but actually supported it. There are many colleagues to thank, but I will mention Dr. Laura Beard and Dr. Vicky Ruetalo, chairs of the Modern Languages and Cultural Studies Department, as well as Dr. Gordon Gow for their support. Discovering that there were Tommy Atkins footprints all over Alberta, including some in Edmonton, led me to collaborate with Kyla Fisher of ECAMP (Edmonton City as Museum Project), Deborah Dobbins of the Shiloh Centre for Multicultural Roots, and Allan Goddard of the Breton Museum. Research assistants at the University of Alberta were a tremendous help, and I managed somehow to get all of them interested in the story. Thank you to Chelsea Ball and Luke Bennett for tracking down documents at NARA Fort Worth and Kansas City, respectively. These RAs helped organize the thousands of court transcripts, interviews, press clippings, and letters associated with the case. Thank you, Kerry Sluchinski, Saman Rezaei, Shahab Nadimi, Wei Zeng, and Josie Baker.

Getting the Tommy Atkins story into a book form started with an assist from Michael Hingston, who helped me refine the proposal. The story caught the eye of Maria Rogers of the Tobias Agency, who helped me tame this wild beast of a story into something that an editor might actually acquire. Thank you, Maria, for your editorial detail and tenacity. Thanks as well to my current agent at Tobias, Jacqueline Lipton, for the encouragement. Several editors were interested, but I could tell Catherine Tung of Beacon Press understood the narrative and its implications for Indigenous, environmental, and regional history. Catherine manages to simultaneously see the Big Picture while also attending to the nuances of language and complicated chronology here. She reshaped the manuscript, refined the prose, and finally convinced me to tell the story straight. My most profound gratitude goes to you, Catherine, for everything you've done on this project. The entire team at Beacon has understood not only the importance of this story but also the importance of telling it the right way; thank you Susan Lumenello and Brittany Wallace for your input and guidance. Kate Scott helped polish the prose, the sources, and the clarity of what you have here. Any errors herein, however, lie at my feet.

I am thankful to *Great Plains Quarterly* and the *Chronicles of Oklahoma* for publishing aspects of the Tommy Atkins story to a scholarly audience, and to colleagues and editors Dr. Kalenda Eaton and Dr. Elizabeth Bass, respectively, for helping set the facts down in a methodical manner, which is entirely contrary to my harebrained modus operandi.

Friends from Alberta to Oklahoma kept my spirits up by listening to my research rants and asking the right questions. Conversations about oil, identity, and greed kept the Power Team Running Club going (Nathan, Sarah, Levi, Omar, and Josie) on occasion. Daniel Laforest, Dave Sauriol, and Evan McIntyre were always ready to listen over beers. Fellow Edmonton scribes and friends Jana Pruden and Danielle Paradis also provided insights, questions, and encouragement.

My brother from another mother (but the same father), Candler Barnett, stepped in to help at the end by tracking down some Charles Page miscellanea. Candler, you broke the Cobb curse! Lastly, I must acknowledge the love and support of my mother, Patricia Songer Cobb (1942–2019), who cultivated an appreciation of Tulsa weirdness in me. The contrarian spirit of my grandmother Dorothy Hogan Bennett (1922–2001) flows through these pages. I know my grand-mère would find it amusing that, after all these years, I ended up writing a book whose timeline begins six miles up the old Texas Road from her resting place in the Checotah Cemetery.

NOTES

Unpublished primary source material from the Atkins trials and investigations are from three main sources.

1. Materials relating to the investigation of R. C. Allen and the subsequent investigation of political interference by Charles Page and R. A. Josey are housed at the National Archives and Records Administration (NARA) main depository in Washington, DC. The complete record for this collection is Central Classified Files (CCF), 1907–1939, Entry 121-A, Record Group 75, Bureau of Indian Affairs, file 83406-1915-154-Creek, National Archives, Washington, DC. Whenever possible, I have given an author, title, and date to specify the file. This collection is cited as CCF, 83406-1915-154-Creek.

2. Materials from the FBI, correspondence with the Atkins family, and other materials relating to the allotment of Tommy Atkins are in three boxes: CCF, 1907–1939, Entry PI-163, Record Group 75, 121A, File 112829-1914-053-Creek, NARA, Washington, DC. This is cited as CCF 112829-1914-053-Creek, with as much detail on names and dates as could be located.

3. For *United States v. Minnie Atkins et al.*, Equity 2131 of the Eastern District of Oklahoma, along with an appeals court proceeding, federal trial records, including court transcripts, correspondence with attorneys, and exhibits for the courtroom are housed at the NARA repository in Kansas City, as of September 2022 (formerly housed at NARA, Fort Worth, Texas). Materials from these boxes are cited by names, dates, and titles when possible. The case is cited herein as *US v. Minnie Atkins et al.* 2131.

Cases in Oklahoma county courts, especially the Creek County Court, generally have little to no presence online. They must be looked up by a courthouse clerk on microfilm and the documents then pulled from a warehouse. I have provided as many detailed records about these cases as possible, but important pieces are missing. The 1929 lawsuit brought by the Atkins family members of African descent alleging the murder of Minnie Atkins by Charles Page or his associates—*Nathaniel Atkins et al. v. A. G. McMillan, District Superintendent of the Five Civilized Tribes, et al.*, District Court of Creek County, Okla., No. 18395—can be looked up at the Creek County Courthouse.

PROLOGUE

1. David McClintick, *Stealing from the Rich: The Home-Stake Oil Swindle* (New York: Evans, 1977); "Top Personalities Reported Bilked in $100 Million Scheme," *Los Angeles Times*, June 26, 1974.

2. Tales of Russell Cobb Jr.'s decadence and profligacy are documented in McClintick, *Stealing from the Rich*. This book sat on the bookshelf of Cobb's widow, Jane Cobb (my paternal grandmother), with an inscription from her about the "son of a bitch" author, a *Wall Street Journal* reporter. Jane was embarrassed by the attention from the book but still displayed it in her living room and brought it down occasionally to demonstrate that the family's ruin was not attributable to her but rather to her husband, an incorrigible rake.

3. Patricia Nelson Limerick, "Land, Justice, and Angie Debo: Telling the Truth to—and About—Your Neighbors," *Great Plains Quarterly* 21, no. 2 (Fall 2001): 264, https://digitalcommons.unl.edu/greatplainsquarterly/2209.

4. Department of the Interior, *Annual Report of the Department of the Interior*, vol. 2 (Washington, DC: Government Printing Office, 1883), 731, https://www.google.ca/books/edition/Annual_Report_of_the_Department_of_the_I/L2IvAQAAMAAJ.

5. David Truer, *The Heartbeat of Wounded Knee: Native America from 1890 to the Present* (New York: Penguin, 2019), 113.

6. "Indian's Artistic Taste Excels in Designing of Fine Motor Cars," *Muskogee Times-Democrat*, May 23, 1925, https://www.newspapers.com/article/muskogee-times-democrat-indians-artisti/130855034.

7. See Suzanne H. Schrems and Cynthia J. Wolff, "Politics and Libel: Angie Debo and the Publication of *and Still the Waters Run*," *Western Historical Quarterly* 22, no. 2 (1991): 185–203, https://doi.org/10.2307/969205.

8. Angie Debo, *And Still the Waters Run: The Betrayal of the Five Civilized Tribes* (Princeton, NJ: Princeton University Press, 2022), https://press.princeton.edu/books/paperback/9780691237770/and-still-the-waters-run.

9. Debo, *And Still the Waters Run*, 274.

10. See Angie Debo and Connie Cronley, *A Life on Fire: Oklahoma's Kate Barnard* (Norman: University of Oklahoma Press, 2021). Cronley documents Barnard's ill-fated attempt to achieve justice for Indian minors.

11. Opal Bennefield Clark, *A Fool's Enterprise: The Life of Charles Page* (Sand Springs, OK: Dexter Publishing, 1988).

12. Debo, *And Still the Waters Run*, 274.

13. Kent Carter, *The Dawes Commission and the Allotment of the Five Civilized Tribes 1893–1914* (Orem, UT: Ancestry Publishing, 1999), 153n131.

14. Carter, *The Dawes Commission*, 153.

15. Ruth Sheldon Knowles, *The Greatest Gamblers* (Norman: University of Oklahoma Press, 1959), 129.

16. "Oklahoma," *U.S. News & World Report*, https://www.usnews.com/news/best-states/oklahoma; US Attorney's Office, Northern District of Oklahoma, "Drumright Man Pleads Guilty to Stealing More Than $400,000 from an Illinois Oil and Gas Company," press release, Feb. 12, 2021, https://www.justice.gov/usao-ndok/pr/drumright-man-pleads-guilty-stealing-more-400000-illinois-oil-and-gas-company.

17. Fernando Coronil, *The Magical State: Nature, Money, and Modernity in Venezuela* (Chicago: University of Chicago Press, 1997).

18. Loren Steffy, "Out of Gas," *Texas Monthly*, July 2016, https://www.texasmonthly.com/articles/the-fall-of-aubrey-mcclendon.

CHAPTER 1: GROWING UP IN THE TERRITORY WITH MINNIE ATKINS

1. Christopher Haveman, *Rivers of Sand: Creek Emigration, Relocation, and Ethnic Cleansing in the American South* (Lincoln: University of Nebraska Press), 11.

2. Mary Jane Warde, "Civil War Refugees," *The Encyclopedia of Oklahoma History and Culture*, Oklahoma Historical Society, https://www.okhistory.org/publications/enc/entry?entry=CI013.

3. Mary Phillips, "Another Buried Treasure Tale Is Uncovered in Oklahoma," *The Oklahoman*, Aug. 29, 2016, https://www.oklahoman.com/story/lifestyle/2016/08/29/the-archivist-another-buried-treasure-tale-is-uncovered-in-oklahoma/60654924007.

4. *Organization of the Territory of Oklahoma*, House Report No. 263 Pt. 2, 50th Cong., 1st Sess. (1888).

5. Pleasant Porter, Applications for Enrollment of the Commission to the Five Civilized Tribes,1898–1914. Record Group 75: Records of the Bureau of Indian Affairs, 1793–1999; National Archives, Washington, DC.

6. Stan Hoig, "Boomer Movement," *The Encyclopedia of Oklahoma History and Culture*, Oklahoma Historical Society, https://www.okhistory.org/publications/enc/entry.php?entry=BO011, accessed Dec. 4, 2023.

CHAPTER 2: "INTO THE LIGHT BEFORE"

1. Augustus Ward Loomis, *Scenes in the Indian Country* (Philadelphia: Presbyterian Board of Publication, 1859), 40.

2. Robert A. Trennert, "From Carlisle to Phoenix: The Rise and Fall of the Indian Outing System, 1878–1930," *Pacific Historical Review* 52, no. 3 (1983): 267–91, https://doi.org/10.2307/3639003.

3. Alice Robertson left her papers to the University of Tulsa, an institution she helped create. For Robertson's correspondence, including a letter from Minnie Atkins, see Papers of the Robertson and Worcester families, 1815–1932, 1931-001, Department of Special Collections and University Archives, McFarlin Library, University of Tulsa.

4. Nettie Terry Brown, "The Missionary World of Ann Eliza Worcester Robertson," PhD diss., University of North Texas, 1978, https://digital.library.unt.edu/ark:/67531/metadc332832/m2/1/high_res_d/1002783639-Brown.pdf.

5. Ben Marshall, "Untitled," *The School News*, vol. 1, no. 9, Carlisle, Pennsylvania, Feb. 1881, Carlisle Indian School Digital Resources Center, https://carlisleindian.dickinson.edu.

6. National Park Service, "The Carlisle Indian Industrial School: Assimilation with Education After the Indian Wars," https://www.nps.gov/articles/the-carlisle-indian-industrial-school-assimilation-with-education-after-the-indian-wars-teaching-with-historic-places.htm.

7. Cecily Hilleary, "Indian Boarding Schools 'Outings': Apprenticeships or Indentured Servitude?" Voice of America, updated Nov. 14, 2021, https://www .voanews.com/a/indian-boarding-schools-outings-apprendiceships-or-indentured -servitude/6300451.html.

8. Genevieve Bell, "Telling Stories Out of School: Remembering the Carlisle Indian Industrial School, 1879–1918," PhD diss., Stanford University, 1998, https://login.ezproxy.library.ualberta.ca/login?url=https://www.proquest.com /dissertations-theses/telling-stories-out-school-remembering-carlisle/docview /304448530/se-2.

9. Tally D. Fugate, "Anti-Suffrage Association," *The Encyclopedia of Oklahoma History and Culture*, Oklahoma Historical Society, https://www.okhistory .org/publications/enc/entry?entry=AN014.

10. "Alleges Extreme Cruelty," *Twice-a-Week Oklahoman*, Apr. 22, 1904.

11. "Woman to Face Larceny Charge—Indian Peddler of Champagne," *Tulsa World*, Nov. 25, 1906.

12. "Arrest Two Women on Robbery Charge," *Daily Oklahoman*, Feb. 2, 1908.

CHAPTER 3: BECOMING A LADY

1. George H. Hyde, Postcard to Richard H. Pratt, July 11, 1884, RG 75, Series 1327, Folder 2485, Box 50, National Archives and Records Administration (henceforth cited as NARA), available online: Minnie Atkins Student File, Carlisle Indian School Digital Resource Center, https://carlisleindian.dickinson.edu /student_files/minnie-atkins-student-file.

2. *US v. Minnie Atkins et al.* 2131, "Brief on Behalf of the Defendants, Minnie Folk (Née Atkins), Charles Page, et al.," memo to US District Court of the Eastern District of Oklahoma.

3. *US v. Minnie Atkins et al.* 2131, "Testimony of Sadie James," p. 23. The following passage is based on Sadie James's testimony. Her testimony is collected in four volumes housed at NARA, Kansas City, Missouri. They are part of a larger collection of a court case from the US District Court for Eastern District of Oklahoma, *United States of America v. Minnie Atkins et al.*, Equity 2131. Quotes from James's testimony are cited by page number. Sadie James Testimony (1) volume 2 from 1 to 79; incomplete, p. 3.

4. Many years later, another noteworthy Oklahoman, Chelsea Manning, would do time at the USDB.

5. "Testimony of Emily Ripley," *US v. Minnie Atkins et al.* 2131.

6. "Government's Case Not Good Says Campbell," *Tulsa World* (Morning Daily Edition), Feb. 27, 1915, https://www.newspapers.com/image/83121993 /?terms=Campbell.

7. "Memorial Page for Mable Peterkin," Find a Grave, https://www.finda grave.com/memorial/14142867/mable-peterkin, accessed Oct. 3, 2023.

8. Mary Jane Warde, *George Washington Grayson and the Creek Nation, 1843–1920* (Norman: University of Oklahoma Press, 1999), 6–7.

9. *Oakland (CA) News*, June 7, 1921, Robertson Collection, Oklahoma Historical Society, quoted in Joe Powell Spaulding, "The Life of Alice Mary

Robertson," PhD diss., University of Oklahoma, 1959, p. 57, https://shareok.org
/bitstream/handle/11244/1402/5902971.PDF.

10. Minnie Atkins to Judge Moore, 1892, 1931.001.2.6.3-7, Papers of the
Robertson and Worcester Families, Alice Mary Robertson Collection, Special
Collections and University Archives, McFarlin Library, University of Tulsa.

11. Minnie Atkins to Judge Moore, 1892.

12. "A Grave Injustice," *Muskogee Phoenix*, June 8, 1905.

13. "Lee Atkins Killed," *The Indian Journal*, Nov. 16, 1894, 1, https://www
.newspapers.com/image/586146254.

CHAPTER 4: "MY NATION IS ABOUT TO DISAPPEAR"

1. Mary Jane Warde, *George Washington Grayson and the Creek Nation,
1843–1920* (Norman: University of Oklahoma Press, 1999), 207.

2. Page v. Atkins, 144, 208 P. 807 86 Okla. 290, case number 12769 (Oklahoma Supreme Court, 1922).

CHAPTER 5: CHARLES PAGE, THE "SECULAR SAINT"
OF MODERN-DAY TULSA

1. "Judge Orders John Pickle Co. to Pay $1.24 Million to 52 Foreign Work-
ers in 'Human Trafficking' Case," US Equal Employment Opportunity Commission, press release, May 26, 2006, https://www.eeoc.gov/newsroom/judge-orders
-john-pickle-co-pay-124-million-52-foreign-workers-human-trafficking-case.

2. "John Nash Pickle Jr., 1937–2021," *Tulsa World*, Sept. 5, 2021, https://
www.legacy.com/us/obituaries/tulsaworld/name/john-pickle-obituary?id
=18504177.

3. Denise Gamino, "Exemptions from Divestiture Law Sought by Oklahoma Foundations," *Daily Oklahoman*, July 1, 1983, https://www.oklahoman
.com/story/news/1983/07/01/exemptions-from-divestiture-law-sought-by
-oklahoma-foundations/62839949007/

4. Ralph Marler, "Sooners' Amendments Adopted," *Tulsa World*, July 23,
1982, https://www.newspapers.com/image/891168967/?terms=%22sand%20
springs%20home%22%20%22david%20boren%22&match=1.

5. Sean Murphy, "Oklahoma Ex-Senator David Boren Accused of Sexual
Misconduct," Associated Press, Mar. 30, 2019, https://news.yahoo.com/oklahoma
-ex-senator-david-boren-accused-sexual-misconduct-192028112.html.

6. "Sand Springs History Dating Back to Charles Page," 2 News Oklahoma,
updated June 15, 2018, https://www.kjrh.com/news/local-news/sand-springs
-history-dating-back-to-charles-page.

CHAPTER 6: THE MAKING OF "DADDY" PAGE

1. Opal Bennefield Clark, *A Fool's Enterprise: The Life of Charles Page*
(Sand Springs, OK: Dexter Publishing, 1988), 11.

2. Josephine S. Hughes, *"Unto the Least of These": A Sketch of the
Life of the Late Charles Page*, pamphlet (Sand Springs, OK: 1939), 11, in
WHC-M-1271, Box H-13, Western History Collections, University of Okla-
homa Libraries.

3. National Park Service, "Forgotten Warriors," https://www.nps.gov/articles/forgotten-warriors.htm.

4. See Hughes, "*Unto the Least of These*," and Carolyn Thomas Foreman and Grant Foreman, *Fort Gibson: A Brief History*, Project Gutenberg eBook, 2015, https://www.gutenberg.org/cache/epub/48240/pg48240-images.html

5. "Chas. Page the Man, and A Life of Human Goodness," *Sand Springs Leader*, June 2, 1949, 2, https://www.newspapers.com/image/904632332; Hughes, "*Unto the Least of These*."

6. Clark, *A Fool's Enterprise*, 12.

7. Variations on this story appear in Clark, *A Fool's Enterprise*; see also John Erling, "Charles Page: Oklahoma Oilman and Philanthropist," interview, *Voices of Oklahoma*, June 2015, https://www.voicesofoklahoma.com/interviews/page-charles, accessed Jan. 25, 2024. In Hughes, "*Unto the Least of These*," Page works his way up from rabbit trapping to the cattle business.

8. Clark, *A Fool's Enterprise*, 13; Erling, "Charles Page."

9. Erling, "Charles Page."

10. Hugh Rockoff, "Great Fortunes of the Gilded Age," National Bureau of Economic Research working paper 14555, Dec. 2008, https://www.nber.org/system/files/working_papers/w14555/w14555.pdf.

11. Jeffrey Michael Bartos, "The Blight of the Federation: James Mcparland, the Pinkerton National Detective Agency and the Western Federation of Miners, 1892–1907," master's thesis, Montana State University, Apr. 2013, https://www.montana.edu/history/documents/papers/2013J.%20Bartos_Thesis.pdf.

12. Hughes, "*Unto the Least of These*," 8.

13. Scott quoted in "Address of Albert R. Parsons," in *The Famous Speeches of the Eight Chicago Anarchists in Court: When Asked If They Had Anything to Say Why Sentence of Death Should Not be Passed Upon Them* (Chicago: Lucy E. Parsons, 1886), 76, https://www.google.ca/books/edition/The_Famous_Speeches_of_the_Eight_Chicago/J_kJAAAAIAAJ.

14. Mathew Stanley, "The Great Railroad Strike of 1877," *Oxford Research Encyclopedia of American History*, accessed Jan. 25, 2024, https://oxfordre.com/americanhistory/view/10.1093/acrefore/9780199329175.001.0001/acrefore-9780199329175-e-931.

15. Clark, *A Fool's Enterprise*, 17.

16. Bartos, "The Blight of the Federation."

17. "Charles Page the Man, and a Life of Human Goodness," *Sand Springs Leader*, June 2, 1949.

CHAPTER 7: OKLAHOMA JOINS THE DANCE

1. Daniel F. Littlefield and Lonnie E. Underhill, "The 'Crazy Snake Uprising' of 1909: A Red, Black, or White Affair?" *Arizona and the West* 20, no. 4 (1978): 307–24, http://www.jstor.org/stable/40168759.

2. Larry O'Dell, "Senate Bill One," *The Encyclopedia of Oklahoma History and Culture*, Oklahoma Historical Society, https://www.okhistory.org/publications/enc/entry?entry=SE017.

3. James M. Smallwood, "Segregation," *The Encyclopedia of Oklahoma History and Culture*, Oklahoma Historical Society, https://www.okhistory.org /publications/enc/entry?entry=SE006.

4. See Brian Frehner, *Finding Oil: The Nature of Petroleum Geology, 1859–1920* (Lincoln: University of Nebraska Press, 2011), and Darren Dochuk, *Anointed with Oil: How Christianity and Crude Made Modern America* (New York: Basic Books, 2019). The mix of Christian theology and petroleum ideology can be seen at the base of Tulsa's *Golden Driller* statue, where a plaque states that "god's abundance" was bestowed on the men of the industry willing to take a chance.

5. Bobby D. Weaver, "Red Fork Field," *The Encyclopedia of Oklahoma History and Culture*, Oklahoma Historical Society, https://www.okhistory.org /publications/enc/entry?entry=RE004.

6. A key document to this era was a pamphlet by the Indian Rights Association, *Oklahoma's Poor Rich Indians* (Philadelphia: Indian Rights Association, 1924), in which researchers told the story of Millie Naharkey, an underage Muscogee girl who was kidnapped before her eighteenth birthday and forced to sell her allotment to an agent of Grant Stebbins, a Tulsa oilman. When she refused, she was raped. She was later sent to Chilocco Indian School, where she had little say over her own affairs. A Tulsa bank continued to control access to her funds into the 1980s. Later, I discuss the murder of Gabriel Emarthla. The Lucinda History Research Institute has documented the suspicious deaths of many of the descendants of Tuckabache.

7. "Regrets the Late Oil Find," *Daily Ardmorite*, July 1, 1901.

8. See Kent Carter, *The Dawes Commission and the Allotment of the Five Civilized Tribes 1893–1914* (Orem, UT: Ancestry Publishing, 1999).

9. Fred Bowers, Testimony before the Dawes Commission, Muskogee, Indian Territory, Aug. 25, 1904.

10. "Creek Indian No. 3718," "In the matter of the application of Minnie Harris," Department of the Interior, Commission to the Five Civilized Tribes," Muskogee, Indian Territory, Feb. 20, 1907.

CHAPTER 8: EMARTHLA OF THE SNAKE FACTION

1. Isparhecher (principal chief, Creek Nation), letter, Oct. 7, 1897, OHS microfilm CRN roll 4, cited in Kent Carter, *The Dawes Commission and the Allotment of the Five Civilized Tribes, 1893–1914* (Orem, UT: Ancestry Publishing, 1999), 30.

2. "'Crazy Snake' Makes Plea for Red Men," *Los Angeles Herald*, Nov. 24, 1906.

3. For Harjo's speech, see Kenneth Waldo McIntosh, "Chitto Harjo, the Crazy Snakes and the Birth of Indian Political Activism in the Twentieth Century," order no. 9402455, Texas Christian University, 1993, 194–200.

4. "Creeks to Mexico," *Houston Post*, Dec. 16, 1906.

5. Daniel F. Littlefield and Lonnie E. Underhill, "The 'Crazy Snake Uprising' of 1909: A Red, Black, or White Affair?" *Arizona and the West* 20, no. 4 (Winter 1978): 307–24.

6. Joseph B. Thoburn, *A Standard History of Oklahoma: An Authentic Narrative of Its Development from the Date of the First European Exploration Down*

to the Present Time, Including Accounts of the Indian Tribes, Both Civilized and Wild, of the Cattle Range, of the Land Openings and the Achievements of the Most Recent Period (Washington, DC: American Historical Society, 1916).

7. See McIntosh, "Chitto Harjo, the Crazy Snakes and the Birth of Indian Political Activism in the Twentieth Century"; Littlefield and Underhill, "The 'Crazy Snake Uprising' of 1909"; Leslie Jones, "Chitto Harjo and the Snake Rebellion," summer 2010, Gateway to Oklahoma History, https://gateway .okhistory.org/ark:/67531/metadc2006506. The tensions around Black identity and Muscogee culture are ever-present and continue to manifest themselves to-day in the struggle for the full enfranchisement of the freedmen within the tribe.

8. It can come as a surprise to some people to learn that Oklahoma, a deeply "red" state, had the most active Socialist Party in the nation in the 1910s. See Nigel Anthony Sellars, "Green Corn Rebellion," *The Encyclopedia of Oklahoma History and Culture*, Oklahoma Historical Society, https://www .okhistory.org/publications/enc/entry?entry=GR022.

9. Jones, "Chitto Harjo and the Snake Rebellion."

10. The reconstruction of the events of the Emarthla deaths comes from the following newspaper clippings: "Real Estate Transfers," *Tulsa Tribune*, June 7, 1910; "Two Intoxicated Indians Killed by Passenger on Katy," *Tulsa Tribune*, July 7, 1910; "District Court Filings," *Tulsa Daily Legal News*, June 8, 1960. On the probate decision in Tulsa County Court, see Tulsa County (Oklahoma), Probate Court Clerk, "In the matter of the estate of Gabriel Emarthla," Probate Records, 1907–1950, index, 1907–1977.

11. R. L. Davidson to R. C. Allen, May 27, 1915, Oklahoma, US Wills and Probate Records, 1801–2008, https://www.ancestry.com/imageviewer /collections/9077/images/007080060_00159?usePUB=true&_phsrc=sCf10& _phstart=successSource&usePUBJs=true&pId=1744610.

12. Opal Bennefield Clark, *A Fool's Enterprise: The Life of Charles Page* (Sand Springs, OK: Dexter Publishing, 1988), 69.

13. This case, like so many others, has been unexamined by professional his-torians. It was brought to my attention by a Muscogee businessman and writer, J. D. Colbert, who has been investigating the case of the Davis murder for years. Colbert provided court documents and leads, many of which were verified by news clippings, including, "Tulsa Man Is Slain in Home of Fiancée," *Parsons Daily Sun*, Dec. 19, 1916; "Love and Sorrow Mrs. Davis' Lot," *Tulsa World*, 1916.

14. "Daisy Carter Sisk Sues for Divorce," *Joplin Globe*, Jan. 9, 1921.

CHAPTER 9: BARTLETT'S QUITCLAIM
1. "Wildcatters in Their Glory in Oklahoma's Great New El Dorado," *Oklahoma State Register*, Jan. 2, 1913.
2. "Valuable Oil Lease Settled," *Guthrie Daily Leader*, Mar. 2, 1914.

CHAPTER 10: "ALL CROOKS AT TULSA"
1. The case of the United States and the Muscogee Nation against Minnie Atkins, Charles Page, and at least twenty other interested parties that is discussed in this chapter was first brought in the US District Court for the Eastern District of Oklahoma in Muskogee, presided over by Judge Ralph Campbell until his

resignation in 1918. This was an "equity case," which prior to the federal judicial reforms of 1938 was the nomenclature for resolving disputes concerning common law rather than criminal law. After 1938, equity cases per se no longer existed, as they were merged into other cases that concern civil procedure. The equity case number 2131 gave rise to an extended hearing on receivership for the Gem Oil Company's operations on Tommy's land. After Judge Campbell ruled in favor of the defendants, the case went to the Eighth Circuit Court of Appeals. NARA has categorized these cases as RG 0021, District Courts of the United States, US District Court for the Eastern District of Oklahoma, OKE03, Muskogee Equity Case Files, 1907–1938, NAID 3371084. There are five archival boxes of court transcripts, currently housed in the NARA, Kansas City, Missouri. In my documentation of the discussion I cite the case as *US v. Minnie Atkins et al.* 2131. The location of cited material is identified by page number.

2. "Tommy Atkins Actually Was, Witnesses Say," *Tulsa World*, Mar. 3, 1915.

3. NARA, RG 0021, District Courts of the United States, US District Court for the Eastern District of Oklahoma, OKE03, Muskogee Equity Case Files, 1907–1938, NAID 3371084.

4. "Judges Scored with McDougal in Pittman Case," *Tulsa Tribune*, July 13, 1913.

5. William O. Beall, letter to C. B. Stuart, May 21, 1918, Cruce, Cruce, and Bleakmore Collection, Papers 1899–1935, General Native American Manuscript Collections, Western History Collections, University of Oklahoma Libraries, Norman, https://archives.libraries.ou.edu/repositories/2/resources/115.

6. Beall, letter to Stuart.

7. *US v. Minnie Atkins et al.* 2131.

8. "Dictograph Tells Now What It Hears," *New York Times*, Apr. 10, 1913, 10.

9. The transcripts of Dlabal's conversations are included with exhibits in the federal government's appeal to Judge Campbell's decision in the US Court of Appeals, No. 5420. The transcripts are stored in RG 75 Records of BIA Miscellaneous Case Files, Minnie Atkins, Box 1, NARA, Kansas City.

10. "The Conflicting Stories of Minnie Atkins" chart is included in several different archives, including the Cruce, Cruce, and Bleakmore Collection, Papers 1899–1935, General Native American Manuscript Collections, Western History Collections, University of Oklahoma Libraries, Norman, https://archives.libraries.ou.edu/repositories/2/resources/115.

CHAPTER 11: MINNIE ATKINS IN SEATTLE

1. Frank Montgomery, Case Notes, untitled and undated, stored with *US v. Minnie Atkins et al.* 2131 files, NARA, Kansas City. The nineteen-page document, his attempt to reconstruct the chaos of events, has no title page and is signed "Frank L. Montgomery, U.S. probate attorney."

2. *US v. Minnie Atkins et al.* 2131, 1373.

3. Frank Montgomery to Cato Sells, Commissioner, Dec. 17, 1914, Central Classified Files (henceforth cited as CCF), 112829-1914-053-Creek, Creek Boxes, 19–21, NARA, Washington, DC.

4. Montgomery, Case Notes, 9.

5. Montgomery, Case Notes, 19 (these are Montgomery's concluding lines).

CHAPTER 12: "UTTERLY UNWORTHY OF YOUR CONFIDENCE"
1. Chief Inspector E. B. Linnen, "Report in Re: Allen Investigation," June 7, 1915, CCF, 83406-1915-Creek-154, NARA, Washington, DC.
2. Linnen, "Report."
3. Linnen, "Report."
4. "'Father' and Forty 'Kids' to See Exposition," *San Francisco Bulletin,* June 12, 1915.
5. "Affidavit of Nat Ligon," July 31, 1915, R. C. Allen Investigation, CCF, 83406-1915-Creek-154, folder 4 (henceforth cited as Allen Investigation), NARA, Washington, DC. Linnen obtained this affidavit in Creek County. Ligon, a probate attorney, said that Josey "made some very bitter remarks" about Allen and Montgomery. He said he would spend Gem Oil Company money to have them both fired, and have Allen disbarred.
6. "Affidavit of Nat Ligon."
7. R. C. Armstrong to Cato Sells, n.d., CCF, 112829-1914-053-Creek, Creek Boxes 19–21, NARA, Washington, DC.
8. Morris Brown, testimony, and R. A. Josey, testimony, Allen Investigation.
9. Bunnie McCorsa to Franklin K. Lane, July 13, 1915, CCF, 112829-1914-053-Creek, NARA, Washington, DC.
10. McCorsa to Lane.
11. "Telegrams," CCF, 112829-1914-053-Creek, NARA, Washington, DC. To my knowledge, this episode has never been written about before. Much of the material was marked "classified" in the National Archives. At some point, it was declassified.
12. On the deception of Chief Tiger through willful mistranslation see "Telegrams." Lumpkin never used a first name and appears to be Allen's hired investigator.
13. William G. Bruner to Cato Sells, July 12, 1915, CCF, 112829-1914-053-Creek, NARA, Washington, DC.
14. William G. Bruner to Cato Sells, May 13, 1915, CCF, 112829-1914-053-Creek, NARA, Washington, DC.
15. "Resolution," Sept. 11, 1914, Allen Investigation.
16. The Nunnery Scene, *Hamlet,* act III, scene 1, Royal Shakespeare Company, https://www.rsc.org.uk/shakespeare-learning-zone/hamlet/language/the-nunneryscene, accessed Oct. 1, 2023.
17. J. E. Richardson to Woodrow Wilson, July 2, 1915.

CHAPTER 13: "THERE IS NO JUSTICE FOR THE WEAK?"
1. "The Plot to Take Money from Indian Minors," *New Britain Herald,* July 24, 1914.
2. "The Plot to Take Money from Indian Minors."
3. Linda Edmondson and Margaret Larason, "Kate Barnard: The Story of a Woman Politician," *Chronicles of Oklahoma* 78, no. 2 (Summer 2000): 172, https://gateway.okhistory.org/ark:/67531/metadc1725776/m1/46/?q=alice%20robertson.
4. US Congress, Senate Committee on Indian Affairs, Indian Appropriation Bill, 64th Cong. 1917, 240–41.

5. "Davenport Hot on Allen Trail," *Muskogee Times-Democrat*, June 1, 1916.

6. "In Re: Cancellation of Enrollment of Thomas Atkins, Creek Indian Roll no. 7913," *US v. Minnie Atkins et al.* 2131. This document is a bound volume in the Creek attorney's files titled "Allen Abstract," which provides a lengthy overview of the case from Allen's perspective. It is labelled "Property of R.C. Allen," but it was addressed to the secretary of the interior.

7. Chief Inspector E. B. Linnen, "Report in Re: Allen Investigation," June 7, 1915, CCF, 83406-1915-Creek-154, NARA, Washington, DC, 3.

8. "Cushing-Drumright Field," *The Encyclopedia of Oklahoma History and Culture*, Oklahoma Historical Society, https://www.okhistory.org/publications/enc/entry?entry=CU008.

9. "Application to the Court for Instructions as to Taking Over Steel Tankage and Contracts for the Sale of Oil," *US v. Minnie Atkins et al.* 2131, NARA, Kansas City. This document is included with other documents for the trial and lays out the receiver's logic for taking over property not on the Atkins lands per se.

10. Response of complainant, untitled, *US v. Minnie Atkins et al.* 2131.

11. "A Contract Is Unnecessary," *Tulsa World*, June 20, 1919.

12. "Mother Admits 'Tommy Atkins' Just a Myth," *Tulsa World*, May 9, 1917.

13. "The World's Blackmailers at Work," *Tulsa Morning Times*, June 11, 1917.

CHAPTER 14: "WHAT A FOOL WE HAVE BEEN"

1. US General Services Administration, "Ed Edmondson U.S. Courthouse, Muskogee, OK," https://www.gsa.gov/historic-buildings/ed-edmondson-us-courthouse-muskogee-ok, accessed Apr. 7, 2023.

2. "Page Witnesses Are Small Army," *Tulsa World* (Morning Daily Edition), May 12, 1917, https://www.newspapers.com/image/71109546.

3. "Minnie Tells Story of Birth and Death of Her Son 'Tommy,'" *Tulsa Morning Times*, May 30, 1917, https://www.newspapers.com/image/883010351.

4. "Too Many Were Abroad, Expert Tells in Court," *Tulsa World* (Morning Daily Edition), July 28, 1915, https://www.newspapers.com/image/83131525.

5. "Page Defense to Open Up Monday," *Tulsa World*, May 11, 1917, https://www.newspapers.com/image/71109249.

6. "Remarks of One Employee," *Tulsa Tribune*, June 24, 1919.

7. "Page Gets Jolt in Atkins Case" *Tulsa World* (Morning Daily Edition), May 4, 1917, https://www.newspapers.com/article/tulsa-world/124229283.

8. *US v. Minnie Atkins et al.* 2131, 2698–99.

9. *US v. Minnie Atkins et al.* 2131, 2698–99.

10. *US v. Minnie Atkins et al.* 2131, 1094.

11. *US v. Minnie Atkins et al.* 2131, 2786–92.

12. *US v. Minnie Atkins et al.* 2131, 2793.

CHAPTER 15: "NANCY SHATTERS OWN CHANCE"

1. *US v. Minnie Atkins et al.* 2131, 565.

2. "Bogus Creek Warrants," *St. Louis Globe-Democrat*, Dec. 3, 1898, https://www.newspapers.com/image/571391736.

3. *US v. Minnie Atkins et al.* 2131, 2648.

4. *US v. Minnie Atkins et al.* 2131, 2709–10.

5. *US v. Minnie Atkins et al.* 2131, 81.

SAM BROWN INTERLUDE

1. Russell Cushman, "Sam Houston: A Legacy of Lost Loves," Navasota Current, Blogger.com, Mar. 7, 2016, https://russellcushman.blogspot.com/2016 /03/sam-houston-legacy-of-lost-loves.html.

2. "Indian, Christian, Military Rites for Aged Chief Today," *Tulsa Tribune*, Feb. 24, 1935, https://www.newspapers.com/image/900148076.

3. "Indian, Christian, Military Rites for Aged Chief Today."

4. Pamela Wallace, "Yuchi Social History Since World War II: Political Symbolism in Ethnic Identity," PhD diss., University of Oklahoma, 1998, 445.

5. "H. B. Folk to S. W. Brown," Nov. 9, 1925, 1992.001, Samuel W. Brown Collection, 1875–1965, Oklahoma Historical Society, Oklahoma City.

6. B. F. Ingraham to S. W. Brown, Jan. 27, 1931, Samuel W. Brown Collection, 1875–1965, Oklahoma Historical Society, Oklahoma City.

7. S. W. Brown Jr. to Paul Estill, Apr. 15, 1957, Brown Family Collection, Oklahoma History Center, Oklahoma City.

8. S. W. Brown, Jr. to Sand Springs Home, "In re: Euchee Tribal Rolls of 1898," Mar. 22, 1957, 1992.001, Samuel W. Brown Collection, 1875–1965, Oklahoma Historical Society, Oklahoma City.

9. Brown v. Evan Durrell, Sand Springs Home, Alice Perryman, United States of America, and Oklahoma Tax Commission, Tulsa County District Court, no. 93252.

10. "Lawyer Kills Child, Then Himself," *Fort Worth Star-Telegram*, February 28, 1931.

CHAPTER 16: "YOU KNOW HOW A WHITE MAN IS ABOUT MONEY"

1. "Exchange National Will Add Four Stories to New Skyscraper," *Tulsa Morning Times*, Jan. 12, 1917.

2. *US v. Minnie Atkins et al.* 2131, 644–45.

3. In *US v. Minnie Atkins et al.* 2131, Sadie James's testimony covers several hundred pages. She spoke at the receivership hearing and later at the main trial. Her testimony in a deposition will also be covered here. When available, I have supplied page numbers from the NARA files located in Kansas City. Some pages are missing from the original archive.

4. "Optimism Masks the Oil Outlook There, Just Snow," *Tulsa Post*, July 31, 1911, 8, https://www.newspapers.com/image/662624812.

5. "'Royal and Loyal Ethiopians' Say They're Happy," *Tulsa Post*, Feb. 17, 1911, https://www.newspapers.com/article/the-tulsa-post-royal-and-loyal -ethiopian/124747232.

6. "Royal and Loyal Ethiopians Say They're Happy," *Tulsa Daily World*, July 5, 1911.

7. "Woman 'Stockinglegger' Arrested with Whiskey," *Tulsa Post*, Dec. 1, 1910.

8. "Woman 'Stockinglegger' Arrested with Whiskey."

9. "Sadie Johnson's Shooting Story," *Tulsa Tribune*, July 15, 1913, https:// www.newspapers.com/article/the-tulsa-tribune-sadie-shoots-agnew/124874091.

10. "Summary Discharge of Panel Demanded After Acquittals of Negroes Charged with Murder," *Tulsa Tribune*, July 15, 1913.

11. Andrew Jackson Smitherman, "Jury Acquits Sadie Johnson," *Tulsa Star*, July 18, 1913.

12. *US v. Minnie Atkins et al.* 2131, 564.

13. *US v. Minnie Atkins et al.* 2131, 546.

14. *US v. Minnie Atkins et al.* 2131, 548.

15. *US v. Minnie Atkins et al.* 2131, 549.

16. *US v. Minnie Atkins et al.* 2131, 553.

17. *US v. Minnie Atkins et al.* 2131, 556–57.

18. *US v. Minnie Atkins et al.* 2131, 560.

19. *US v. Minnie Atkins et al.* 2131, 574.

20. *US v. Minnie Atkins et al.* 2131, 584

21. "Accuser of Page Broke Attorney's Nose, He Declares," *Muskogee Daily Phoenix and Times-Democrat*, March 3, 1915.

22. *US v. Minnie Atkins et al.* 2131, 609.

23. *US v. Minnie Atkins et al.* 2131, 609.

24. *US v. Minnie Atkins et al.* 2131, 611.

25. "Sadie Confesses Page Relations," *Tulsa World*, June 9, 1917.

26. *US v. Minnie Atkins et al.* 2131, 678.

27. This address will be familiar to Tulsans. It is the home of the U-Haul building, an Art Deco building with a spinning U-Haul truck on the top. The building also contains a plaque to Tulsa musician Bob Wills, who was inspired to write the song "Take Me Back to Tulsa" at this intersection. In the song, Wills, a white man, sings about being dropped off at Archer Street and walking down to the heart of Greenwood, presumably for some of the pleasures Charles Page also sought.

28. *US v. Minnie Atkins et al.* 2131, 828.

29. *US v. Minnie Atkins et al.* 2131, 680.

30. "Sadie Confesses Page Relations."

31. "Statement of Mayor Hubbard," *Tulsa World*, Apr. 4, 1919.

CHAPTER 17: "ANYTHING TO GET THE COIN"

1. The *Coffeyville Daily Journal*, May 25, 1919, noted a "nervous breakdown" as the cause of death, as did the *Anadarko American Democrat*, June 5, 1919. The *Tulsa Tribune*, May 24, 1919, claimed that Minnie had been ill "about three weeks" and died of heart failure. Other newspapers, from Kansas to Mississippi, noted simply that she had died suddenly. Many of these reports were full of inaccuracies, including claims that Minnie was a "wealthy Indian" (she had little wealth at her own disposal) and was a citizen of the Muscogee Nation (she had been stricken from the tribe's rolls).

2. "Minnie Atkins' Death Brings New Claimants for Millions," *Tulsa World*, May 25, 1919.

3. "Charlie Page, Tax Dodger," *Tulsa World*, June 21, 1919.

4. "Here's Mr. Page's Letter in Which He Tells of Much Water," *Tulsa World*, June 17, 1919.

5. Nathaniel Atkins et al. v. A. G. McMillan, Sand Springs Home, et al., Creek County District Court, State of Oklahoma, 18395, CCF, 1907–1939,

Entry PI-163, Record Group 75, 121A, File 112829-1914-053-Creek, NARA, Washington, DC. The case documents are available on microfiche.

6. *Nathaniel Atkins et al. v. A. G. McMillan.*

7. CCF, 1907–1939, Entry PI-163, Record Group 75, 121A, File 112829-1914-053-Creek, NARA, Washington, DC.

8. Albina Dlabal, second conversation, July 27, 1915, CCF, 112829-1914-053-Creek, NARA, Washington, DC.

9. "Did You Know? Osage Murders, the Reign of Terror," The Osage Nation (website), https://www.osagenation-nsn.gov/news-events/news/did-you-know-osage-murders, accessed Feb. 26, 2024.

10. Ruth Sheldon Knowles, *The Greatest Gamblers* (Norman: University of Oklahoma Press, 1959), 129.

CHAPTER 18: FROM BLOOD QUANTUM TO LIQUID GOLD

1. Nathaniel Atkins to Office of Indian Affairs, Nov. 18, 1922, CCF, 112829-1914-053-Creek, NARA, Washington, DC.

2. "Richard Atkins, Creek Enrollment Cases, 617283, Applications for Enrollment of the Commission to the Five Civilized Tribes, 1898–1914, 24, Record Group 75: Records of the Bureau of Indian Affairs, 1793–1999," NARA, Washington, DC.

3. "Richard Atkins, Creek Enrollment Cases, 617283."

4. "Says She's Mother of Tommy," *Tulsa World*, Apr. 18, 1919.

5. Frank B. Long to C. B. Stuart, Apr. 4, 1917, Box 54, Cruce, Cruce and Bleakmore, Western History Collections, University of Oklahoma, Norman.

6. Billie Byrd, "An Interview with Alex Haynes," May 21, 1937, Indian-Pioneer Papers, Western History Collections, University of Oklahoma, https://digital.libraries.ou.edu/cdm/ref/collection/indianpp/id/987.

7. Long to Stuart.

8. Long to Stuart.

9. "Wright Told of Fortune," *Tulsa Tribune*, Aug. 25, 1921.

10. "Charged Sapulpa Jurist Took Bribe," *Sapulpa Herald*, July 14, 1921.

11. "Death Threat in Bribe Case," *Tulsa Tribune*, July 28, 1921.

12. "Death Threat in Bribe Case."

13. "Frame-Up Says Wright's Lawer" and "Sheriff Slept Through Tulsa Riot," *Tulsa World*, July 15, 1921.

14. "Page Is Victorious in Tommy Atkins Case," *Harlow's Weekly*, May 4, 1922; *US v. Atkins*, 260 U.S. 220 (1922).

15. See Nathaniel Atkins et al. v. A. G. McMillan, Sand Springs Home, et al., Creek County District Court, State of Oklahoma, 18395, CCF, 1907–1939, Entry PI-163, Record Group 75, 121A, File 112829-1914-053-Creek, NARA, Washington, DC.

16. "Memory of Charles Page, Sand Springs Founder, Will Live in Bronze; Work of Celebrated Sculptor, Larado [sic] Taft, Will Be Unveiled Soon," *Tulsa Sunday World*, Nov. 2, 1930, https://www.newspapers.com/image/884640635.

17. Alaina E. Roberts, *I've Been Here All the While: Black Freedom on Native Land* (Philadelphia: University of Pennsylvania Press, 2021).

CHAPTER 19: "BUT INSISTS HE HAS NEVER DIED"

1. Orin Jordan, letter to Commissioner Collier, Dec. 6, 1937, CCF, 112829-1914-053-Creek.

2. David Felix to Indian Office, Department of the Interior, August 23, 1939. 112829-1914-053-creek.

3. J. Allen Gulick to Jerry Voorhis, Aug. 28, 1937, CCF 112829-1914-053-Creek.

4. A. Mitchell Palmer to John Barton Payne, Jan. 7, 1921, CCF 112829-1914-053-Creek.

INDEX

Checotah, OK: Atkins and Hogan
families in, 24–25, 31; Creek
Cemetery, 54–55
Cherokee Nation: borders of, 7;
James's mother's birth in, 182; as
one of the Five Tribes, 3; per cap-
ita payments, 183; taxes paid by
settlers to, 49
Cherokee Strip area, 183
Cheyaha Town (Muscogee),
Atkinses in, 52, 223
Chickasaw Nation, 3, 26, 141
Childers, Anderson, 223
Childers, Ellis: background, 166–67;
corruptibility, 167, 237; inter-
preter work, 169–70; relationship
with Allen, 142–43; support
for Nancy Atkins's claim, 105,
154–56, 166–68, 226
Choctaw Nation, 3, 5, 26, 95, 141
Clark, Opal Bennefield, 10, 76, 116
Cleaver, Barney, 184, 186
Clinton, Fred, 85
Cobb, Candler, 2
Cobb, Elena, 2
Cobb, Jane, 257n2
Cobb, Mattie, 111, 195
Cobb, Russell, Jr., 2, 185, 257n2
Cobb, Russell, Sr., 1–2, 185, 247
Cobb, Russell, III, 2, 5
Colbert, J. D., 263n13
Collier, John, 238–39
Colorado, People's Party, 75
Comanche peoples, 37, 43
"The Conflicting Stories of Minnie
Atkins" (Allen), 115
Cook, Fred, 94
Covington, Gina, 15, 45, 218
Coweta Realty Company, 123,
127–28
Coweta Town (Muscogee), 23,
26–28, 123, 223
Crawley, Mr. (government agent),
205
"Creek," as a term, 8n
Creek (Crook) County, OK, 17–18, 58
Creek County Court: accessing
records from, 256; cases involv-
ing Tommy Atkins leasehold, 14;

case records from, 256; and the
permitting of guardian "borrowing" from Indian wards, 98; trials
involving Tommy Atkins's allotment, 14, 106, 116, 154, 216
Creek Indian #7913, association
with Creek Nation enrollment
card 2707, 142–43. *See also*
Atkins, Thomas "Tommy";
Dawes Commission/Dawes Rolls
Creekmore, Bill, 181–82, 184, 200
Crilley, George, 110–11, 195
"Crook County," naming of, 1
Crowell, Sarah Elizabeth "Bettie,"
38, 40–41
Cruce, Lee, 16, 244
"cult of true womanhood," 39–40,
48, 86, 139
Curtis Act. *See* Act for the Protection of the People of Indian Terri-
tory (1898)
Cushing, E. R., 223
Cushing-Drumright Field. *See* oil
industry

Davenport, James, 142, 151
Davidson, R. L., 98–99
Davis, Ethel, 97, 99–101
Davis, John, 165, 217, 217n, 228
Davis, Josiah, 107
Davis, Mary Jane, x
Davis, Sam, 82, 97, 98, 101, 263n13
Dawes, Henry, Dawes Act, 4–6
Dawes Commission/Dawes Rolls:
Allen's attack on, 145–46;
Thomas Atkins's name on, 10,
145; efforts to find Minnie,
89–90, 163; enrollment decisions,
12, 83, 163, 183, 224; forced
enrollments, 54, 87, 96; goals,
6; handling fraud, 141; Hold Up
Book, 55; lasting impacts, 4–6,
55; oral testimony collected by,
87; "paper genocide," 6, 82. *See
also* Atkins, Thomas "Tommy";
Bixby, Tams
Dawes Severalty Act, 1887, 79
"dead Indian," in land titles, 83,
97, 99

PHOTO INSERT
CREDITS

Page 1, Minnie Atkins: Dickinson College Archives & Special Collections

Page 1, Chitto Harjo: Photograph by Duncan, retrieved from Library of Congress, Prints and Photographs Division

Page 2, Statue of Charles Page: Stuart Hetherwood, a Tulsa-based artist and designer

Page 2, Alice Robertson: Oklahoma Historical Society, Oklahoma City

Page 2, Enrollment Card: Creek Nation, Dawes Roll card number 2707, National Archives and Records Administration

Page 3, Tullahassee Creek Indian Cemetery: Stuart Hetherwood

Page 3, Certificate of Selection: Files of Equity #2131, National Archives and Records Administration branch, Kansas City, MO

Page 4, Muscogee girls: Dickinson College Archives & Special Collections

Page 4, Sand Springs Railway line: Russell Cobb

Page 5, *Tulsa World* cartoon: *Tulsa World*, June 20, 1919

Page 5, Wilson telegram: NARA Central Classified Files collection on the Creek Nation (1907–1939), Washington, DC

Page 5, "World's Champion Santa": *Wichita Beacon*, December 25, 1921

Page 6, Nathaniel Atkins: Collection of Bobbi West, descendent of Sally and Richard Atkins

Page 6, Oaklawn Cemetery: Russell Cobb

Page 6, "Sadie Confesses Page Relations," *Tulsa World*

Page 7, Oil field remains: Russell Cobb

Page 7, *Panorama of Petroleum*: Russell Cobb

Page 7, Minnie Atkins's house: Russell Cobb

Page 8, Oil fire at Drumright: Oklahoma Historical Society, Oklahoma City

Page 8, stuck car: Russell Cobb

Page 58, Indian Territory Map 1890: Oklahoma Digital Maps Collection, Oklahoma State University

Page 92, Hastain's allotment map: *Hastain's Town Plats of the Creek Nation*

ABOUT THE AUTHOR

Russell Cobb, PhD, descended from three generations of Tulsa oilmen, is a professor in the Faculty of Arts at the University of Alberta and the author of *The Great Oklahoma Swindle*, which won the 2021 Director's Award at the Oklahoma Book Awards. His research on the mega-preacher Carlton Pearson appeared on *This American Life* and was subsequently adapted into the film *Come Sunday*, distributed by Netflix. He lives in Edmonton, Alberta, Canada, with his wife, Rachel, and two sons, August and Henry.